Published by Applied Research and Design Publishing, an imprint of ORO Editions
Gordon Goff: Publisher

www.appliedresearchanddesign.com
info@appliedresearchanddesign.com

Author:
María Bellalta

Art Direction:
María Bellalta

Production Team:
María Bellalta, Daniela Coray, and Erica Rayworth

Project Manager:
Jake Anderson

All photographs are the author's unless otherwise stated.

10 9 8 7 6 5 4 3 2 1 First Edition

ISBN: 978-1-943532-68-1

Color Separations and Printing: ORO Group Ltd.
Printed in China.

AR+D Publishing makes a continuous effort to minimize the overall carbon footprint of its publications. As part of this goal, AR+D, in association with Global ReLeaf, arranges to plant trees to replace those used in the manufacturing of the paper produced for its books. Global ReLeaf is an international campaign run by American Forests, one of the world's oldest nonprofit conservation organizations. Global ReLeaf is American Forests' education and action program that helps individuals, organizations, agencies, and corporations improve the local and global environment by planting and caring for trees.

SOCIAL URBANISM

Reframing Spatial Design • Discourses from Latin America

MARÍA BELLALTA

CONTENTS

CONTENIDO

ACKNOWLEDGMENTS

Stemming from Colombia, Mexico, the U.S., and Chile, this project, through shared narratives, drawings, and photographs unfolds the dynamics of space across borders and through various cultural reads, to explore ideas on social urbansim fueling a broader dynamic for unraveling the spatial opportunities that lie before us.

I am grateful to so many people who have believed in the premise of this work and for their generous contributions to this project. Alejandro Echeverri Restrepo, director pf URBAM at EAFIT University, whose instrumental work on social urbanism in Medellín I admire, has been tremendously supportive over the value of this project, offering his insights from the field and illuminating the extensions for developing regions elsewhere. Lina Escobar Ocampo, a dear colleague and director of the Universidad Pontificia Bolivariana (UPB), Master of Landscape Architecture program, has tirelessly extended her classroom and the hidden corners of the city in order to understand the parameters of urbanization in Latin America more fully, without whom these studies could not have been realized. To all my energetic Boston Architectural College (BAC) students who have joined me over the years in the expeditions to learn from Medellín, I am grateful for their curiosity and for grappling with the scale and complexity of the planning issues we have explored, expanding the knowledge of the design disciplines further afield. I am, likewise, thankful for the opportunity to engage with and share these studies with UPB's design students, and for the unforgettable chance to meet the people of Medellín and the many comunas that make up this amazing city. I offer a special thank you to Daniela Coray, BAC, for her research and production assistance toward the realization of this endeavor. My gratitude to Erica Rayworth, BAC, for her diligence as research/project assistant.

The studies in Medellín would not have been the same without Juan Camilo Jaramillo who guided our field trips, as a naturalist in Colombia, teaching us and advocating for the deep ecology of the region. Samuel Vélez González, director of architecture faculty, UPB, has welcomed my students each year, as well as shared his perspectives on the city's history and urban development. Jorge Pérez Jaramillo, architect and former planning director for the Municipality of Medellín, has been instrumental in disclosing his deep knowledge of the city's planning frameworks, including his memory of the collective institutional processes that have carried Medellín forward. Gabriel Gutierrez, architect, extended great enthusiasm over this book, connecting me to others in the city, including former mayor and governor Sergio Fajardo, who offered hidden points of view, including the invaluable community participation that has driven the political discourse explored through this project. Jared Green, D.C. journalist, and Elizabeth Ferry, anthropology professor at Brandeis University in Boston, each provided their diverse perspectives as Americans whose experiences in Latin America expand on the relevance of cultural spaces and customs through concepts on city branding and gold, stimulating the multi-dimensional ideas offered. Stephen Ferry, photo journalist in Bogota, shared spectacular images of the native inhabitants and miners of Colombia, illustrating the magic of their habitats and practices. Theresa Williamson, from Rio de Janeiro, has provided awareness on new community and city structures, deepening models for urbanization and providing a worldview perspective. Ongoing collaborations with Francisco Luna Ugarte and Carlos Ruiz de Chávez in Mexico City, through Buró Verde Arquitectura and Centro Metropolitano de Arquitectura Sustentable (C+), have provided insight into the nuances of neighboring and dense cities of the globe and their firsthand understanding of indigenous cultures, widening the view of this study. To Alexandra Bellalta and Josefina Letelier Bellalta, my dear sister and niece in Santiago who shared their inspiring photographs of the Andean landscape, I am grateful as these reveal the unmatched power behind the geography of the region. I owe Gloria Aponte García, founder of the Landscape Architecture program at UPB in Medellín, a special thank you for extending me my first invitation to visit the city in 2014, as the genesis of this work, and for the memories of this visit that I hold dear.

I would be remiss not to offer a truly special thank you to my loving family, Damon—my husband, and my children, Sara and James, for supporting me throughout this project, and to whom I dedicate this work.

AGRADECIMIENTOS

Derivada desde Colombia, México, Brasil, los Estados Unidos y Chile, este proyecto, por medio de una narrativa colectiva, acompañada por dibujos y fotografías, releva las dinámicas que existen a través de los bordes y las diferentes culturas, explorando ideas sobre el urbanismo social, así fortaleciendo las opotunidades sobre las intervenciones de los espacios que existen por delante de nosotros.

Agradezco a tantas personas que han creído en las premisas de este trabajo y por sus generosas contribuciones a este proyecto. Alejandro Echeverri Restrepo, director de URBAM, Universidad EAFIT, cuyo trabajo Instrumental sobre el urbanismo social en Medellín admiro, ha ofrecido su gran apoyo sobre el valor de este proyecto, con deas desde el campo, iluminando la importancia de este trabajo para areas en desarrollo regionales. Lina Escobar Ocampo, querida colega y directora del la Maestría de Arquitectura del Paisaje, Universidad Pontificia Bolivariana (UPB), ha extendido inagotablemente su taller de estudio, dirigiéndome a los rincones más escondidos de la ciudad, para comprender los parámetros de la urbanización en América Latina de manera más completa, sin quien estos estudios no podrían haberse realizado. A todos mis enérgicos estudiantes del Boston Architectural College (BAC), que se han unido conmigo a lo largo de los años en las expediciones de aprendizaje en Medellín, estoy agradecida por su curiosidad y por lidiar con la escala y la complejidad de los problemas de planificación que hemos explorado, expandiendo el conocimiento de la disciplina del diseño aún más allá. Asimismo, estoy agradecida por la oportunidad de participar y compartir estos estudios con los estudiantes de diseño del UPB, así como por la inolvidable ocasión de conocer a la gente de las comunas de Medellín, quienes forman parte de esta increíble ciudad. Le agradezco a Daniela Coray, BAC, por su asistencia con la investigacion y realización de este complejo proyecto. Mi agradecimiento a Erica Rayworth, BAC, por su diligencia como asistente de investigación y de proyecto. Los estudios en Medellín no habrían sido los mismos sin Juan Camilo Jaramillo, quien guió nuestras excursiones, como naturalista en Colombia, enseñándonos y abogando por la intensa ecología de la región. Samuel Vélez González, director de la Facultad Arquitectura del UPB, ha dado la bienvenida a mis alumnos cada onde ha compartido sus puntos de vista sobre la historia de la el desarrollo urbano. Jorge Pérez Jaramillo, arquitecto, ex-

director de Planificación, Municipalidad de Medellín, ha ofrecido su profundo conocimiento sobre los marcos de planificación de la ciudad, añadiendo su memoria de los procesos institucionales colectivos que han llevado a Medellín hacia adelante. Gabriel Gutiérrez, arquitecto, extendió su entusiasmo por este libro, conectándome con otros en la ciudad, particularmente con el ex-alcalde de Medellín y gobernador de Antioquia Sergio Fajardo, quien ofreció puntos de vista claves para esta investigación, incluyendo la invaluable participación comunitaria que ha impulsado el discurso politico explorado en este proyecto. Jared Green, periodista en Washington, D.C., y Elizabeth Ferry, profesora do antropología en Universidad de Brandeis en Boston, compartieron sus diversas perspectivas con respectivos estudios en América Latina. Estos han ofrecido ideologías sobre el significado de los espacios y las costumbes culturales reflejados mediante la ciudad y el oro, estimulando ideas multidimensionales sobre el tema del desarrollo urbano. Stephen Ferry, periodista fotográfico en Bogotá, compartió imágenes espectaculares de los nativos y mineros de Colombia, ilustrando la magia de sus hábitats y de sus trabajos. Theresa Williamson, desde Río de Janeiro, ha compartido valiosa información sobre nuevas estructuras comunitarias, profundizando modelos para los centros de urbanización. Colaboraciones continuas con Francisco Luna Ugarte y Carlos Ruiz de Chávez en la Ciudad de México, a través de Buró Verde Arquitectura y Centro Metropolitano de Arquitectura Sustentable (C+), han impartido información relevante a otras ciudades latino americanas junto con las maravillas de las culturas indígenas, ampliando la visión de este estudio. A Alexandra Bellalta y Josefina Letelier Bellalta, mi querida hermana y sobrina en Santiago quienes compartieron sus bellas fotografías del paisaje andino, les agradezco por captar el poder inigualable que ofrece la geografía de la región. Le debo a Gloria Aponte García, fundadora del programa de Arquitectura del Paisaje, UPB, en Medellín, un agradecimiento especial por extenderme mi primera invitación para visitar la ciudad en 2014, como la génesis de este trabajo, y por los recuerdos que esta visita marca.

Esta obra no estaría completa sin ofrecer mi profundo agradecimiento a mi querida familia, a Damon—mi marido, y mis hijos Sara y James, por apoyarme a lo largo de este proyecto, y a quienes les dedico este trabajo.

PROLOGUE

Alejandro Echeverri

The urban transformation of Medellín during the past 20 years has made it possible to break our isolation, permitting us to come together to take part in a broader conversation. In our city, researchers, political leaders, and academics have joined arms in search for answers to the challenges presented by urbanization and the extreme and unstable conditions these pose, as problems we share with so many cities of the Global South.

Through this period of renewed dialogue I met María, a few years ago at URBAM (our academic institute, which is part of EAFIT University), during one of her first studio visits to the city. I recall her sensitivity and her commitment to the social and urban challenges we are faced with, her ability to explore and understand the reality of communities in the northern neighborhoods of our city, and her energy and passion for guiding students through these unusual experiences. Our city and processes for tackling social and urban issues have garnered interest and are explored in this publication.

This book is a critical reflection, stemming from intense personal and intellectual experiences, in search of solutions to the realities of our contexts today. María, as an urbanist and trained as a landscape architect, was raised in Chile and forced into exile with her family during Pinochet´s dictatorship. Her studies in environmental psychology, coupled with her dedication and quest for social equity and spatial justice through design, permit her to re-contextualize the premises framing the social urbanism processes derived from Medellín, and to broadly apply these perspectives to similar social and urban conditions elsewhere.

This is an ambitious book as it explores a unique theory regarding the evolution of urbanization in Latin America, based on the geographical splendor and the unequivocal qualities of the continental landscape, and situating the processes of social urbanism as a practical reference for framing a vision of inclusive urban development. It provides valuable information for urbanists, urban designers, landscape architects, architects, and academics. The book offers a historical analysis of the urbanization processes and social exclusion of our city. It questions how a reality that begins with Medellín's deep and complex crisis manages to change course in order to arrive at a more conceivable existence.

Without a doubt, one of the most valuable contributions of this work derives from the diverse data and quality of spatial representation, at various scales, through unseen cartographic interpretations. The extensive quality of this material is an invaluable contribution to the region as well as the city. We ask ourselves how to represent our realities in order to see ourselves more clearly. María explores and draws the geography, the landscape, and, through this process, comes across a multitude of information. This is a journey in search of a clearer understanding, through the representation of our environment, of the social and cultural realities in Medellín.

Some of the most important cues regarding what has transpired in Medellín are embedded within the process of building a cultural landscape, as part of the geographical impacts made by human action, and by the nuances of the regional geography that define the identity and the behavior of its society. The visual quality of this book makes an asserted contribution to comprehending these dynamics more deeply.

We have reached a critical moment with respect to cities that requires a profound shift. The socio-environmental crisis, the urban explosion, and inequality are moving us toward a future that is no longer viable. Unfortunately, we confront the challenges ahead with no simple or universal answers. Our experience in Medellín has offered some suggestions, such as the extraordinary capacity imparted through local management; the relevance of the achievements reached through our social consensus; the power borne through our dialogue that has helped to build trust; the value of spatial design toward creating spaces for encounters; and the strength in leadership and the capacity of local communities. Each is a complex process that requires consideration and time, which are incredibly fragile aspects given that these also demand continuity as a condition–too often missed in the political sphere.

PRÓLOGO

Alejandro Echeverri

La transformación urbana de Medellín durante los últimos 20 años hizo posible romper nuestro aislamiento y permitió que nos integráramos a una conversación mas amplia. En nuestra ciudad han confluido investigadores, líderes políticos y académicos en la búsqueda de respuestas para nuestros retos urbanos en condiciones extremas e inestables, problemas que compartimos muchas de las ciudades del sur global.

En este proceso de creación de nuevos diálogos conocí a María hace algunos años en URBAM, nuestro centro de estudios de la Universidad EAFIT, en una de sus primeras visitas de estudio a la ciudad. Me impactó su sensibilidad, su compromiso hacia nuestros retos sociales y urbanos, su capacidad para adentrarse y comprender la realidad de las comunidades de los barrios del norte, tanto como su energía y pasión para llevar a sus estudiantes hacia experiencias únicas. Nuestra ciudad y nuestro proceso urbano y social fueron conquistando un espacio cada vez mayor en sus intereses que se traducen en esta publicación.

Este libro es una reflexión crítica y propositiva como consecuencia de una experiencia de vida personal e intelectual intensas, en la búsqueda de soluciones para realidades propias de nuestros contextos. María, quien tiene una formación de urbanista y arquitecta de paisaje, tuvo forzosamente que exiliarse con su familia de Chile, su país, durante la dictadura Pinochet. Sus estudios de psicología ambiental y su compromiso y búsqueda de la equidad y justicia espacial a través del diseño, le han permitido re-contextualizar los fundamentos del proceso de urbanismo social en Medellín para construir unas perspectivas de aplicación amplias en contextos sociales y urbanos similares.

Este es un texto ambicioso, al desarrollar una idea propia sobre el proceso de urbanización en Latino América a partir del esplendor geográfico y la singularidad del paisaje continental; y al localizar el proceso de urbanismo social en Medellín como referente práctico de una visión de desarrollo incluyente, como laboratorio de trabajo para urbanistas, diseñadores urbanos, paisajistas, arquitectos y académicos. Elabora un análisis histórico y espacial del proceso de urbanización y de exclusión social de nuestra ciudad. Cuestiona, como una realidad que

parte de una crisis profunda y compleja de una ciudad fracturada, y logra iniciar un cambio de rumbo hacia un relato posible.

Sin duda, uno de los aportes más relevantes de este libro es la capacidad de representación espacial de procesos y datos diversos a escalas variables con la producción de una cartografía única y propia. La calidad y extensión de este material es un aporte invaluable tanto para la región como para nuestra ciudad. Siempre nos cuestionamos como representar nuestras realidades para vernos con mayor claridad. María explora y dibuja nuestra geografía, nuestro paisaje, y en este proceso cruza informaciones y datos múltiples. Es un viaje hacia la búsqueda de una lectura más certera, con la representación de nuestro entorno geográfico atravesado por nuestras realidades culturales y sociales.

Las claves más importantes del proceso de Medellín están en el proceso de construcción de su paisaje cultural, en los impactos geográficos de la acción humana, en la incidencia de las condiciones propias de la geografía del territorio para definir la identidad y el comportamiento de nuestra sociedad. El material gráfico de este libro hace un aporte decisivo para comprender esto con mayor precisión.

Estamos en un momento crítico en nuestras ciudades con una necesidad urgente de un viraje profundo. La crisis socio-ambiental, la explosión urbana y la inequidad nos llevan hacia un futuro inviable. Desafortunadamente para enfrentar estos retos no hay respuestas simples ni formulas universales. Nuestra experiencia en Medellín nos ha dejado algunas claves tales como la extraordinaria capacidad de la gestión local; la relevancia de lograr un relato, un consenso social; el poder del diálogo para la construcción de confianza; el valor del diseño urbano y del paisaje hacia escenarios para el encuentro de las personas; y como fortalecer y visibilizar el liderazgo y la capacidad de las comunidades locales. Estos son todos procesos complejos que necesitan decisión y tiempo, y por esto son inmensamente frágiles pues exigen continuidad, una condición que es excepcional en nuestras realidades políticas.

INTRODUCTION

The geographical splendor and enigmatic nature of Latin America's terrain has offered us an endless fountain of wealth and glory. Overlooked as the source of frivolous whims, triggering its own subordination, the traditional narrative of Latin America has oft omitted a much deeper understanding of the ecological and spatial relationships forged in these territories. Behind the powerful, rugged mountains, along the abundant watersheds, and from the rich flora and fauna, natural resources produced by the arduous labor of indigenous people and enslaved cultures have provided Europe and the United States with commodities and a high standard of living, of which the locals are not permitted to delight. In response to such a divisive ploy, this work provides an alternate view, where the magical allure of the landscape is not the culprit, rather, one where the landscape is a "cultural space," formed and influenced by the regional geography, providing lasting meaning to its community and allowing a productive exchange between habitable space and the social values of humankind to coexist.

This book provides insight into 21st-century frameworks for a more equitable view of development for politicians, urbanists, landscape architects, architects, faculty, and students, as well as for communities who believe that the future of living spaces must be reconsidered in order for us to provide for, and partake in, a more humane, global arena. Social urbanism, defined as a socio-political and practical approach to urban globalization, derives from a planning strategy and a portfolio of built projects initiated as a response to the social crisis in Medellín, Colombia during the last decades of the 20th-century. Through the work presented here, social urbanism is expanded as a worldview that considers the cultural values of a given place as interconnected to the geographical landscape of the region, and therefore, as the driving forces behind future models of globalization and urban growth.

A journey through Latin America's robust landscape reveals how the interruption between geography and culture has led to the belittlement of indigenous and Latin American cultures and communities, and to the negligence of resulting planning frameworks for well over five centuries. The imposition of Spanish Colonization and European Imperialism are unearthed, to comprehend how over time the magnitude of corruption stemming from international development strategies have steadily super-seded distinct and inclusive agendas that should be geared toward regional progress. Driven by greed, through foreign extraction of the land's purest resources, and of its people, a clearer understanding of why local development in Latin America has failed comes into view. The United States's political and economic interests, as the sequel plot, is explored through capitalist ventures that have dominated Latin American territories for over a century, and which continue to burden this region's resources, oppressing its communities to this day.

In order to dig deeper, Medellín, located in central Colombia in the Valle de Aburrá, is explored in detail in order to analyze how its geographical location, as well as its mountainous tributary character, relates to this prominent city's historical, political, and economic evolution. The migration patterns of the agrarian Aburrae people down from the mountains to the valley, along the Medellín River, and their return to the mountainside are traced, indicating a natural course and settlement pattern that has been interrupted as a result of invasive development schemes. The outcomes have led to erratic frameworks and to a place where the community has been left physically and culturally disconnected, having to instead surrender their livelihood to violence and terror.

The revitalization outcomes of Medellín have been renowned worldwide. Initially recognized as the pit of the earth, and most recently, as a designer's dream hub, this is a trending city where projects and tactics in urbanism abound and are referenced as being on the cusp of solving the Latin American development dilemma. It is through a bilateral participatory process among city leaders and the Medellín community, together with an array of strategic planning projects, transit systems, buildings and cultural programs, that social urbanism offers valuable lessons for transforming a politically, economically, and socially broken city into a veritable renaissance.

While the marvels of Medellín's epoch over the past 10 years provide significant insight into future plans for urban development, these are then scrutinized against longer-term planning parameters to understand the full value and replicability for neighboring and/or comparable urbanizing areas. In Medellín, the inclusive focus and the planning and architectural projects implemented through this social urbanism approach, have signaled the way toward a socio-cultural shift, yet these maneuvers have not managed to resolve the discord of the city, nor of the country, for prolonged periods of time. The truth of the matter is that the investment interests remain in the hands of the Global North, over a local focus, recreating past scenarios where the community and the region's resources continue to be violated, therefore repeating similarly disjointed socio-economic practices, and only perpetuating a misaligned spatial paradox.

Through a broader view of social urbanism, implemented not only through political processes and a targeted list of urban projects geared toward the community, yet also by an emphasis on the unique character of the regional and local geography as inherent elements of urban development, the necessary re-contextualization of space is unfolded. This gives way to a plausible direction forward, where the intimacy between landscape and culture are restored. The realization that we are today all connected through our "collective culture," through global ecologies, economies, and overlapping socio-political spheres, the possibility for an integrated framework derives, providing a renewed vision for eradicating the divide that has delineated the Global North from the Global South for so long. An ideal moment of grounded perspectives affecting urban development is identified, reframed through our mutual agency, where global equity can be reconsidered.

A pedagogical process for guiding spatial designers and emerging professionals in cross-contextual experiences, moreover, considers these social urbanism practices and projects further. Academic studies situated in Medellín, Colombia, conducted between local design students from Colombia and the United States, examine the expanding spatial patterns in the urban, peri-urban, and rural contexts of the city. These studies fixate on the underlying principle that future models for urban development must be informed through a deeper analysis and understanding of the regional, geographical landscape, as well as through direct interactions with the local community that reveals the delicate nuances and roots of their customs.

Six years of international academic collaborations have invited students of spatial design to consider the distinct socio-political, economic, and environmental parameters of Medellín and its environs. The unique qualities of the regional landscape and of its communities are considered through the mutual assessment of local, as well as international in-situ experiences, and, as a result, offer valuable insights into urgent ideologies geared toward a global design paradigm.

The points of view of multiple colleagues and experts across differing fields provide introspection on the value and implementation of social urbanism. Stemming from a range of disciplines, including spatial theorists, urbanists, politicians, scientists, anthropologists, and community leaders with whom I have collaborated and admire, the greater impacts and applications of social urbanism are evaluated. These shared opinions strengthen the significance of this work and affirm our joint values and visions for the global urbanization challenges we are confronting in the 21st-century, and which continue into the future.

In the end, these perceptions reflect on firsthand experiences that further support the premises of social urbanism. Born in London to a family of Chilean and British descent, and having lived in Santiago during my childhood and adolescent years, to have later been exiled to the United States during the Nixon-Pinochet era, I offer my own ideas over how the landscape shapes us. As a foreigner and as an urbanist in search of responses to the challenges confronting spatial planning in our time, the principles behind social urbanism provide an alternative vision, as well as the impetus for a global, social movement, for practicing and teaching the intricate connections between geography and social equity, and therefore for redirecting us toward a transformative new world.

By the time I had finished writing this book, the COVID-19 (Coronavirus) pandemic became a global syndrome affecting communities worldwide. The publishing deadline and restrictions at the time prevented me from ably expounding on these issues, although it seems clear that the advocacy for social and spatial reform through this work has been heightened by the detriment of our social distancing and isolation. We are understanding through this ultimate environmental crisis that we can only move forward through our mutual best practices, where "we are all in this together", as we explore the possibilities for the future.

INTRODUCCIÓN

El esplendor geográfico y la naturaleza enigmática del terreno de Latino América nos ha ofrecido una fuente inagotable de riqueza y gloria. Olvidada como un capricho, culpable por su propia subordinación, la narrativa tradicional sobre Latino América ha omitido frecuentemente una comprensión más profunda sobre las relaciones ecológicas y espaciales forjadas en estos territorios. Detrás de las poderosas montañas escarpadas, a lo largo de las abundantes cuencas hidrológicas, y de la rica flora y fauna, los recursos naturales producidos por la ardua labor de los pueblos indígenas y las culturas esclavizadas, le han proporcionado a Europa y a los Estados Unidos comodidades y un alto nivel de vida inalcanzables para el disfruto del pueblo. En respuesta a una posición tan dividida, este trabajo ofrece una visión alternativa, donde el encanto mágico del paisaje no es el culpable; sino donde existe un "espacio cultural," formado e influenciado por la geografía regional, dándole significado a su comunidad y permitiendo la coexistencia de un intercambio productivo entre el espacio habitable y los valores sociales de la humanidad.

Este libro sugiere nuestros nuevos compromisos con el Siglo XXI, ofreciendo una visión más equitativa sobre el desarrollo urbano, para informar a ciertos políticos, urbanistas, arquitectos y paisajistas, profesores y estudiantes, así como para las comunidades que creen que el futuro de nuestros espacios públicos debe ser reconocidos mutuamente para que podamos proveer y participar en un escenario global más humano. El urbanismo social, definido por medio de un enfoque socio-político y un acercamiento práctico para la globalización urbana, deriva de una estrategia de planificación y un portafolio de proyectos en respuesta a la crisis social en Medellín, Colombia durante las últimas décadas del Siglo XX. Por medio del trabajo expuesto aquí, el urbanismo social se expande como una visión global que considera los valores culturales de cada dado lugar como interconectados con el paisaje geográfico de la región, y, por lo tanto, como las fuerzas impulsoras detrás de los futuros modelos de globalización y expansión urbana.

Un viaje a través del paisaje robusto de Latino América revela cómo la interrupción entre la geografía y la cultura ha llevado a la degradación de las sociedades Indígenas y Latina Americanas, y a la negligencia de los marcos de planificación resultantes durante más de cinco siglos. Se entiende como la imposición de la colonización española y el imperialismo europeo, y la magnitud de la corrupción derivada de las estrategias de desarrollo internacional, han superado constantemente las agendas locales e inclusivas que deben orientarse hacia el progreso regional. Impulsados por la codicia de estranjeros, a través de la extracción de los recursos más puros de la tierra y de su gente, se ve una historia más clara de cómo el desarrollo local en Latino América ha fallado por tanto tiempo. Los intereses políticos y económicos de los Estados Unidos, como el siguiente capítulo, se presentan a través de los intereses de empresas capitalistas que han dominado los territorios Latinoamericanos por más de un siglo, y que continúan aprisionando los recursos de esta región, oprimiendo a sus comunidades hasta hoy en día.

Para profundizar, Medellín, situada en el centro del Valle de Aburrá en Colombia, es explorada en más detalle para analizar cómo su ubicación geográfica, tal como sus montañas, su carácter tributario, por ejemplo, se relacionan con su evolución histórica, política y económica. Los patrones de migración del pueblo agrario de los Aburrae, desde las montañas hasta el valle, a lo largo del Río Medellín, y su regreso a la ladera, indican un curso natural y un modelo de asentamiento que han sido interrumpidos como el resultado de esquemas de desarrollo invasivos. Los resultados han llegado a soluciones erráticas y a un lugar donde la comunidad ha quedado desconectada física y culturalmente, teniendo que, en vez, rendirse al crimen, la violencia y al terror.

Los resultados de revitalización de Medellín han sido reconocidos mundialmente. Inicialmente como el peor lugar del mundo, y más recientemente, como un sueño urbanístico; esta es una ciudad donde abundan proyectos y tácticas en el urbanismo, haciendo referencia a ellos como si fueran a la cúspide de resolver el dilema del desarrollo en Latino América. Por medio de un proceso participativo, bilateral entre los líderes de la ciudad y la comunidad de Medellín, junto con una serie de proyectos de planificación estratégica, sistemas de tránsito, edificios y programas culturales, el urbanismo social ofrece lecciones valiosas para transformar una ciudad económica, social y políticamente fracturada, en un verdadero renacimiento.

Mientras las maravillas de la época de Medellín en los últimos 10 años imparten una visión importante hacia los planes futuros para el desarrollo urbano, estos se analizan en función a los parámetros de planificación de más largo plazo para comprender el valor fundamental y la replicabilidad de estas tácticas hacia zonas de urbanización comparables. En Medellín, el enfoque inclusivo y los proyectos de planificación y arquitectura implementados a través del urbanismo social, han señalado una pauta hacia un cambio sociocultural, pero estas maniobras aún no han logrado resolver la discordia de la ciudad, ni del país, por períodos prolongados. La verdad del asunto es que los intereses de inversión permanecen en las manos del Norte Global, sobre un interés local, recreando escenarios del pasado donde la comunidad y los recursos de las regiones continúan siendo violados, por lo tanto, repitiendo prácticas socioeconómicas igualmente desarticuladas, y perpetuando una paradoja espacial desalineada.

A través de una visión del urbanismo social más amplia, implementado no sólo por medio de procesos políticos y de una multitud de proyectos urbanísticos para el conforme de la comunidad, sino que también con un énfasis crítico hacia la geografía regional y local, se encuentran los elementos inherentes para el desarrollo urbano; aquí ocurre la re-contextualización necesaria del espacio. Esto permite una dirección plausible donde se restaura la intimidad entre el paisaje y la cultura. Además, al darnos cuenta de que hoy estamos todos conectados por una "cultura colectiva," con ecologías globales, economías y esferas sociopolíticas superpuestas, se abre la posibilidad hacia un marco integrado, con una visión renovadora para erradicar la brecha que ha delineado una división entre el Norte con El Sur Global. Aquí se identifica un momento ideal formado dentro de perspectivas colectivas para afectar el desarrollo urbano, reformulado por nuestra mutua agencia, donde es posible reconsiderar la equidad espacial.

Un proceso pedagógico que guía a diseñadores urbanos y a profesionales emergentes con experiencias de multi-contextos, aporta a estas prácticas y proyectos de urbanismo social. Estudios académicos ubicados en Medellín, Colombia, realizados entre estudiantes de diseño de Colombia y de los Estados Unidos, examinan ciertos esquemas de urbanismo y de la expansión en los ámbitos rurales, rurales-urbanos, y urbanos. Estos estudios se fijan en el principio subyacente de que los futuros modelos del desarrollo urbano deben ser informados por un análisis y una comprensión más profunda sobre el paisaje geográfico y regional, donde estos serán influenciados por la comunidad, revelando sus delicados detalles, y las profundas raíces de sus costumbres.

Seis años de participación en estas colaboraciones académicas, internacionales, han invitado a estudiantes a considerar los distintos parámetros sociopolíticos, económicos y ambientales de Medellín y sus alrededores.

Las cualidades únicas del paisaje regional, y de las comunidades, se consideran, tal como las experiencias in-situ, ofreciendo valiosa y pertinente información sobre las urgentes ideologías orientadas y respondiendo hacia un paradigma de diseño global.

Los puntos de vista de múltiples colegas y expertos en diferentes campos dictan una introspección sobre el valor y la implementación del urbanismo social. Compartiendo disciplinas, e incluyendo teóricos urbanísticos, ciertos políticos, científicos, antropólogos y líderes comunitarios con quienes he colaborado y a cuales admiro, se evalúan los mayores impactos y aplicaciones del urbanismo social. Estas opiniones refuerzan la importancia de este trabajo y afirman nuestros valores y visiones colectivos, para los desafíos de urbanización que enfrentamos en el Siglo XXI y que continúan en nuestro futuro.

Al final, estas ideas reflejan experiencias de primera mano que respaldan aún más las bases sobre el urbanismo social y sus meritos. Nacida en Londrés de una familia de ascendencia chilena e inglesa, y habiendo vivido en Santiago, Chile durante mi infancia y adolescencia, para luego haber sido exiliada a los Estados Unidos durante la era de Nixon-Pinochet, ofrezco mis propias ideas sobre cómo el paisaje nos forma. Como extranjera, y como urbanista en busca de respuestas a los desafíos que enfrenta la planificación espacial en nuestro tiempo, los principios detrás del urbanismo social definen una visión alternativa, así como el impulso para un movimiento social global; para guiar y emprender las conexiones inseparables que existen entre la geografía y la equidad social, y, por lo tanto, para poder redirigirnos hacia un nuevo mundo transformativo.

Cuando terminé de escribir este libro, la pandemia de COVID-19 (Coronavirus) se convirtió en un síndrome global que ha afectado a todas las comunidades del mundo. Las fechas y restricciones de publicación en ese momento me impidieron exponer hábilmente sobre estos temas, aunque es evidente que la propuesta de la reforma social y espacial expuesta en este trabajo se hace mas relevante por nuestro aislamiento y distanciamiento social. A medida que entendemos que esta es una crisis del medio ambiente sin precedentes, queda claro que solo se podrá resolver por medio de nuestra colaboración, donde "estamos todos juntos en esto", mientras exploramos las posibilidades para el futuro.

LATIN AMERICA

A Geographical Overview

1

LATIN AMERICA
a Geographical Overview

As partners of the great North American continent, the United States and Mexico share a lengthy sliver of land, measuring over three thousand kilometers.[1] With the U.S. sitting to the north, and Mexico to the south, the dry and barren desert-soil characterizes both sides, as the landscape runs through the two countries, sharing similar ecologies derived from one universal, natural system. El Rio Bravo del Norte marks a pronounced stretch, of over two thousand kilometers[2] separating Mexico from the U.S. El Rio Grande is the line in the sand.

Representing not only a clear geographical boundary between El Paso, Texas, and Ciudad Juárez, Mexico, the Rio Grande delineates the broader division established by the political supremacy of one country, over the socio-economic development and autonomy of another. The fracture results from a narrow view of power, ruled by political consequences rather than by the strength of geographical and cultural virtues.

The Brandt Line separates the Global North from the Global South, based on GDP per capita. It was first proposed by Willy Brandt, former German Chancellor, in the 1980s. The line is drawn primarily at 30°N above the equator, with deviations due north and south, suggesting all countries south of the line are less developed than those to the north.

Preceding page: Sketch of Latin America's coastal elevation profile and dominance of the Andes Mountains, *María Bellalta*.

By contrast, this exact band across the U.S.-Mexico border also marks the northernmost perimeter forming the amalgamation and union among North, Central, and South America, together with the Caribbean Islands, constituting Latin America.[a,3] Unlike the uniform character between El Paso and Ciudad Juárez, however, the eco-regions that describe these north-central-south land masses and sister islands fluctuate noticeably.

From aquatic species, to varied soil composition and geomorphology; from high to low topographic features resulting in intensive hydrological patterns and distinct biomes throughout, the composition of Latin America is based on the ecological and social diversity derived from these shared landscapes.

Mexico, shaped by the Pacific Ocean to its west, and the Gulf Coast brushing with the Yucatan Peninsula and the Caribbean Sea to the east, is demarcated by the rocky Sierra Madres running vigorously down, from the west and east sides, framing the central plateau in the heart of the Mexican Altiplano. Ancient civilizations ruled here over two thousand years ago,[4] where rituals and sacrifices befitting the Mayan and Aztec gods, together with pyramids, temples, and brilliant minerals, have for long recalled this as a golden region.

Though by a slighter seam, North America tightly connects to Central America at the southern border of Mexico, genteelly joining with neighboring Guatemala and Belize. These countries share similar characteristics and customs, coastal and arid mountainous regions, with volcanic soil and ruins, before meeting with El Salvador and the Mosquito Coast of Honduras and Nicaragua.

El Rio Grande is the line in the sand. Representing not only a clear geographical boundary between El Paso, Texas, and Ciudad Juárez, Mexico, the Rio Grande delineates the broader division established by the political supremacy of one country, over the socio-economic development and autonomy of another.

a   There has been deep debate over the term "Latin America," from Napoleon III's desire to claim the French occupation of Mexico (1830), over British Imperialism, through a shared Latin background with former Spanish and Portuguese colonies; to Latin America being initially referenced by Chilean writer and sociologist Francisco Bilbao during his speech in Paris on June 22, 1865, proclaiming that "the union is the true patriotism of the Americans of the South.... This union which takes the form of a confederation of the South, watered by the Amazon and the Plata and shaded by the Andes, is the picture of the American and Latin identity, which will perpetuate the race and permit the creation of the great American nation.... Only this union...can hold back the imperialism of the United States."

Amid the vast Pacific Ocean and Caribbean Sea, with extended arms, Costa Rica and Panama link Central America to South America through the Darién forest, brilliantly green and lush, with tropical fruits and birds of paradise. To the northeast, between Central and South America, Latin America welcomes the Caribbean Islands, including Cuba, Haiti, Puerto Rico, the Dominican Republic, Trinidad and Tobago, and many more, floating preciously in the calypso sea, where exotic food, lively music and dance have traversed from Europe, the Americas, and afar from Africa.

Over seven thousand kilometers[5] of frisky Pacific coastline crush against the insistent, contoured edge of the rugged Cordillera de los Andes, outlining Latin America's distinct topographic traits along its Southern Cone. As the longest mountain range, this geographical wonder begins in northern Venezuela, running through Colombia and Ecuador, down to Peru in honor of Inti (Incan sun god), to Argentina where the Aconcagua summit reaches nearly seven thousand meters,[6] before arriving to the end of the world, in the southern tip of Chile. The omnipresence of this landscape sets it apart, in many respects, protecting South America with a contiguous, pronounced frontier, as with a seductive veil, creating a warm and quiet aura, to perfect the wine-filled valleys, hidden behind.

In the interior, at one thousand meters high,[7] the towering Angel Falls flow toward Venezuela's Orinoco River before reaching the Atlantic; and through Colombia, the ridges of the Andes open wide, splitting into several strands, peaking at Ecuador's Chimborazo mountain, with over six thousand meters[8] in altitude. The lowlands collect the heavy rainfall from the tropics, depositing the fresh water into the Magdalena and Esmeralda Rivers, northbound, toward the Caribbean. The Guianas and Suriname, together with Peru and Bolivia, flow in the opposite direction, gathering runoff from over one thousand tributaries that travel east, feeding one-fifth of the area's prominent river basin. As the final confluence of multiple rivers carrying over 20% of the globe's ravine discharge,[9] and as the widest and longest stream-bed, the Amazon River in Brazil is formed, before finally arriving to the vast Atlantic. Here too, Latin and Afro-descendants characterize the colorful and exuberant region, distinguishing a profuse area of South America, where the Amazon Forest reigns. Brazil occupies the largest area of any country in Latin America, with 8.5 million square kilometers of land;[10] 60% is classified by forest floors, including rivers, and 30% by agricultural production,[11] providing the country and Earth with the richest, most diverse biosphere in existence.

Along this eastern port, the region stretches, descending, becoming low, to meet the Atlantic Ocean, where the highlands of the New World were once made to bow to the European kingdom of the Old World. El Río de la Plata, between Argentina and Uruguay, provides the hidden passage into the heart of the hinterland, crossing the grassy pampas before reaching the marsh plains of landlocked Paraguay. Bolivia, surrounded as well, sits high up over the deep ores that lie below, where long ago the secret key to the fountain of silver once filled the Spanish coffers of Potosí.

Latin America traverses fourteen thousand kilometers from north to south,[12] with a shifting landscape of arid desert, volcanic, rugged mountains, onto wetlands and tropical forests, to expansive lake districts and culminating in brisk pine forests. Transcending from coast to coast, imprinting the connections of people to the landscape, transformative values are framed, expressed through the camaraderie of Latin American communities, who together celebrate the higher culture of this part of the world.

Roraima Savanna
Guianan Uplands/ Tepuis
Rupununi Savanna
Guyana Low Mountains
Amazon Estuary
Tocantin Hills/Tablelands
Gurupi Plains
Northern Maranhão Plains
Northern Piauí Plains
Northeastern Caatinga
Roraima Plains
Upper Rio Negro/ Campinas
Váreza/Igapó
Amazon Flat Plains
Amazon Upland Plains
Southwestern Amazonian Plains
Mixed Forest Plains
Upper Xingu Depression
Mato Grosso Savanna
Araguaia Depression
Guapore Plains/Hills
Pantanal
Southern Cerrado Tablelands
Northern Humid Chaco
Western Inland Atlantic Mixed Forest
Araucaria Tablelands
Campos/Northern Pampas
Uruguay Lowland
Northeastern Cerrado
Caatinga transition
Western Caatinga
Diamantina Hills/ Low Mountains
Eastern Inland Atlantic Mixed Forest
Brazilian Atlantic Coastal Forest

Amazon and Coastal Lowland
Mixed Forest and Savanna
Cerrado/Caatinga

ECO-REGIONS OF BRAZIL

250
0   500km

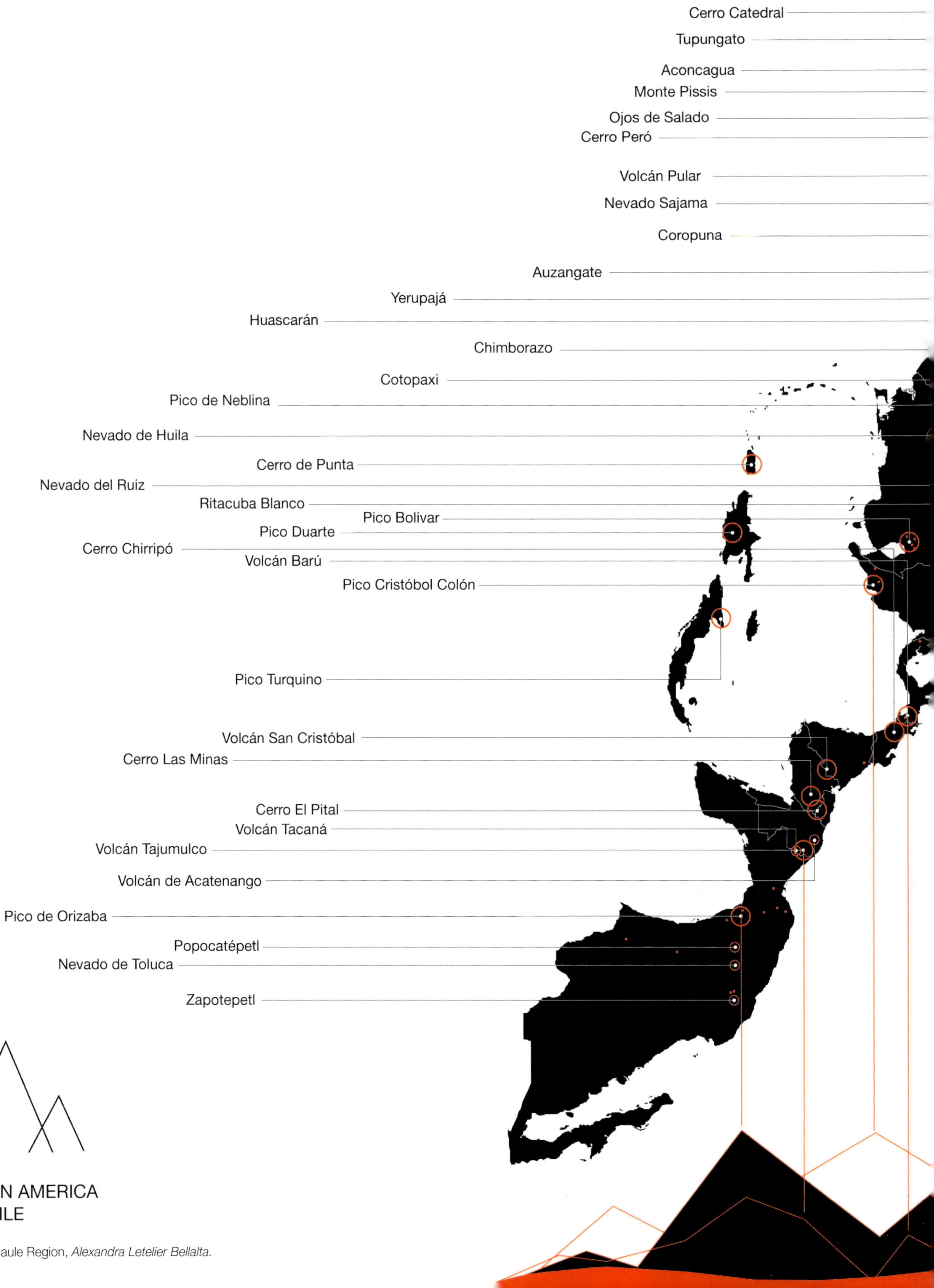

Cerro Catedral
Tupungato
Aconcagua
Monte Pissis
Ojos de Salado
Cerro Peró
Volcán Pular
Nevado Sajama
Coropuna
Auzangate
Yerupajá
Huascarán
Chimborazo
Cotopaxi
Pico de Neblina
Nevado de Huila
Cerro de Punta
Nevado del Ruiz
Ritacuba Blanco
Pico Bolivar
Pico Duarte
Cerro Chirripó
Volcán Barú
Pico Cristóbol Colón
Pico Turquino
Volcán San Cristóbal
Cerro Las Minas
Cerro El Pital
Volcán Tacaná
Volcán Tajumulco
Volcán de Acatenango
Pico de Orizaba
Popocatépetl
Nevado de Toluca
Zapotepetl

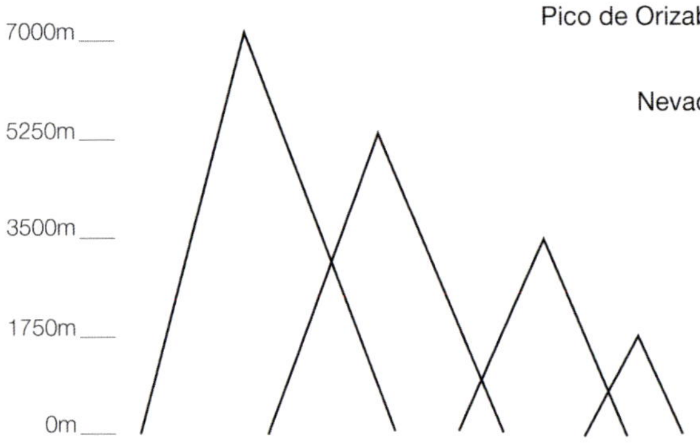

7000m
5250m
3500m
1750m
0m

MAJOR MOUNTAIN PEAKS OF LATIN AMERICA
NORTH / SOUTH ELEVATION PROFILE

Preceding Pages: Reserva Nacional Altos de Lircay, Maule Region, *Alexandra Letelier Bellalta*.

500
0   1000km

7000m
5250m
3500m
1750m
0m

TERRAIN PROFILE OF LATIN AMERICA

500

0   1000km

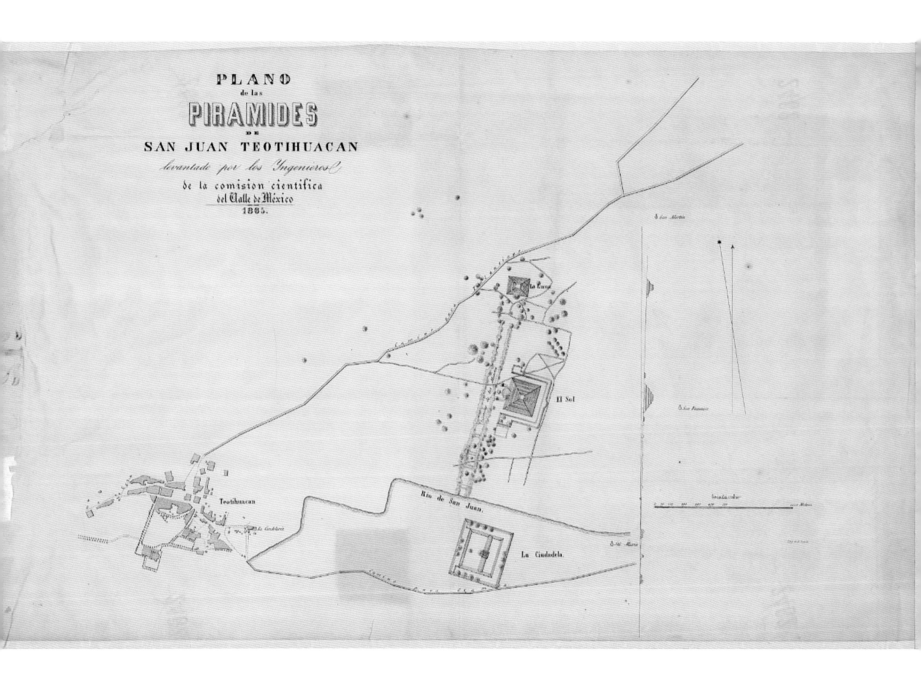

1865 plan and section of Las Pirámides de San Juan Teotihuacán, *Ramon Almaraz, Mapoteca Manuel Orozco y Berra.*

FIG-22

MAPA DE TECCIZTLAN, ACÓLMAN, TEOTIHUACAN, Y TEPECHPAN, CORREGIMIENTO DE TECCIZTLAN, ARZOBISPADO DE MEXICO, 1580

1580 map of Tecciztlán, Acólman, Teotihuacán, and Tepéchpan in Mexico, *Mapoteca Manuel Orozco y Berra.*

Conquests of the 15th Century

Spanish and European Conquistadores did not imagine that their invasion of Latin America would transform everyday life for eternity. When they plundered off in search of land and resources with which to expand their kingdom, the New World in the west was not recognized as a place inhabited by native communities who celebrated rituals derived from the form and composition of this intriguing landscape. The splendid character of the region was missed beyond the immediate monetary value and wealth it could provide the masters of the Old World. Concerned over their dependence for commodities from the Far East, from the mundane to the insidious, from salt and pepper, herbs and spices, pearls and cloth, to arms, Spanish Catholics instead aimed to further their reign by acquiring greater assets, even over the forgone destiny of those to whom the land truthfully belonged. As a continuation of the Holy Inquisition and as part of the crusading wars of medieval Spain, in 1492 Pope Alexander VI appointed Queen Isabella of Castile the owner of the New World, "extending God's reign over the earth,"[13] forevermore disrupting and usurping the origins of Latin America.

During the Treaty of Tordesillas[b] in 1494, the Pope drew a simple, "imaginary line,"[14] decreeing this the west-most point of which would belong to New Spain. Portugal would thereby occupy Latin American territories east of the Canary Islands, where Martim Affonso de Sousa established the first Portuguese communities on Brazil's east coast. Hernán Cortés, Spanish conquistador and first governor of New Spain, first arrived to Cuba before making his way to Mexico, where together with Pedro de Alvarado, the intrusion through Central America continued. Alvarado was appointed governor of Guatemala, as he successfully continued with the takeover of Honduras, El Salvador, and Guatemala. The multiple points of entry made for a clever invasion, infiltrating from the top, into the central regions, then reaching Cuzco of the Inca Empire (modern Peru), to the Atacama Desert, where Pedro de Valdivia eventually conquered Santiago de Chile. At long last, Ferdinand Magellan and his men, at the very south, returned home to Spain with mesmerizing news of vivid wonders, all the glitter and gold, encountered through navigating the immense Atlantic and Pacific Oceans.

Despite the fact that these European invasions reflect upon an over-simplification of the profound traditions of long-established communities and the broader ecological value of their Latin American nations, elsewhere, connections to the landscape have abounded since the beginning of time. Evidenced in Mexico, and extending as far back as the 1st-century CE, Teotihuacán,[15] the City of Gods, was erected as a religious center characterized by astonishing architectural forms made of 60-meter-tall pyramids reaching up to the sky, built from the local stone and hand-made adobe bricks covered in brightly colored limestone. These practices influenced Mayan and later Mesoamerican cultures of the pre-Columbian era, who adopted similar customs of building pyramids as temples and tombs to commemorate the gods. With associations to the natural essence of the area, the indigenous people drew celestial inspiration from the cosmos and the eclipsing sky, from the red and light tones of the earth, the open sea, and the grassy reeds that sprouted, providing maize, beans, chilies, chocolate, and later sugar. Crops were cultivated using a raised bed system to collect irrigation and yield the harvest. Gold and silver, along with colorful bird feathers, were worked to create decorative jewelry for adornment, and as art pieces, indicative of the region's natural soil capacity to provide lustrous and exotic resources.

Following similar traditions, built by Aztecs much later during the 12th-century, Tenochtitlán, the city-state sitting over the central lake plateau in Mexico, was viewed by the conquistadores much differently; not as an ancient city nor agricultural society having been established from the roots of the ground upon which it stood, but rather as an idealized place. Filled by desirable ephemera, made of "floating gardens, zoos of exotic tropical animals, and an enormous privileged religious and political elite, bedecked in gold, jewels and exotic feathers...no city in Europe could rival (Tenochtitlán) in wealth, power, beauty and size."[16] The Spanish quest was irresistible; the revenue, not to mention opulence, drawn from these territories benefitted Spain and its entire Kingdom of God. Employing several forms of brutality for the takeover, a quarter of a million indigenous people were killed; murder, starvation, and disease was worth nothing less than pure gold, and nothing more than pure greed. Those who survived were forced to surrender and serve on encomiedas,[c] working tirelessly with inadequate food or pay. The same stones used to build the pyramids were tumbled, only to be reused by the Aztecs themselves as they were forced to build Spain's Catholic Cathedral.

b   Pope Alexander VI drew a line of colonial demarcation in 1493, at 38° longitude. The Treaty of Tordesillas moved the line east to 46° longitude, after Portugal's King John II negotiated for more territory in the Americas, while maintaining Portuguese rule over the Eastern coast of Africa.

c   The Spanish forced the indigenous populations into a form of labor called encomienda, whereby they had to provide services in farming, mining, building construction, domestic work, and monetary tributes in exchange for protection, Christian doctrine, and decent treatment. The reality involved brutal exploitation and the removal of indigenous lands from their rightful owners.

de Almagro 1535
Pizarro 1531/33
Magellan 1519
Cortés 1510
Columbus 1502
Columbus 1498
Columbus 1496
Columbus 1492

Aztec, Maya, Inca Empires

Spain

Portugal

ROUTES OF SPANISH and PORTUGESE CONQUEST

500

0   1000km

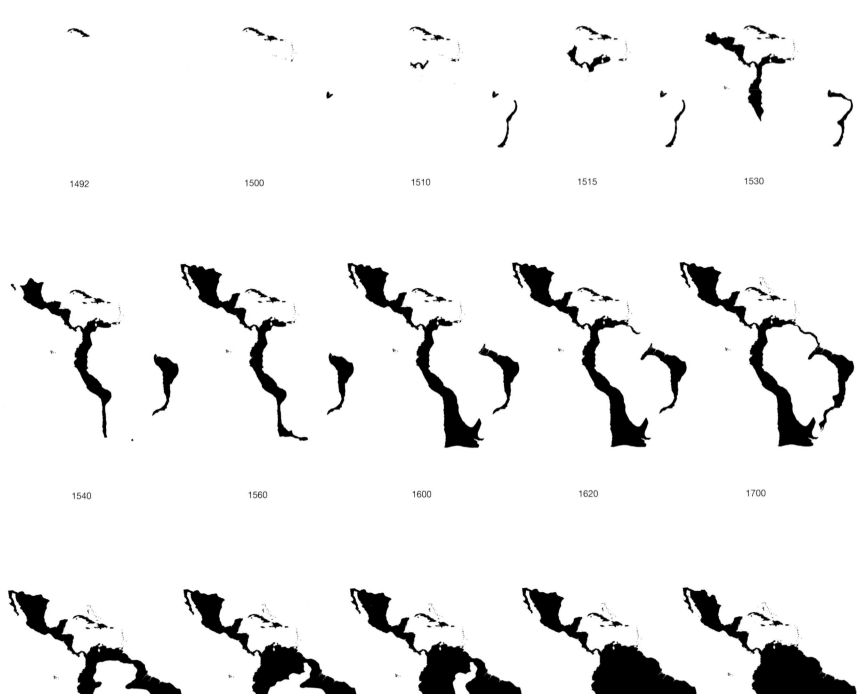

1492   1500   1510   1515   1530

1540   1560   1600   1620   1700

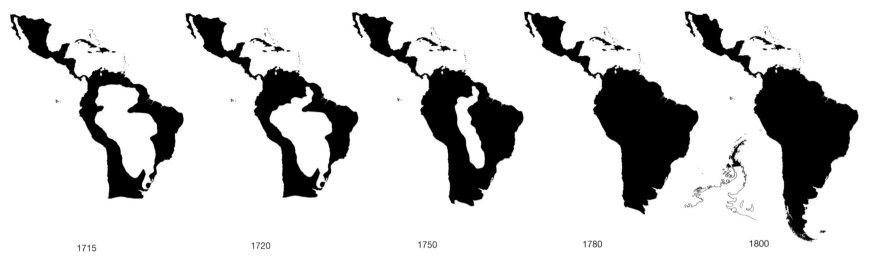

1715   1720   1750   1780   1800

SPANISH and PORTUGESE COLONIZATION 1492-1800
THE NEW WORLD

2500

0   5000km

SPANISH and PORTUGESE COLONIZATION
EXTENTS BY 1800 IN LATIN AMERICA

500
0   1000km

In the end, Tenochtitlán was put to rest under the footprint of colonial Mexico City, while digging for gold and silver ensued with jewels and decorative arts swapped by the Spanish in place of shiny currency stolen from the earth, allowing the conquerors to impose ultimate power on the land.

These practices marked the "New Era," with land takeovers, services, and valuable goods transported by sea from the New World back to the Old, benefitting far away lords and ladies to relish among their late 16th-century coteries.

The colonial patterns initiated by the Spanish and Portuguese were pronounced, with multiple points of origin and sources being identified throughout Latin America. Not only gold (Au), but silver (Ag) were mined in exorbitant quantities in Zacatecas and Guanajuato, Mexico, and in Potosí, Bolivia.[17] Beaten down miners dropped to the ground from not only having their souls plucked, but from exhaustion, cracked skin, and the poisonous, sparkling silica. For the colonist, on the other hand, these rich elements provided valuable sources used for coins and mercantilism; for phenomenal status symbols, from armor, statues, and fine jewelry to fanciful tableware. The precious metals went on to tease and quench the appetites of the French, Dutch, and English imperialists who had arrived, overruling the Spanish and claiming the throne while collecting the merchandise. The quest only intensified during the late sixteen to mid-seventeen hundreds, with captured and displaced slaves forced to mine every last carat of metallic ores to appease the frenzy. Uprooted, violated, and often killed, indigenous people with distinct cultures were shipped from Africa to Central and South America, and to the Caribbean Islands, ensuring the speed of production. The trend continued, with slave trafficking directly from Africa to Britain, furthering the economic development in Europe through low costs of local labor and production.

Right: Small-scale gold mining using the traditional Batea, *Stephen Ferry.*

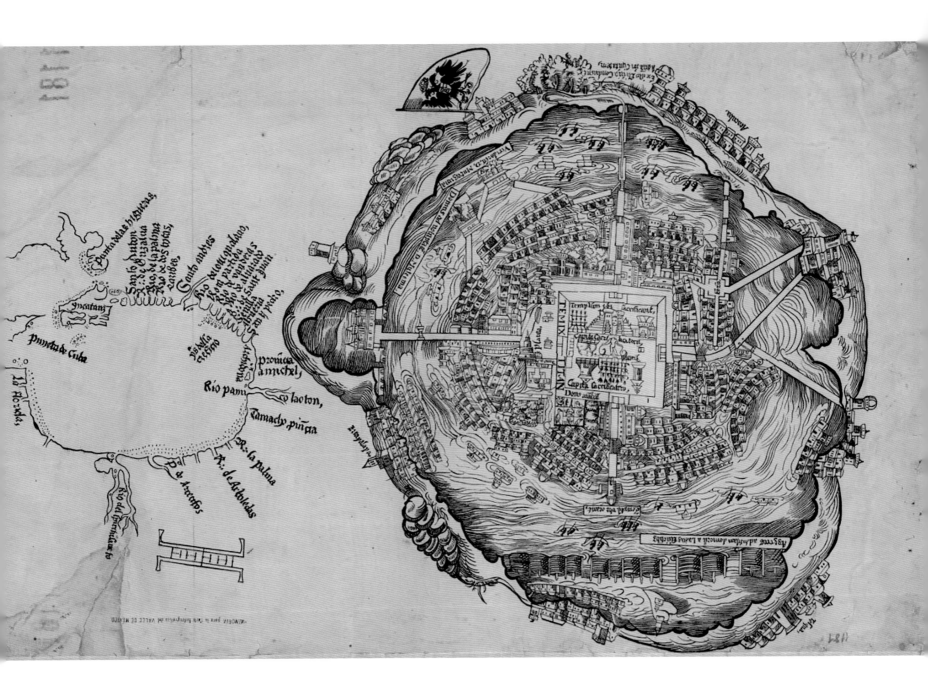

44 Above: 1523 map of Tenochtlán, attributed to *Hernán Cortés, Mapoteca Manuela Orozco y Berra.*

Sonora
Los Alamos (Canada)
AuRico (Canada)

Zacatecas
Minera San Javier
Glamis Gold (Canada)
Metallica Resources (Canada)

Colima
GABFER (Canada)
Consorcio Minero Benito Juarez
Peña Colorada
Ternium (Italy)
Mittalstel

Morelos
Alamos Gold (Canada)

San Luis Potosi
Glamis Gold (Canada)

Cocula
Media Luna
Teck Resources (Canada)

Guatemala
Kappes Kassiday (USA)
Exploraciones Mineras
Entre Mares (Canada)
Goldcorp Inc. (Canada)
Glamis Gold (Canada)
Minera San Rafael (Canada)
Tahoe Resources (Canada)

Nicaragua
B2 Gold Corp. (Canada)
Corazon Gold Corp. (Canada)

Costa Rica
B2 Gold Corp. (Canada)
Glencair Gold Corp. (Canada)
Metales Procesados

Panama
Iberian Resources Corp. (Canada)
Petaquilla Minerals
Inmet Mining Corp. (Canada)
Minera Panama
Korea Panama Mining (Korea)
Teck Resources (Canada)

Ecuador
Ecuacorriente S.A.
CRCC-Tongguan (China)
Tongling Nonferrous Metals (China)
China Railway Corp. (China)
Int'l African Mining Gold Corp. (Canada)
INV Metals (Canada)
Kinross-Aurelian (Canada)
Junefield (China)

Peru
Newmont Mining Corp. (USA)
Compañía Minera Buenaventura
Barrick Gold Corp. (Canada)
Minera Yanacocha
Sumitono Corp. (Japan)
Hochschild Mining
Doe Rn (USA)

Chile
BHP Billiton (Australia)
Asarco Inc.
CODELCO
Angle American (UK)
Rio Tinto (Australia)
Freeport McMoran (USA)
Barrick Gold Corp. (Canada)
Sumitono Corp. (Japan)
Minera Nevada
Pan Pacific Copper (Japan)
Teck Resources (Canada)
Dayton (Canada)
New Gold (Canada)
Goldcorp Inc. (Canada)

Dominican Republic
GoldQuest (Canada)
Barrick Gold (Canada)
Goldcorp Inc. (Canada)

Honduras
Mineras La Capa
Velomato
Glamis Gold (Canada)
Entre Mares
Goldcorp Inc. (Canada)
Greenstone Minera (Canada)
Yamana Gold Inc. (Canada)
Aura Gold (Canada)

Colombia
Gran Colombia Gold
Sunward Resources (Canada)
Muriel Mining Corp. (USA)
Rio Tinto (Australia)
Jupiter S.O.M (Canada)
Continental Gold (Canada)
Anglo Gold Ashanti (S.Africa)

Brazil
Vale
Rio Paracatu Mineracao
Kinross Gold (Canada)
Nexa Resources
Votorantim Metais
Minorte
Ourominas

Peru
Brazil
Mexico
Colombia
Chile
Argentina

0 metric tons
80 metric tons
167 metric tons

1950 2020

GOLD (Au) EXTRACTION IN LATIN AMERICA

500
0   1000km

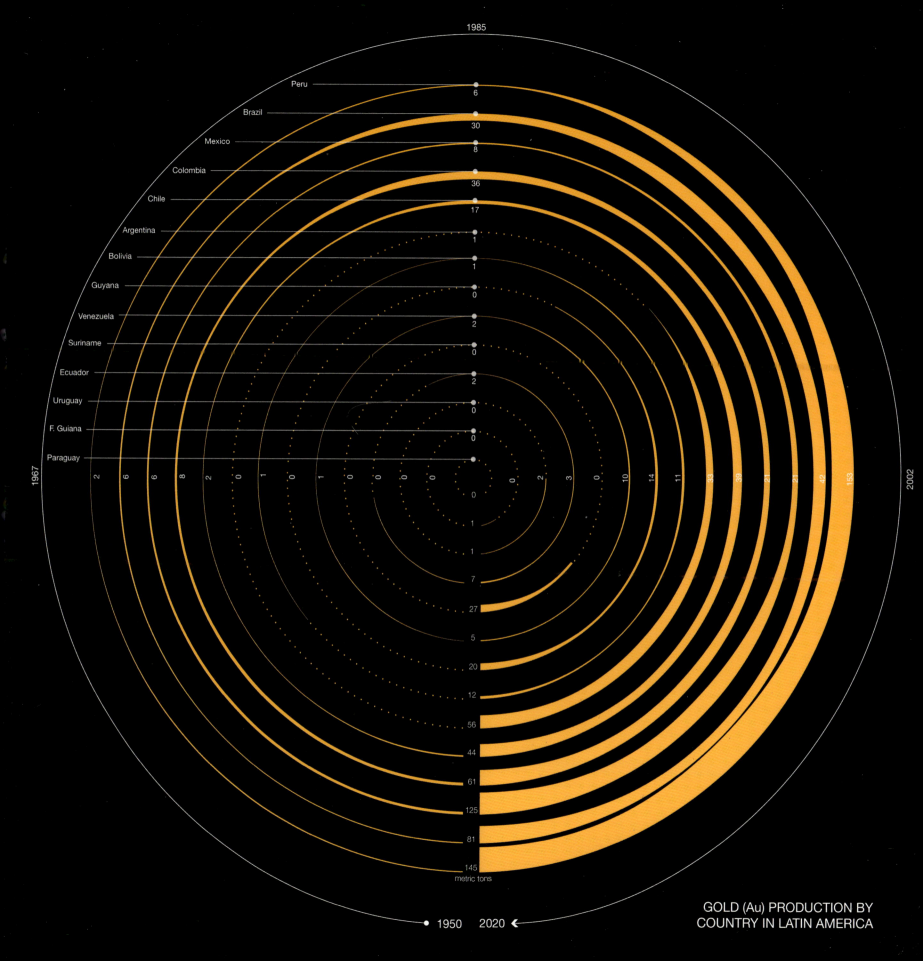

1985

Peru 6
Brazil 30
Mexico 8
Colombia 36
Chile 17
Argentina 1
Bolivia 1
Guyana 0
Venezuela 2
Suriname 0
Ecuador 2
Uruguay 0
F. Guiana 0
Paraguay

1967

2 6 6 8 2 0 1 0 1 0 0 0 0 0 2 3 0 10 14 11 33 39 21 21 42 153

2002

0
1
1
7
27
5
20
12
56
44
61
125
81
145
metric tons

1950   2020

GOLD (Au) PRODUCTION BY
COUNTRY IN LATIN AMERICA

Chihuahua
Mag Silver (Canada)
Minefinders Corp. (Canada)

Zacatecas
Pan American Silver Corp.
(Canada)
Minera Real de Angeles
ORCA mine tailings
Grupo Mexico
Goldcorp Inc. (Canada)

Pitarilla, Durango
Silver Standard (Canada)

Wirikuta Natural Reserve
Revolution Resources Corp.
First Majestic Silver Corp.

San Luis Potosi
Glamis Gold (Canada)

Michoacán
Grupo Mexico

Oaxaca
Continuum Resources
Fortuna Silver mines
Sundance Minerals Ltd. (Canada)

Santa Barbára
Breakwater
Oracle Energy Corp (Canada)
Nyrstar (Belgium)

Miramar
Glencair Gold (Canada)
Metales Procesados
B2 GOLD Corp (Canada)

San Miguel Ixtahuacan
Goldcorp Inc. (Canada)

Jutiapa
Goldcorp Inc. (Canada)

Uren River, Talamanca
Grupo Sureño

Santander
Greystar open pit mine (Canada)

Antioquia
Caramanta Conde mine (Canada)
Solvista Gold Corp. (Canada)
Medoro Resources (Canada)
B2 GOLD Corp. (Canada)
Anglo Gold Ashanti (S. Africa)

Bolivar
Salazar Resources
Curimining
Union Mining

South Ecuador
Int'l Minerals Corp. (Canada)
Cornerstone (Canada)
Int'l African Mining Gold Corp. (Canada)
INV metals (Canada)

Northern Peru
Minera Shahuindo
Rio Alto Mining ltd. (Canada)
Tahoe Resources (Canada)
Newmont Mining Corp. (USA)
INCA ONE GOLD Corp. (Canada)

Central Peru
Compañía Minera Buenaventura
Cie Minera Caudalosa
Minera Chinalco (China)
Compania Minera Antamina
Xstrata Cooper (Switzerland)
BHP Billiton (Australia)
Teck Resources Ltd. (Canada)
Mitsubishi (Japan)

Atacama Desert
BHP Billiton (Australia)
Rio Tinto (Japan)
Kinross Gold (Canada)

Potosí
Couer Mining Inc. (USA)
COMSUR
Corporacion Minera de Bolivia

San Cristobal
Sumitono Corp. (Japan)

La Joya
Newmont Mining Corp. (USA)

Dalence
Corporacion Minera de Bolivia

Caçapava do Sul
Nexa Resources
Votorantim Metais

Huasco
Barrick Gold Corp. (Canada)
Minera Nevada

Pirquitas, Jujuy
Sunshine Argentina
Silver Standard Resources (Canada)

Southern Argentina
Pan American Silver Corp. (Canada)
Tritón
Minera Santa Cruz
Hochschild Mining

Mexico
Peru
Chile
Bolivia
Argentina
Guatemala

0-100 metric tons
3,000 metric tons
6,000 metric tons

1980 2020

SILVER (Ag) EXTRACTION IN LATIN AMERICA

500

0   1000km

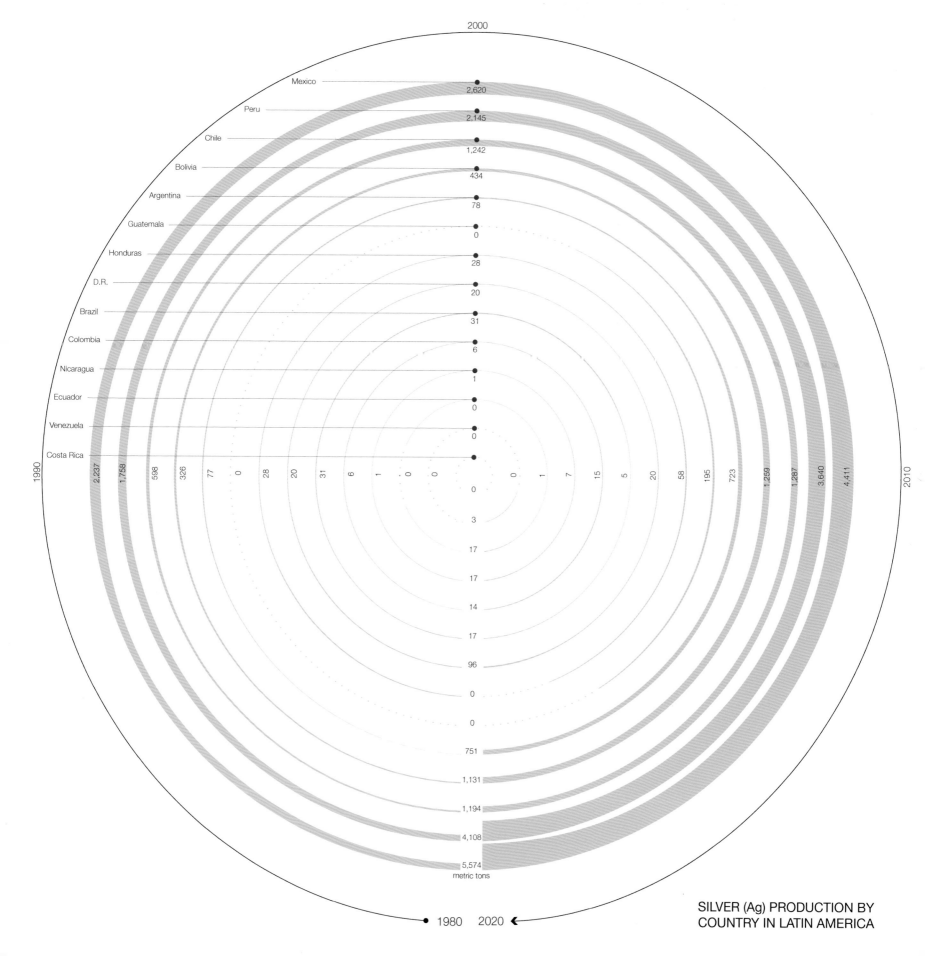

2000

Mexico 2,620
Peru 2,145
Chile 1,242
Bolivia 434
Argentina 78
Guatemala 0
Honduras 28
D.R. 20
Brazil 31
Colombia 6
Nicaragua 1
Ecuador 0
Venezuela 0
Costa Rica .....

1990

2,237 | 1,758 | 598 | 326 | 77 | 0 | 28 | 20 | 31 | 6 | 1 | 0 | 0

0 | 1 | 7 | 15 | 5 | 20 | 58 | 195 | 723 | 1,259 | 1,287 | 3,640 | 4,411

2010

0
3
17
17
14
17
96
0
0
751
1,131
1,194
4,108
5,574
metric tons

● 1980   2020 ←

SILVER (Ag) PRODUCTION BY
COUNTRY IN LATIN AMERICA

Above: Sketch of predominant trade and slave routes between the Old and New Worlds, *María Bellalta*.

THE INDUSTRIAL LANDSCAPE
The Industrial Revolution of the 18th–19th Centuries

Across the ocean, Puritans later sailed in search of the New World, far away from the narrow views of the Church of England. By resorting to the tried, albeit corrupt practices, of trading slaves from Africa for molasses in the Caribbean, only to sell West Indies rum made in Boston, the settlers gained political and economic strength. The system was repeated; "the whole process was a pumping of blood from one set of veins to another: the development of the development of some, the underdevelopment of others."[18] The slave trade provided the revenue necessary to evolve, with foundry and naval industry in Providence and Newport along the East Coast, supplying the artillery for the American Revolution, and at long last, for the independence from England.

This breaking off from the mother country meant that the monopoly of Latin America's assets benefitting Britain had reached its fulcrum. The slave triangle had broadened, resulting in riskier voyages and greater commercial competition. What the rest of Europe and New England could produce at reduced costs through slave labor, England had to exceed in order to maintain leading mercantilism and economic power. Increased productivity through manufacturing, the introduction of labor wage earnings and the promotion of international trade markets was a way to expand the enterprise. The wealth distribution shifted from the hands of a few to those of many, fueling local manufacturing, innovation, and the birth of the Industrial Revolution in Britain. As technology was invented in order to make money, Britain invested in technology that could offset the cost of production. Iron, then steel, became the new precious metals necessary to construct the machines that would duplicate human labor. With England's abundance of fossil fuels, coal became the common denominator, as the least expensive raw material to ignite the steam engines. This permitted the mechanization of labor; it fast-forwarded production and enabled Britain to regain its strength through industrial leadership. Britain's economic development plan thus shifted from one dependent on slave trade to one that relied on local manufacturing and industry instead.[19] Steam engines replaced people; engines powered machinery and, eventually, a superior industry flourished. Through the telegraph and the steam locomotive, for instance, communication and transportation transformed daily operations, providing commodities and accessibility for a preponderance of artifacts and operations delivered at unimaginable speed. These and other advanced systems influenced the labor structure, educational standards, as well as the evolution of science and industry. An era of even greater goods and services had arrived; a period, moreover, where people were magically transported farther from the origins of a slower agrarian landscape, and into the hands of the bustling, promising city.

The United States followed Britain's enterprising market, soon becoming the leading cotton producer in the world, over India, supplying England and the world's demand in the textile industry. New England factories worked seamlessly, ingeniously powered through spinning machines and looms that required less human energy. The railroad drastically changed typical life scenarios through the speed of travel, transporting dwellers from one place to another, increasing the number of people who settled, and later shaping the fabric of the city. The slaves, forced to pick the southern cotton under the foreboding sun remained a part of the antiquated equation, leaving the darkest scars that the Civil War could not abolish nor heal.

THE POLITICAL LANDSCAPE
The World Wars of the 20th Century

Three primary wars and acts of extreme aggression in the first half of the 20th-century shaped what became the Modern World and had longstanding political ramifications worldwide. The progress of the 19th-century directly led to the peril, which erupted at the turn of the 20th-century, with World War I between European countries questioning their individual prosperity as a result of the limitations of colonial and imperial land acquisition, speculating and projecting over the quantity and character of acquired colonies providing materials and services for production. As the Industrial Revolution progressed, the initial drive of status and wellbeing was overtaken by a thirst for greater technology and innovation. World War II went beyond these ideals, fiercely infiltrating into foreign territories through nuclear weapons, devastating forms of artillery produced by the very means derived from innovation and technology. And finally, the hateful genocide in the Nazi death camps against those of Jewish descent, the Roma, gypsies, people with disabilities, and other sub-cultures within the German territories was a chilling epoch of civilization. Reminiscent of the destruction by colonists of indigenous communities of the Aztec and Inca worlds of pre-Columbian times, this remains an unpardonable paradox of humankind, seeking glory, profit, and progress, but which often leads to the destruction of landscape and human life.

Right: Bombing of La Moneda presidential palace, Chilean Coup d'etat, 1973, *Biblioteca del Congreso Nacional de Chile.*

THE AGRARIAN LANDSCAPE
The Mid-20th Century

Though there has been a shift over time in the manner in which prestige and power have been produced, from the barbaric colonial and imperial land appropriations and demand for forced labor on foreign land, to later becoming a factor of Latin American resources unfairly extracted and exported in order to supply European and U.S. industry, the heavy hand inflicted upon Latin America has remained consistent. Indigenous serving *encomenderos* through forced mining and agricultural work later had their properties whisked away, having been collected and transferred to a select, fortunate group of land owners through the *latifundio*[d] land reform practices. They dictated what crops would be grown on the land, and what food would remain for the original families to survive from after harvesting the fields. The latifundistas became the new masters, only this time the lords were members of Latin American countries, men who had risen to the top as foreign agents, enticed by greed, with their destitute workers turned into peons. What is more, the land reform created a new class of slaves reincarnating the bottom of a top-tiered social hierarchy hinged to economics that were permitted to trickle down, slowly, if ever, from industrialists in the Northern Hemisphere to the latifundistas, and downward along the class pyramid. The latifundio men ensured the price of labor for harvesting the exported crops would remain unjustly low, maintaining foreign buyers' interests, while at the same time promoting a higher standard for themselves.

Agricultural products for food consumption, en masse, with bananas and sugar from Cuba and the Caribbean islands, coffee and cacao from Colombia, Venezuela, Guatemala, El Salvador, and Haiti, as well as wheat from Argentina, and later cotton from Brazil and Mexico for textiles, were harvested and exported to Europe and the U.S. Abroad, the abundance of these sweet, soft products became easily attainable not only to high-ranking bankers or industry owners, but to ordinary consumers.

The highly desirable and affordable market prices were designed to promote consumption through low importation costs, secured through tariffs imposed on Latin American countries, therefore preventing price escalation.

As industries and manufacturing expanded, products abounded, extending the real benefits of consumerism into the hands of foreign interests. The business agendas of international investors laid back at home, far removed from the economic advancement of Latin American countries. The transactions resulted in skewed international exchanges, based on the manufacturing resources and cheap labor provided by these nations for U.S. benefits, where return on local investment was purposely manipulated, if not overlooked.

---

d   The latifundio system involved large landholders holding estates of, typically, over 500 hectares, where indigenous populations and slave labor were forced to work for little to no pay. The landholders were of an elite class, and they monopolized land acquisition to maintain control over land, labor, water, markets, infrastructure, technology, and political influence.

Right: Maguey fields, Hacienda de San Antonio, Tlachotlaco, Mexico.
Following pages: Cloud forests of the Central Andes, Colombia, *Juan Camilo Jaramillo.*

Suriname
Guyana
Panama
Belize
Brazil
Peru

55% total land forest area
77.5% total land forest area
100% total land forest area

1990 2015

Biodiversity hotspot

Forest cover

Grass and Shrubland

NATIVE FOREST AND GRASSLAND IN LATIN AMERICA

500

0   1000km

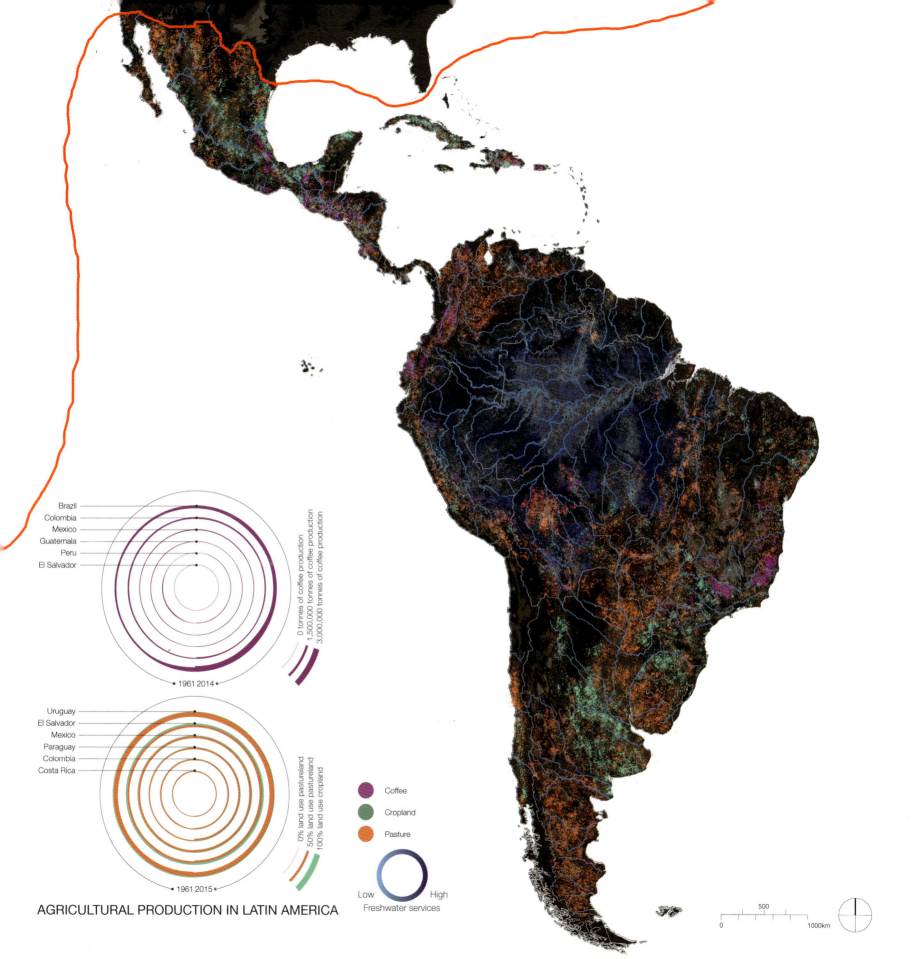

Brazil
Colombia
Mexico
Guatemala
Peru
El Salvador

0 tonnes of coffee production
1,500,000 tonnes of coffee production
3,000,000 tonnes of coffee production

1961 2014

Uruguay
El Salvador
Mexico
Paraguay
Colombia
Costa Rica

0% land use pastureland
50% land use pastureland
100% land use cropland

1961 2015

Coffee

Cropland

Pasture

Low   High
Freshwater services

AGRICULTURAL PRODUCTION IN LATIN AMERICA

500

0   1000km

Argentina*
Bolivia
Colombia
Venezuela
Peru
Mexico

0 sq. km of deforestation
1,750 sq. km of deforestation
3,500 sq. km of deforestation
*Brazil not shown, with an average outlier
of 21,266 sq. km of deforestation

1990 2020

500
0   1000km

AGRICULTURAL IMPACT ON LATIN AMERICAN NATIVE ECOSYSTEMS

Preceding pages: Millenary larch trees in the Reserva Nacional Alerce Costero, Valdivia, Chile, *Josefina Letelier Bellalta*.
Right: Small-scale farming outside Medellín, Colombia.

THE MANUFACTURING LANDSCAPE

Not only quality resources, but more of them, were required to fuel industry and to gain control of the world economy. Amidst industry and world wars, manufacturing of useful products was likewise in high demand, with rubber production and exportation, for instance, of pneumatic tires from Brazil, and slicker, faster cars mass-produced for inexpensive material costs and low wages in Brazil and Mexico, to be driven elsewhere. Steel, iron, tin, and petroleum became the next selection of ores and liquid gold for extraction, used to drive the growth in public works, roadways, and bridges in the U.S., fueling the "American Dream," and painting the country as the land of plenty. Higher employment numbers in the U.S., in turn, fed into a frantic consumer system, exponentially cultivating a vicious cycle of one class over another, proliferating a weaker labor system throughout Latin America.

In fact, the immensely diverse, agrarian landscape throughout Latin America was turned into a veritable production machine. The bountiful soil once sowed with delicious, varied fruit and vegetable crops was replaced by endless monoculture fields that could instead increase the yield of high demand products called for by other countries. The negative impact of these agrarian practices was twofold. On the first hand, an increase in coffee production through monoculture for the purpose of supplying the U.S. severely compromised the biodiversity of Latin American agrarian regions; jungles, forests, mountains, highlands, pampas, and water basins, among many more geographical features, were ecologically disturbed, while at the same time limiting the daily food of poor workers at home who were left eating low protein diets made of beans and corn. Secondly, rather than raising wages for farmers who worked overtime in the latifundios to increase production in order to supply international demand, the price of coffee was astutely lowered by foreign buyers. Maintaining the low cost of the product provided the assurance that the consumer would continue to purchase it, guaranteeing the investors' margin of profit. As the U.S. controlled the market, they too could determine the value of products, not to mention the wages set for manufacturing labor.

The practice of monoculture latifundios has continued; according to the Food and Agricultural Organization, within the current latifundio socio-agrarian structure, almost 72% of cultivated land in Latin America is owned by less than 1.5% of landowners.[20] Latifundios have become land holdings providing employment for more than a dozen workers, whose landlords have foreign interests in mind, and are therefore focused on the demand of monoculture production with food items such as coffee or sugar; minifundios, by contrast, are small farms barely sufficient for a family of two people, yet make up a substantial portion of Latin American agrarian workers. These farmers alone are certainly unable to uphold the biodiversity of the greater region.

Tijuana / 1.5 mil

Ciudad Juarez / 1.5 mil

Havana / 2.1 mil

Toluca / .5 mil

Mexico City / 21.6 mil

Santo Domingo / 3.3 mil

Guatemala City / 2.1 mil
San Salvador / 6.45 mil

Tegucigalpa / 1.1 mil

Barranquilla / 1.2 mil

Caracas / 3 mil

Managua / 1 mil

San Jose / 1.4 mil

Valencia / .9 mil

Medellín / 3.8 mil

Bogotá / 8.2 mil

Cali / 2.4 mil

Quito / 1.8 mil

Belém / 1.4 mil

Guayaquil / 2.6 mil

Manaus / 2.2 mil

Fortaleza / 4 mil

Recife / 4 mil

Maceió / 1 mil

Lima / 10.5 mil

Brasilia / 3.1 mil

La Paz / .8 mil

Cochabamba / .9 mil

Belo Horizonte / 2.6 mil

Rio de Janeiro / 13 mil

São Paolo / 12 mil

Asunción / 1.5 mil

Curitiba / 1.9 mil

Porto Alegre / 1.5 mil

Córdoba / 1.6 mil

Valparaiso / 1 mil

Santiago / 5.3 mil

Montevideo / 3.46 mil

Concepción / .8 mil

Buenos Aires / 15 mil

Densest cities per capita

"100 fastest-growing cities", 2018

URBAN CENTERS
IN LATIN AMERICA

500

0   1000km

San Pedro

Balsas

Rio Grande

Usumacinta

San Juan

Magdalena

Orinoco

Negro

Putumayo

Amazonas

Madeira

Xingu

Sao Francisco

Paraná

Paraguay

Uruguay

● Hydroelectric dam
● Irrigation dam
● Water supply dam
● Flood control dam
● Navigation dam

LOW

HIGH

Freshwater services

500

0   1000km

WATER RESOURCES AND MAJOR RIVERS IN LATIN AMERICA

Right: Lago Villarrica - Mallalafquén, Province of Cautín, Chile.
Following pages: Lagunas Altiplánicas, San Pedro de Atacama, *Josefina Letelier Bellalta*.

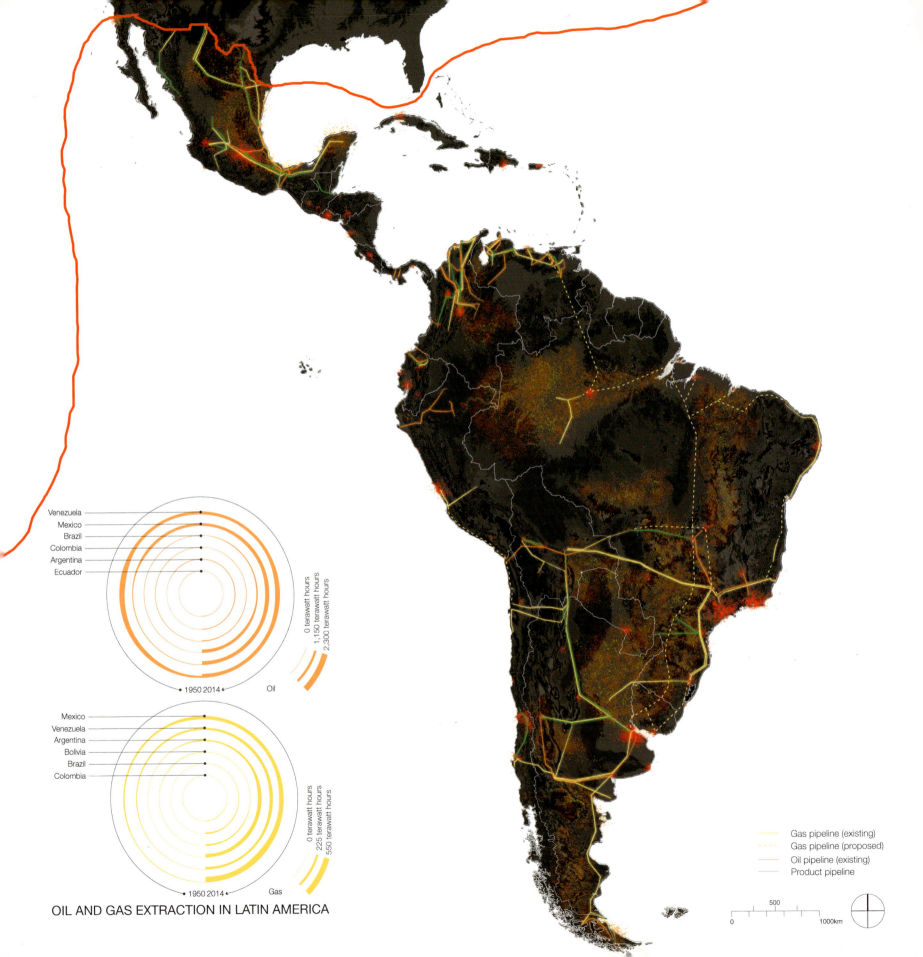

Venezuela
Mexico
Brazil
Colombia
Argentina
Ecuador

0 terawatt hours
1,150 terawatt hours
2,300 terawatt hours

1950 2014 ← Oil

Mexico
Venezuela
Argentina
Bolivia
Brazil
Colombia

0 terawatt hours
225 terawatt hours
550 terawatt hours

1950 2014 ← Gas

Gas pipeline (existing)
Gas pipeline (proposed)
Oil pipeline (existing)
Product pipeline

OIL AND GAS EXTRACTION IN LATIN AMERICA

500
0   1000km

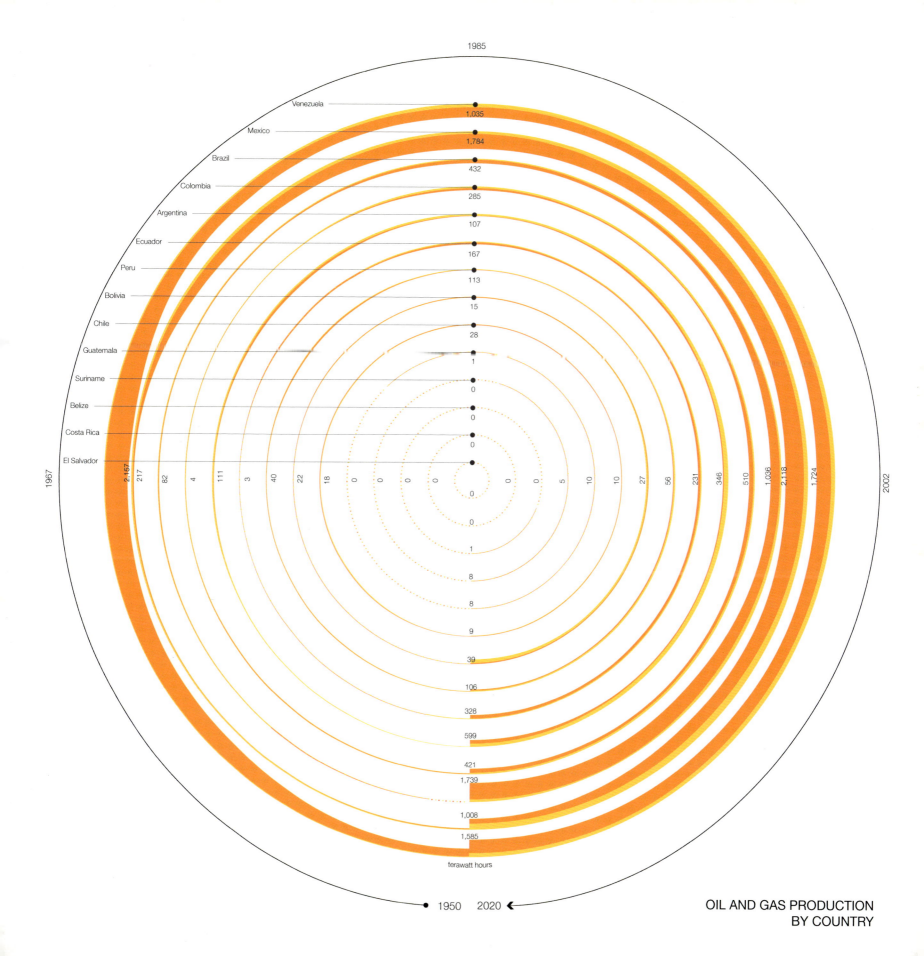

1985

Venezuela 1,035
Mexico 1,784
Brazil 432
Colombia 285
Argentina 107
Ecuador 167
Peru 113
Bolivia 15
Chile 28
Guatemala 1
Suriname 0
Belize 0
Costa Rica 0
El Salvador 0

1967

2002

2,157 217 82 4 111 3 40 22 18 0 0 0 0 0 0 5 10 10 27 56 231 346 510 1,036 2,118 1,724

0

1

8

8

9

39

106

328

599

421

1,739

1,008

1,585

terawatt hours

1950   2020

OIL AND GAS PRODUCTION
BY COUNTRY

CAPITALIST OVER NATIONALIST LANDSCAPES

In his 17th-century inquiry into the *Wealth of Nations*, Scottish political economist Adam Smith theorized that the free market would encourage prosperity while balancing losses through voluntary collaborations between producers and consumers. Planned economies dating back to the 15th-century, however, have demonstrated that feudal processes of resource extraction and exploitation of indigenous people in Latin America have perpetually deviated to the far right, disallowing a state of equilibrium between the purveyor and the buyer, or the producer and the consumer. The imbalance has instead been an advantageous formula, founded on a top-down political economy, for bolstering U.S. and Western European economic development. Even while Latin American countries reached the international forum during the mid-20th-century, albeit less apparently forced to participate in commercial trade negotiations than in the past, the invitation to partake in or receive essential benefits from their agreements in the world economic market remained tenuous. Being permitted to "sell" their agricultural and industrial materials, or receive meager pay for the manufacturing labor and hard sweat Mexican, Brazilian, and other Latin American citizens expended, may have tilted the needle slightly; marginally, though not transformationally. The crooked scheme persisted.

Several new forms of coercion ensued, with communities that remained on their farms being evicted, pushed far away into the harsh jungle to start over again or subsist, only to make room for building one more industrial plant to increase manufacturing quotas and international revenue, squeezing every last drop of energy from the locals and the land. Tantalizing, moreover, were the never-before-seen products created through manufacturing stations deployed on Latin American soil; the factories and assembly lines the local workers would mundanely operate to construct foreign automobiles, televisions, refrigerators, and the endless stream of banal artifacts serving little function to the simple life of a *campesino*.[e] These earnest farmers had once reveled in their productive landscape, otherwise living from the Earth's harvest, cultivating the generous farm-crops that would be no more.

The rise of Western Europe had always depended on the civilization of the Old World, and this period was to be no different, as capitalism had reared its head once again. In fact, since the inception of colonialism, erroneously or consciously, the primary role of the Latin American economy has been as a function of international capitalism.[21] Unfair trade tariffs were imposed on Latin American exportations, as well as on importation costs. Their natural product—were coffee, steel, petroleum, or even fresh red meat from Argentina—were purchased by the foreign market for next to nothing; the labor wages for manufacturing products for exportation, moreover, were unduly low. Taken together with the intensive costs of importing superfluous plastic products that were becoming part of the modern world and commodities in Latin America, the international operation functioned flawlessly.

The truth was that neither Central and South American countries, nor the Caribbean islands would ever prosper individually, in their own right, so long as they remained subsidiaries to the forces from the North. Pressured to reach up and to take part in the modern world's economic structure, the largest Latin American countries, Argentina, Brazil, and Mexico, for instance, envisioned economic independence from the U.S. through international investment that would enable their own industry and development. The only alternative was the nationalization of industries, branding production to boost the local economy, therefore enhancing the market opportunities, the standard of living, and thus the wellbeing of its communities. Owning its own industry meant that Latin American countries would be released from the limiting manufacturing role these nations had been relegated to in service of the North, and nationalism in Latin America, at last, could promote a thriving economy for its nations. Yet, this approach was likewise framed within an uneven playing field. National companies had to operate through huge loans, heavily weighted with high interest rates, restricting the purchase of modern technology necessary to support significant levels of local innovation and industry. Hard restrictions, moreover, were imposed on any type of national patents developed, despite how rudimentary, on the basis that because these new inventions relied on foreign parts, the new equipment proceeds should be shared with all its contributors, domestic, as well as international ones, and thus limiting local progress.

The syndrome persisted, with the production and exchange of goods passed through the "free market" favoring the prosperity of the American or European investors, though never those who owned the materials being sold, nor whom had manufactured or patented any new

---

e   Campesino typically refers to rural farmers in Latin America, and translates literally as "person of the countryside."

products. Neither the U.S. nor other European countries were interested in promoting the socio-economic development of these nations, disregarding educational opportunities and health standards that could have led to Latin America's upward mobility. The Western Block, as part of the free world era of capitalist countries, had superimposed itself again, remaining steadfast over its political and economic oligarchy, gloating, clinching its fists ever so tightly.

The ability for Brazil, or any other Latin American country that attempted to negotiate the fair sale of its products through free trade agreements failed; reaching a mutually beneficial agreement was simply impermissible. As these developing countries searched for ways to broaden and diversify their exportation market, they also fell short; their internal frameworks were compromised through imposed structural changes, impeding the ability to compete in negotiations, and therefore disallowing the countries from breaking off.

As in the past, through coercive persuasion by international thieves, those select men who had climbed to the top through the latifundio land reforms were once more enticed to conspire with foreign intruders. This time, as empowered dictators, they executed the military coup d'etats orchestrated by Washington, D.C. politicians. Others who had financial profits in the scant number of national industries, unknowingly, or perhaps blinded by evil enterprises, sold their shares to international investors, who later became the primary holders with greater assets and power, perpetuating an international rule and monopoly of the financial system. The nationalization of industry in these regions came to a halt; an excruciating era of political suppression against socio-economic reform had also come to a stop, and with it had died further notions of economic prosperity and cultural freedom.

The political coups in Latin American countries have been notorious as part of U.S. coalitions on military aid, assisting developing nations against the malignant, communist-leaning groups that have formed over the years. The truth, of course, is that these were not terrible entities; rather, these were socialist, united fronts, attempting to rescue their countries from the unstoppable oppression and extortion from the North. Guised as saviors on foreign soil to triage and provide damage control for the financial instability of international enterprises, the military paralyzed internal systems with dread, murdering thousands of innocent citizens, kidnapping others, making them disappear, while pointing the finger to the far left. The defeat of Perón in Argentina in 1955, the murder of Vargas Goulat, President of Brazil in 1954, and the later military take-over in 1965, were strategic international operations, from within, geared toward destabilizing and de-nationalizing countries in this part of the world. The communities went on struggling to become independent, as the quest for remedying the underserved living conditions in which they have been cast continued. In Chile, the nationalization of the copper industry posed a threat to foreign investors, with the economy in the hands of the people, and Chuquicamata in Antofagasta as the largest open-pit copper mine in the world.[22] Initially acquired by the Guggenheim family during the early 20th-century, the mine later fell into the hands of Anaconda as a subsidiary of Standard Oil, removing over four billion dollars of Chilean copper. During the early 1970s, Chuquicamata was finally confiscated from Anaconda, becoming nationally owned by Codelco as a result of Chile's socialist movement. In 1973, through a democratically held election, the Unidad Popular party succeeded in seating Chile's first Socialist president. Only three years into his presidency, Salvador Allende was overthrown and assassinated in Santiago by Augusto Pinochet, Chilean military dictator of Spanish descent, as part of a U.S. covert operation backed by the CIA, and implemented through the Chicago Boys' neo-liberal ideals of socio-economic reform.[f] Before Allende, the Chilean economy had been dominated by multinational corporations. "From 1971 to 1973, most of the monopolistic and oligopolistic industries were nationalized and transferred to the public sector…Real Gross Domestic Product (GDP) contracted during 1975 by nearly 15% to its lowest level since 1969, while, according to the IMF, real national income dropped by as much as 26%, leaving real per capita income below its level ten years earlier."[23] In the end, in 1976, in silent journey, many of us were exiled, escaping these nightmares, forever separated from an indigenous landscape that has fundamentally formed us.

---

f   The Chicago Boys were a group of Chilean economists who were trained at Chicago University under the tutelage of Milton Friedman and Arnold Harberger in the 1970s. They were entrenched in the military coup in Chile of 1973, arguing for an economic blueprint for a privately-controlled free market system as the only "medicine" for the country's future prosperity. Orlando Letelier, "The Chicago Boys in Chile: Economic Freedom's Awful Toll," Libcom (blog), August 28, 1976, https://libcom.org/library/chicago-boys-chile-economic-freedoms-awful-toll.

Several countries have passed through similar horrors, with U.S. military invasions in San Salvador during the 1980s, arriving in order to contain the slightest potential for Cold War alliances with Cuba that could disturb the dominion exercised over tiny Latin American nations as part of the Third World. Similarly, "freedom fighters"[24] in Nicaragua landed in support of Contra rebels to fend off leftist Sandinistas, who as so many leftist ideologists, merely fought back to protect the rural populations being uprooted during the countries' social reforms. The Plan Colombia in 2001,[25] aimed as a war on drugs to stabilize the region, is indicative of the malady invoked on these struggling countries, who have looked to the North as the patron of modernization, when it has in fact been the heavy, dark shadow behind the development of these nations. The international debt crisis in the early 1980s shook the Colombian market, depleting investment and leaving the economy to dwindle, just as the thirst for modernization had reached the palms of the poor Colombians' hands. Caught in the tropical storm, they harvested the coca to stay alive; only then the cyclone gained force becoming symptomatic of the long centuries of foreign intrusion, of its residue, manifested by the ongoing internal conflicts. Neighboring Venezuela, led by Hugo Chavez for 14 years, created the Comunidad de Estados de America Latina y el Caribe, to precisely counter U.S. influence in the region. Once one of the richest countries providing petroleum, iron, and natural gas, the capital city of Caracas boomed, investing its assets in highway infrastructure for the masses who ran to the growing city. The national budget multiplied, yet suddenly Standard Oil, Shell, and British Petroleum pulled out, dividing its subsidiaries into what became Mobil Oil, Gulf, and Texaco, severing Venezuelan wealth and negotiations. The country had been pulled in to serve, only to be later discarded as it sought its nationalization. Venezuela is, today, on the brink of extinction.

Through the North American Free Trade Agreement (NAFTA) between the U.S., Canada, and Mexico in 1988, Mexico gained strength through its historically low labor wages, as a competitive advantage for maintaining cheaper production, and therefore threatening U.S. labor.[26] The driving force behind trade agreements has remained economic, all along.

Enterprises that could be jeopardized by trade negotiations would, by default, impose stricter barriers; those who might benefit have eased the restrictions. The World Trade Organization (WTO) in 1994 opened the flood gates on trade bargains, permitting the economic development of countries to flourish by creating free and equitable exchanges between countries who earlier had not been admitted. Finally, in 2003, the U.S. signed a free trade agreement with Chile, a smaller country at roughly three hundred square miles, and only two thousand miles long by roughly two hundred wide, yet with an extraordinary geographic profile as the basis for its own development; a nation blessed by its virtuous agricultural production and copper industries, and which has held one of the most prosperous economies in Latin America.

Chile represents a nation that has consistently been inclined toward a democratic distribution of wealth, as evidenced by the country's left-leaning groups and socialist movement of the early 1970s, circumspect of infiltration, yet receptive to and with the stamina for engaging in international negotiations as components to modernization. The protection of private investment as part of the top-tier sect, however, has resurfaced. On the one hand, Chile has diversified its international business profile by expanding beyond the U.S. and engaging in trade with China and European nations,[g] but the control of this capital is again held by the 1.0%. Same scheme, broader playing field. As government spending is reduced, and the private sector holds control of industry, the country's level of inflation increases, again negatively impacting poorer citizens.

g   "In 2017, Chile sent 27.5% of its exports to China, 14.4% to the U.S., and 12.7% to the European Union." "Chile Trade Agreements," Export.gov. International Trade Administration, 11/01/2018. https://www.export.gov/article?id=Chile-Trade-Agreements.

Cuba
1961 – US troops attempt invasion to overthrow Fidel Castro

Honduras
1963 – Military coups ousts elected President Morales

Haiti
1994 – US troops restore constitutional government

Dominican Republic
1961 – Assassination of dictator Rafael Trujillo
1963 – Coup ousts elected President Bosch
1965 – US Armed Forces occupy Santo Domingo

Venezuela
2019 – President Trump recognizes Juan Guaido as interim president in attempted coup against Maduro

Grenada
1983 – US Armed Forces occupy island

Guyana
1953 – CIA aids British overthrow of democratic government

Guatemala
1954 – CIA organizes armed force to oust President Arbenz
1963 – US supports coup vs President Ydigoras
1982 – US supports coup vs General Lucas Garcia
1983 – US supports coup vs General Rios Montt

El Salvador
1961 – Coup ousts reformist civil-military junta
1979 – Coup ousts President General Humberto Romero
1980 – US aids new military junta government, leading to 12 year civil war

Nicaragua
1979 – US pressures President Somoza to leave
1981-90 – U.S. funds Contras in war against Sandinistas

Panama
1941 – US supports coup ousting elected President Arias
1969 – US supports coup by General Torrijos
1989 – US Armed Forces oust Manuel Noriega

Colombia
1999 – US signs Plan Colombia into law to fight drug cartels and left-wing insurgents

Peru
1990 – CIA sponsors government of Alberto Fujimori, accused of human rights abuses

Bolivia
1963 – Military coup ousts elected President Paz Estenssoro
1971 – Military coup ousts General Torres, brings dictator Banzer to power

Brazil
1964 – U.S. supports coup against President Joao Gilbert

Paraguay
1965 – U.S. supports coup, dictator Stroessner brought to power

Chile
1973 – Military coup supported by U.S. President Nixon and CIA ousts elected President Salvador Allende
1989-90 – U.S. provides financial aid to support overthrow of Augusto Pinochet after 17 years of military dictatorship

Uruguay
1973 – U.S. backs dictatorship of Juan María Bordaberry

Argentina
1976 – U.S. backs overthrow of President Perón

○ Indirect involvement

○ Direct involvement

UNITED STATES INTERVENTION IN LATIN AMERICA

500
0   1000km

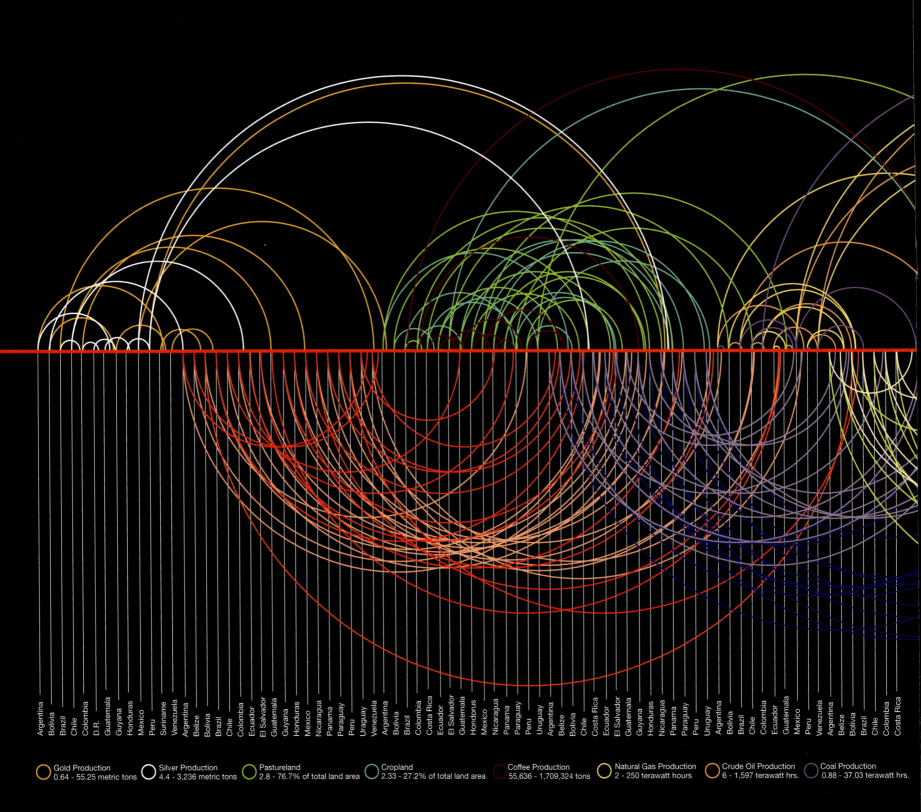

Argentina Bolivia Brazil Chile Colombia D.R. Guatemala Guyana Honduras Mexico Peru Suriname Argentina Venezuela Belize Bolivia Brazil Chile Colombia Ecuador El Salvador Guatemala Guyana Honduras Mexico Nicaragua Panama Paraguay Peru Uraguay Venezuela Argentina Bolivia Brazil Colombia Costa Rica Ecuador El Salvador Guatemala Hondorus Mexico Nicaragua Panama Paraguay Peru Uruguay Argentina Belize Bolivia Chile Costa Rica Ecuador El Salvador Guatemala Guyana Honduras Nicaragua Panama Paraguay Peru Uruguay Argentina Bolivia Brazil Chile Ecuador Colombia Guatemala Mexico Peru Venezuela Argentina Belize Bolivia Brazil Chile Colombia Costa Rica

Gold Production
0.64 - 55.25 metric tons

Silver Production
4.4 - 3,236 metric tons

Pastureland
2.8 - 76.7% of total land area

Cropland
2.33 - 27.2% of total land area

Coffee Production
55,636 - 1,709,324 tons

Natural Gas Production
2 - 250 terawatt hours

Crude Oil Production
6 - 1,597 terawatt hrs.

Coal Production
0.88 - 37.03 terawatt hrs.

NATURAL RESOURCES AND SOCIOECONOMIC IMPACTS IN LATIN AMERICA

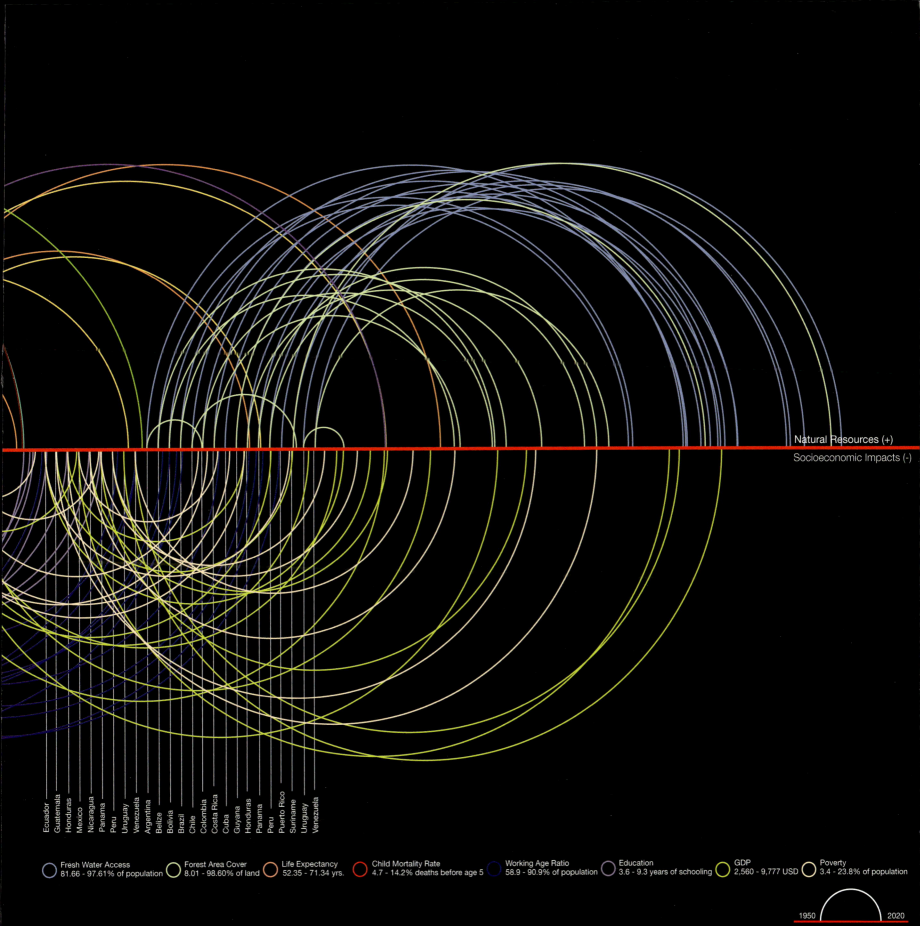

Natural Resources (+)

Socioeconomic Impacts (−)

Ecuador
Guatemala
Honduras
Mexico
Nicaragua
Panama
Peru
Uruguay
Venezuela
Argentina
Belize
Bolivia
Brazil
Chile
Colombia
Costa Rica
Cuba
Guyana
Honduras
Panama
Peru
Puerto Rico
Suriname
Uruguay
Venezuela

Fresh Water Access
81.66 - 97.61% of population

Forest Area Cover
8.01 - 98.60% of land

Life Expectancy
52.35 - 71.34 yrs.

Child Mortality Rate
4.7 - 14.2% deaths before age 5

Working Age Ratio
58.9 - 90.9% of population

Education
3.6 - 9.3 years of schooling

GDP
2,560 - 9,777 USD

Poverty
3.4 - 23.8% of population

1950   2020

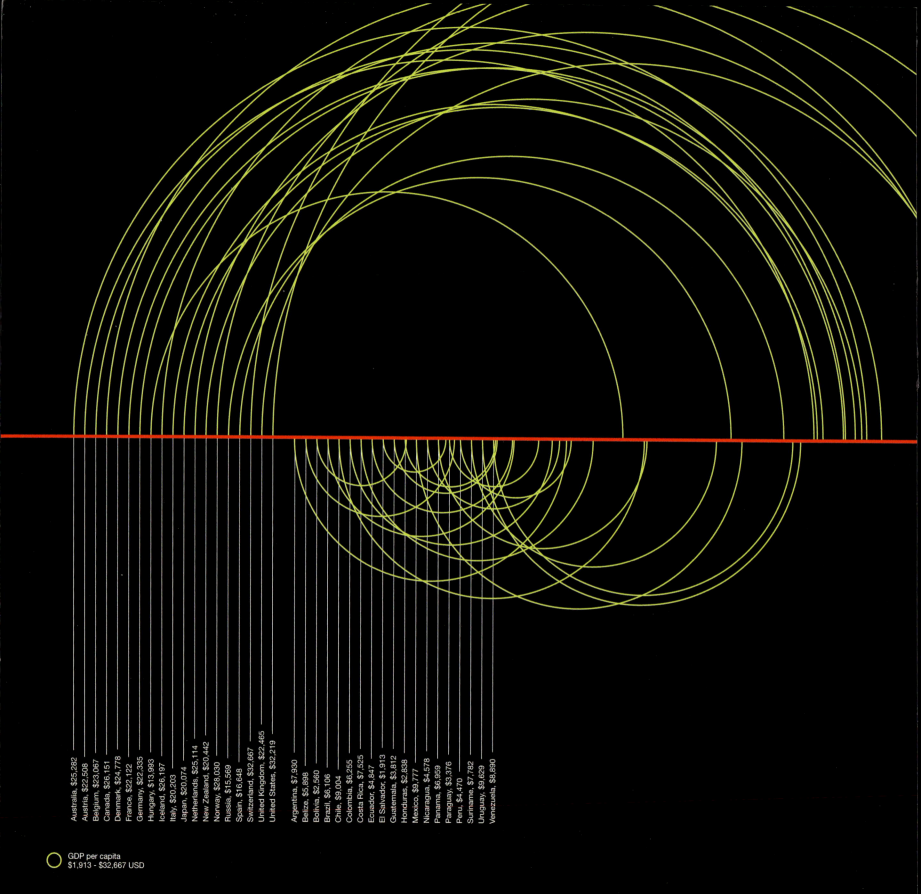

GDP per capita
$1,913 - $32,667 USD

Australia, $25,282
Austria, $22,508
Belgium, $23,067
Canada, $26,151
Denmark, $24,778
France, $22,122
Germany, $22,335
Hungary, $13,993
Iceland, $26,197
Italy, $20,203
Japan, $20,074
Netherlands, $25,114
New Zealand, $20,442
Norway, $28,030
Russia, $15,569
Spain, $16,648
Switzerland, $32,667
United Kingdom, $22,465
United States, $32,219

Argentina, $7,930
Belize, $5,898
Bolivia, $2,560
Brazil, $6,106
Chile, $9,004
Colombia, $6,255
Costa Rica, $7,525
Ecuador, $4,847
El Salvador, $1,913
Guatemala, $3,812
Honduras, $2,838
Mexico, $9,777
Nicaragua, $4,578
Panama, $6,959
Paraguay, $3,376
Peru, $4,470
Suriname, $7,782
Uruguay, $9,629
Venezuela, $8,890

COMPARISON OF AVERAGE GDP PER CAPITAL - GLOBAL NORTH vs. GLOBAL SOUTH (Latin America)

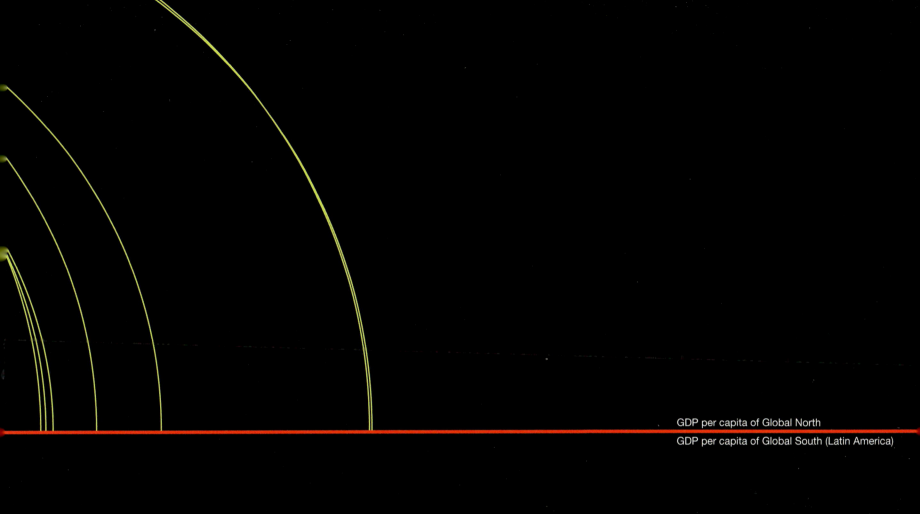

GDP per capita of Global North

GDP per capita of Global South (Latin America)

1950   2020

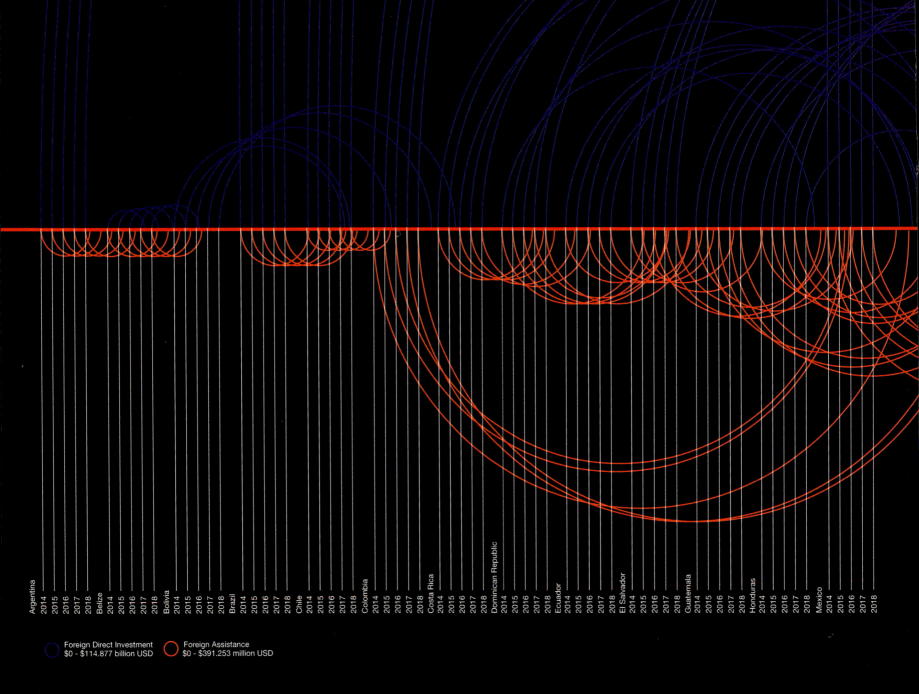

Argentina 2014 2015 2016 2017 2018 Belize 2014 2015 2016 2017 2018 Bolivia 2014 2015 2016 2017 2018 Brazil 2014 2015 2016 2017 2018 Chile 2014 2015 2016 2017 2018 Colombia 2014 2015 2016 2017 2018 Costa Rica 2014 2015 2016 2017 2018 Dominican Republic 2014 2015 2016 2017 2018 Ecuador 2014 2015 2016 2017 2018 El Salvador 2014 2015 2016 2017 2018 Guatemala 2014 2015 2016 2017 2018 Honduras 2014 2015 2016 2017 2018 Mexico 2014 2015 2016 2017 2018

Foreign Direct Investment
$0 - $114.877 billion USD

Foreign Assistance
$0 - $391.253 million USD

RATIO OF FOREIGN DIRECT INVESTMENT vs. FOREIGN ASSISTANCE (U.S.A.) IN LATIN AMERICA

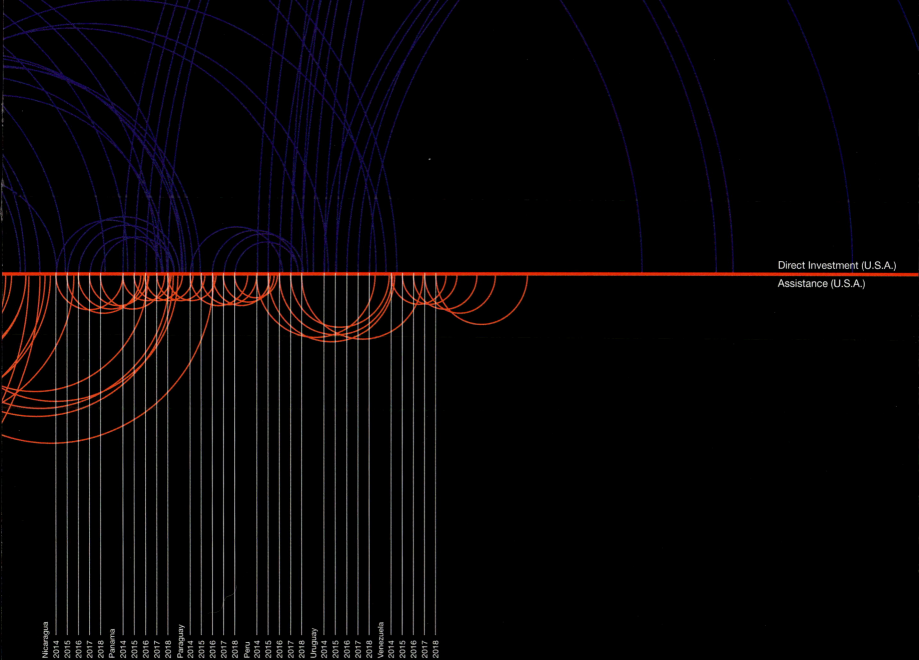

Direct Investment (U.S.A.)

Assistance (U.S.A.)

Nicaragua 2014 2015 2016 2017 2018 Panama 2014 2015 2016 2017 2018 Paraguay 2014 2015 2016 2017 2018 Peru 2014 2015 2016 2017 2018 Uruguay 2014 2015 2016 2017 2018 Venezuela 2014 2015 2016 2017 2018

In the fall of 2019, Chilean citizens protested in Santiago, uprising against subway fare increases emblematic of ensuing policies of inequality, and the citizens' unwillingness to accept a proliferation of the privatization of enterprise and public services, as indicative of a dangerous return to a burdensome schema. The protesters focused on education access, revealing truths in the economy, and replacing the current constitution that had been adopted under Pinochet's dictatorship as a means of shedding the weight of his tumultuous era. Since Pinochet's 17-year military dictatorship, which ended in 1990,[h] presidents from a coalition of center-left political parties have continued with these trends, with what could result in closer ideals for Chile's social reform. The jury is still out.

The U.S. and its far-right leaning administration are opting to annul the NAFTA agreement, as a sanction for the number of Mexican and Central American immigrants who seek asylum from the complex political conflicts created by international entanglements in Latin American countries.

Donald Trump, the feudal head of the United States, only envisions his golden trophy through "America First". Individualism, bigotry, ignorance, and discrimination expressed through the country's withdrawal from the Paris Climate Accord, drawing inflexible lines through a harsh border wall, and separating the landscape between Mexico and the United States will disconnect any remaining natural resources, vetoing the world's pursuit for social equity. The natural wonder of these Latin American countries remains an enigmatic quest to the North, viewed as the underbelly of the powerful, capitalist world. Yet, as the essential economic structure, and as the foundation defining the cultural norms of Latin American communities, the splendidly rich geography is worth so much more.

---

h   Although Pinochet stepped down as dictator in 1990, he continued to be the head of the Chilean army until his removal in 1998, whereby he then maintained a position as senator until 2004.

PRECEDING ARC DIAGRAMS

Natural Resources and Socio-Economic Impacts, Latin America
As an exploration of the natural resources extracted most readily from Latin America, in comparison to socio-economic impacts, this diagram considers numerous datasets, including rates of gold and silver extraction, agricultural and energy-related production, and water resources, against poverty rates, education access, and employment, among others. The diagram uses relative arcs to describe the range of values for each dataset, and demonstrates a relationship between the levels of socio-economic impacts as affected by natural resource extraction.

Average GDP per capita, Global North vs. Global South (Latin America)
Focusing on average Gross Domestic Product (GDP) per capita, this comparison between countries of the Global North and Latin American countries of the Global South spans from 1950 to 2020. This relationship demonstrates a significant disparity in standards of living between the Global North and Global South that has persisted for decades.

Ratio, Roreign Direct Investment (U.S.) vs. Foreign Assistance (U.S.) in Latin America
Over the last five years, Foreign Direct Investment from the United States into Latin American countries has significantly outweighed Foreign Assistance from the United States to the same countries. Foreign Direct Investment includes investment in manufactoring and services, retail development, infrastructure, and natural resource extraction, while Foreign Assistance includes peace initiatives, security, development efforts, and humanitarian relief.

Notes

1 U.S. Census Bureau, U.S.-Canada and U.S-Mexico Border Lengths. Statistical Abstract of the United States, 2011.
https://www2.census.gov/library/publications/2010/compendia/statab/130ed/tables/11s0359.pdf

2 Ibid.

3 Arturo Ardao, *Genesis de la Idea y el Nombre America Latina* (Caracas: Centro de Estudios Latinoamericanos Rómulo Gallegos, 1980).

4 Arlen F. Chase, Diane Z. Chase, and Michael E. Smith, "States and Empires in Ancient Mesoamerica," *Ancient Mesoamerica* 20 (2009): 175–182.

5 "The World Factbook," *Central Intelligence Agency*, last modified October 22, 2019, https://www.cia.gov/library/publications/the-world-factbook/geos/ar.html.

6 Ibid.

7 *National Geographic Atlas of the World*, (National Geographic Society, 2014).

8 "The World Factbook," 2019.

9 "Water Resources," *Food and Agriculture Organization of the United Nations*, last modified 2016, http://www.fao.org/nr/water/aquastat/countries_regions/profile_segments/amazon-WR_eng.stm.

10 "The World Factbook," 2019.

11 Ibid.

12 *National Geographic*, 2014.

13 Eduardo Galeano, *Open Veins of Latin America* (New York: Monthly Review Press, 1973, 1997),12.

14 Richard Lee, *Globalization, Language and Culture* (New York: Chelsea House Publishers, 2006) 1–8.

15 George L. Cowgill, *Ancient Teotihuacan, Early Urbanism in Central Mexico* (New York; Cambridge University Press, 2015).

16 Victor Davis Hanson, *Carnage and Culture: Landmark battles in the rise of western power* (New York: Double Day, 2000), 208.

17 Kendall W. Brown, *A History of Mining in Latin America: From the Colonial Era to the Present* (Albuquerque: University of New Mexico Press, 2012), 15–45.

18 Galeano, *Open Veins,* 83.

19 Robert C. Allen, *The British Industrial Revolution in Global Perspective: How Commerce Created the Industrial Revolution and Modern Economic Growth* (Cambridge: Cambridge University Press, 2009).

20 Cristobal Kay, "Latin America's agrarian reform: lights and shadows," *Land Reform* (Food and Agricultural Organization, 1992) 9–28.

21 Celso Furtado, Economic Development of Latin America: A Survey from Colonial Times to the Cuban Revolution. (Cambridge: University Press, 1970), 11.

22 Nicholas Valencia, "Presentan la historia del campamento de Chuquicamata, la mina a cielo abierto más grande del mundo," *Plataforma Arquitectura*, 2018. https://www.plataformaarquitectura.cl/cl/888156/presentan-la-historia-del-campamento-de-chuquicamata-la-mina-a-cielo-abierto-mas-grande-del-mundo.

23 Orlando Letelier, "The Chicago Boys in Chile: Economic Freedom's Awful Toll," *Libcom* (blog), August 28, 1976, https://libcom.org/library/chicago-boys-chile-economic-freedoms-awful-toll.

24 John, Ross, "Thugs, Not Freedom Fighters," Harvard Crimson, 1986. https://www.thecrimson.com/article/1986/3/17/thugs-not-freedom fighters-pbjbudging-by/.

25 Michael Shifter, "Plan Colombia: A Retrospective," *Americas Quarterly,* (2012), accessed August 28, 2019. https://www.americasquarterly.org/node/3787.

26 I.M Destler, "America's Uneasy History with Free Trade," Economics and Society, *Harvard Business Review*, 2016. https://hbr.org/2016/04/americas-uneasy-history-with-free-trade.

MEDELLÍN

An Urbanist Perspective

2

MEDELLÍN

An Urbanist Perspective

The historical geography of Colombia offers vivid highlights that reveal the archetypal agendas of the colonial conquests, descending through centuries, marking the footprints of land and resource thievery with lasting effects on the socio-economic and spatial development of this naturally rich country and region of the world. As the protagonist, Colombia is representative of many physical qualities shared by Latin American nations, which together with the social and political similarities these countries also have in common, reveal a consistent line of imposition. Colombia forms part of an ecological chain, together with five other Latin American countries, including Panama, Ecuador, Peru, Brazil, and Venezuela, along with its coastal edges, the Pacific and Atlantic Oceans and the Caribbean Sea. It is blessed with an interior framed by prominent mountain ranges, valleys, and streams that pronounce its exceptional terrain and bountiful biodiversity. The organic and structured layers of urban growth, as evidenced in the central region of the country, suggest a recurring theme, as the pendulum continues to swing, between the intricacies of natural systems driving the values of a given community, and the oppressing tendencies created by far away forces.

The Cordillera Occidental, as part of the Andes mountains, enters Colombia from the southwest, as the lowest peaks, then opening into two long strands: the Cordillera Central, as the central and tallest range; to then the Cordillera Oriental, as the widest on the eastern side. Vigorous rivers run through, the Cauca, aligning the western valley, and the Rio Grande de la Magdalena, between Tolima and Huila as the only two departments whose boundaries are crossed by both the Central and Eastern Cordillera, approximately 1,500 km (930 mi) along the Magdalena River Valley on the east. The two reach their confluence in the north near Mompox, before the mouth of the Magdalena at Bocas de Ceniza, where it finally extends out to the warm Caribbean Sea.

This river is recognized for its long tradition of riverine commerce, its fast-flowing currents, and as the greatest source of freshwater fishing in the area. Intensive ecosystems characterize the Magdalena Valley, among them the upper dry forest, the mid-range rainforest, the lower wetlands and swamps, as well as the special alpine tundra, or typical Colombian "páramo,"[1] with its distinct rosette flowers, grasses, and tropical species growing in rare hot spots at high elevations. The Orinoco and Amazon Rivers form the two major basins of the northern and eastern extents, where the area becomes tropical, lit with green hues, and a spectra of blossoms and birds. Colombia is categorized by six distinct geographical regions, including the Andean region, Caribbean/Atlantic coastal region, Pacific, Amazon, the "Llanos" (Eastern Plains), and the Caribbean Insular Island region. The country occupies an area of approximately 1,142,000 km² (441,000 mi²). With a population of roughly 49 million, Colombia has an average density of 43 people per km² (118 per mi²), with Bogotá, Medellín, and Cali currently representing the principal urbanized centers.[2,a]

---

a   See page 257 for chart of comparable Latin American cities.

Right: Geomorphology of Colombia.

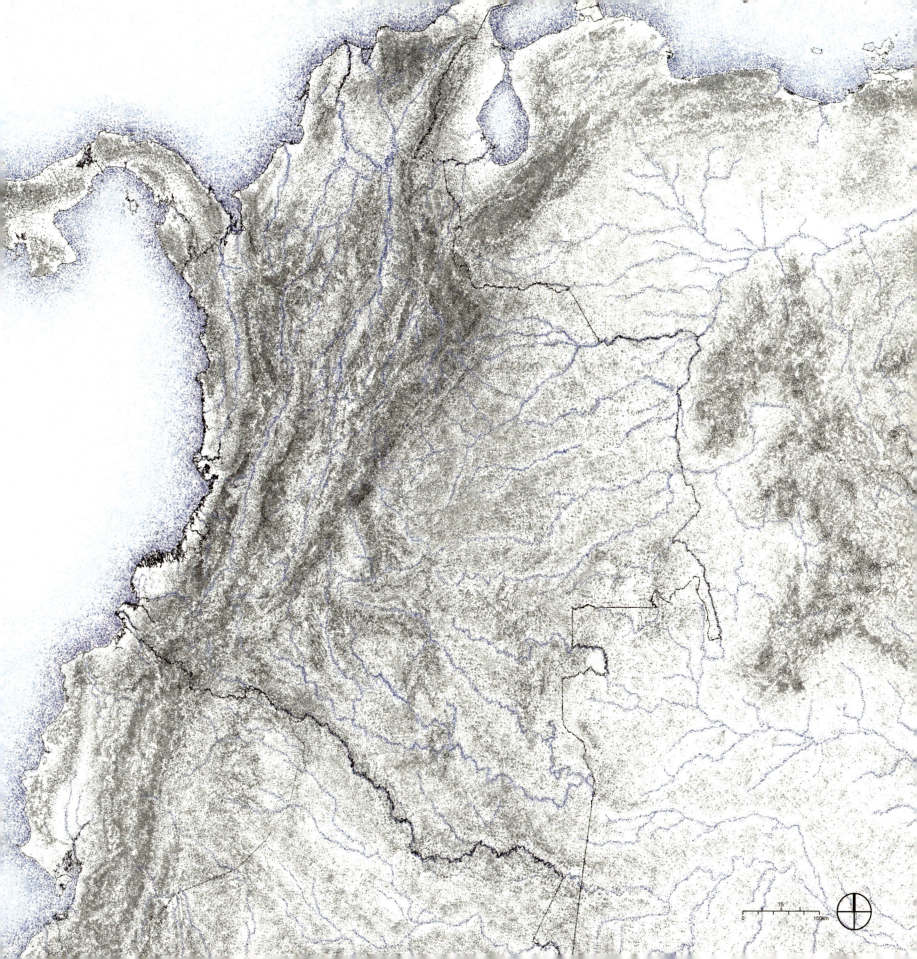

A SYMBOLIC LANDSCAPE
The 16th Century

As early as 1500,[3] Spanish conquistadores arrived to Colombia along the southern Andes, fervidly captivated by the hidden landscape that unfolded before their eyes, as they recognized the fortuity of their greedy quest. Antioquia, the central department of Colombia, extending to the Caribbean, and across the Western and Central Cordilleras of the Andes, was then predominately populated by numerous indigenous Caribs, each with distinct customs as influenced by the unique geographical zone they inhabited. Some of these included the Nutabes and Tahamies along the Nechí and Cauca Rivers, Yamesies and the Guamocoes near the Nechí and Cimitarra Rivers, and the Aburrae,[4] who over the mountain peaks, beyond a distant gaze, had settled in the Valle de Aburrá, quietly hidden, tranquil, in the palm of Antioquia. Loosely sprinkled over the surrounding slopes, mountaintops, and across the alluvial basins, they sustained themselves, independently, through agricultural customs. Indigenous farms were laid throughout the plains and along the fertile borders of the Quebrada Aná, as the principal eastern stream, and along the Aburrá, or Medellín River, running south to north as the apex of the valley. As mountaineers, the Aburrae presided over full views of the horizon. They were an isolated, stout, and dominant group as a result of the canyons and crevices of the grandiose landscape that set them apart, while also affording them seclusion and protection from oncoming foreign invaders. As far back as the 5th-century, in fact, indigenous groups such as the Yamesi, Peque, Ebejico, Norisco, Mani, as well as the Aburrae[5] had engaged in agriculture, weaving, salt commerce, and gold-smithing.[6] These tribes moved along transport routes reliant on mules to reach Puerto Berrio on the Magdalena, northbound, as well as the western Cauca Valley, and the southern Caldas region. The methods employed by natives early on were directly linked to the topographical and hydrological profile of the area, later becoming strong propellers of the region's future growth.

The Cordillera Central, along the eastern shoulder of the Valle de Aburrá is a mountain range composed of clay soils and metamorphic rock, which together with an ideal location and climate near the equator, has provided essential components for the area's development, both favorable and ostentatious. On the one hand, the soil structure, largely comprised of a thin clay strata, makes a perfect combination with the moisture and heat coming from the trade winds. This has resulted in a range of sprouting forests, from the humid premontane, humid-tropical, to the very-humid premontane forests.[7] The clay-based soils, moreover, formed the basis for the original agricultural layout of the land, naturally, along the lower slopes, plateaus, and adjacent to the stream-beds and ravines, where the cultivation of crops prospered. Fruit-bearing trees, including Guanabana (soursop fruit, *Annona muricata*), Aguacate (*Persea americana*), Papaya (mountain papaya, *Vasconcellea pubescens*), and pineapple grown from terrestrial bromeliads;[8] tubers, such as yucca, Arracacha, (Creole celery, *Arracacia xanthorrhiza*), and garlic; together with corn, beans, and chiles were typically grown in the region.[9] These and other delicious species were complemented by small animal husbandry and fishing along the streams to provide a nutritious and varied diet for the natives. The fact that the Central Mountains were formed during the Mesozoic Era and Cretaceous period some 145.5 and 65.5 million years ago respectively,[10] on the other hand, means that parts of Colombia, and central Antioquia in particular, are made up of metamorphic rock, with a high gold mineral content, making this a significant element of the spatial and social evolution of the Valle de Aburrá.

THE LANDSCAPE OF IMPOSITION
The 16th–17th Centuries

Jerónimo Luis Tejelo in 1541 explored the region and identified the valley[11] as an ideal place from which to spread Spanish dominion over the territory and native groups settled there. The Aburrae were first sited adjacent to the Aburrá River and the Aná stream-bed, in the heart of the hollow. Given its inferior gold deposits, however, the Valle de Aburrá was bypassed, and the Spaniards forwent initial ideas of settling in this location. They instead traveled northeast and founded the Villa de Santa Fe, later becoming the capital of the Department of Antioquia, where gold mining activities were found to be more prominent.[b] As part of their "encomiendas,"[12] the colonists were to repay the "Indios"[13] for their arduous work with specks of gold, with land protection, and with teachings of the sacred Christian religion. It seems unlikely that this happened, since only 10 years later, in 1551, decreed as the

---

b   See map of gold deposits in Latin America, pg. 47

Spanish New Kingdom of Nueva Granada,[14] the indigenous living in the region were consolidated, grouped together, outcast, and forced to live elsewhere—south of the Quebrada Aná. Under the pretext of protecting the Aburrae from the abusive "encomenderos,"[15] the Crown had given the order to relocate, while at the same time mining slave labor was perpetuated. The tiny Aburrae villages were confiscated and the agricultural and native land was redistributed among the Spanish conquerors. These settlements included: Bello, Barbosa, Copacabana, Girardota, and Piedras Blancas, north and northeast of the Central Valley; La Aguacatala, centrally sited; Envigado and La Granja, located just south; with Itagüí, La Estrella, and El Prado, also known as San Antonio, southwest, once crossing the Medellín River. There had been 1,000,000 indigenous who inhabited Antioquia in the year 1500 during pre-colonial times. By 1550, of the remaining 600,000 indigenous, 120,000 were already mining slaves in Antioquia, a number that rapidly declined further due to disease, starvation, and slavery to somewhere between 25,000 and 30,000 by 1580.[16]

Bogotá was the ruling center over bordering Venezuela, Ecuador, and Panama, yet with Antioquia becoming a province of the Spanish New Kingdom of Nueva Granada in 1576, with a geographical location that would coincide with its ever-growing prominence. This diverse central region of Colombia, extending out to many seas, with heavenly temperatures, biodiversity, and precious minerals, mountains, and streams, along the Magdalena River, marked the major route for international transport. Given these assets, Antioquia was identified as a significant core early on. Within this context, explorer Francisco de Herrera y Campuzano founded the first Spanish settlement in Antioquia in El Poblado de San Lorenzo in 1616, a village largely composed of the displaced Aburrae whose land had been unjustly stolen. San Lorenzo de Aburrá, as the settlement was also named, connotes a mixture between two worlds and concepts: one stemming from Spanish Catholicism, and the other relating to the autochthonous Aburrae people.[17] From these two extremes, of foreign interference and land-based traditions, lie the incongruent influences that have affected the configuration of the city and the behavior of the community over the centuries.

Three major transformations were at play as the indigenous land was usurped. To begin, being rid of their farmland and moved away from the water's edge, from both the Aburrá River and the Aná stream, caused a significant change not only in their traditional work, but to the layout of the farms, and therefore also to the quality of their diets. The indigenous of the Central Valley were once proficient goldsmiths, who un-intrusively collected gold deposits that flowed down the rivers and streams, then used for trading goods and as decorative adornments, as emblems of the natural and exotic materials of the area. They were also prolific agricultural farmers. Once accustomed to foods based on an assortment of vegetables, fruits and grains, they were later reduced to becoming largely dependent on corn and beans, which could be cultivated in more abundant quantities. Secondly, as their land passed into Spanish hands, the reconfiguration of the lots allowed for more economical farming, with orthogonal lines extending over the fields and into the forests, devoid of topographical or hydrological considerations.

The Spaniards' intent was simply to maximize the plantation area, as a means to an end, that could produce the greatest quantities of feed to minimally sustain many more indigenous, who would then be forced to incessantly work the gold mines in Santa Fe and nearby areas of the region. The newly scored plots, of course, also accommodated grazing for cattle and other livestock that the Spaniards brought over with them, in order to supply their own aristocratic diets, practices that were grossly unlike the Aburrae mountaineer traditions. The destiny of the land was thus not used for that which it was most suitable; its primary benefits, as contributing to the greatest number of people, for the longest period of time, were overlooked, if not purposefully passed over.[18, c] Lastly, as the changes to the utilization of the land took place, so did the nutrients and composition of the ground. Forests were depleted as the Spanish constructed striking two-story colonial houses, larger and taller than any other in the area, built from the felled timber, further compromising the stability of the steep slopes, as well as the overall quality of the soil. These once fertile farms were, in effect, not only ripped away from the indigenous owners of the Valley de Aburrá, but the customs that were innately connected to their regional landscape were also severed. It is important to note, furthermore, that prior to this historical period, there is no evidence that reveals an improper use of the soil, causing its deterioration, nor over the use of substances that could generate pollutants that would modify the physical or chemical structure of the earth. The harmonious relationship the indigenous people had toward the land through their mindful planning and delicate ecological practices is directly contradicted, if not violated, by the tragic disruption to the region.[19]

---

c   The most detrimental aspect of the Colonial conquest is directly related to the extinction of indigenous groups through shutting off the chain of sustenance, through the disruption of agricultural practices, and the (re)-configuration of indigenous land.

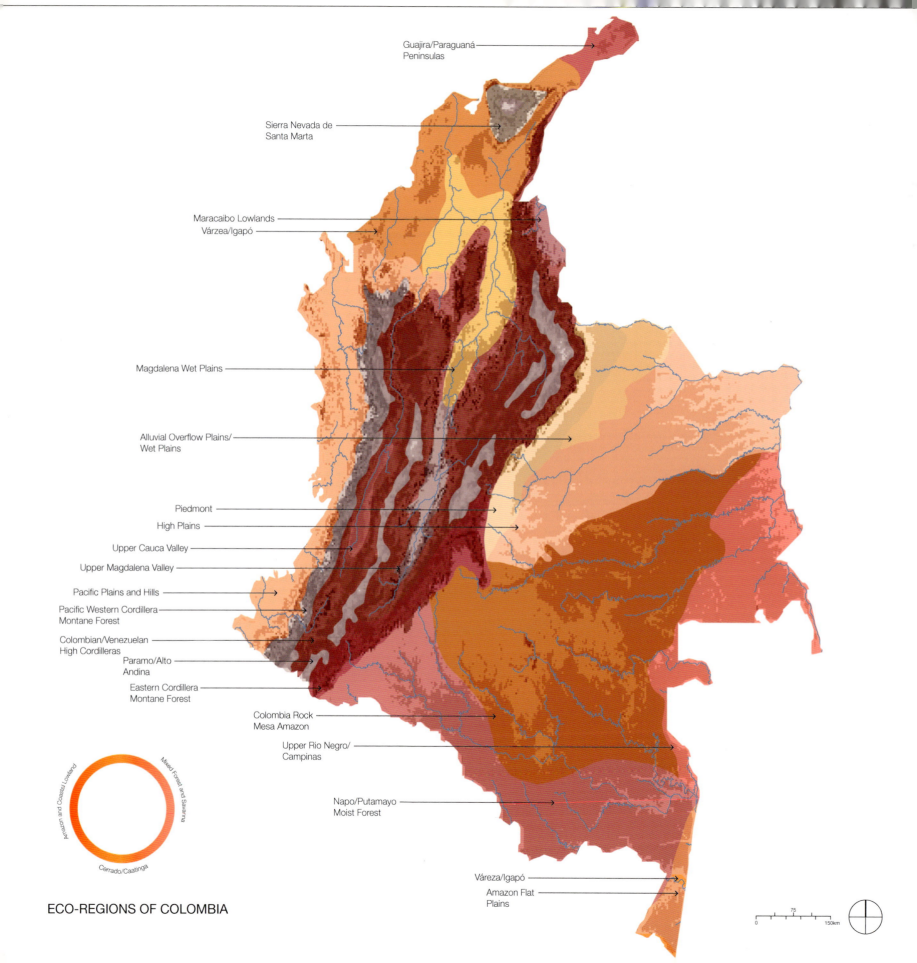

Guajira/Paraguaná
Peninsulas

Sierra Nevada de
Santa Marta

Maracaibo Lowlands
Várzea/Igapó

Magdalena Wet Plains

Alluvial Overflow Plains/
Wet Plains

Piedmont

High Plains

Upper Cauca Valley

Upper Magdalena Valley

Pacific Plains and Hills

Pacific Western Cordillera
Montane Forest

Colombian/Venezuelan
High Cordilleras

Paramo/Alto
Andina

Eastern Cordillera
Montane Forest

Colombia Rock
Mesa Amazon

Upper Rio Negro/
Campinas

Napo/Putamayo
Moist Forest

Váreza/Igapó

Amazon Flat
Plains

Amazon and Coastal Lowland
Mixed Forest and Savanna
Cerrado/Caatinga

ECO-REGIONS OF COLOMBIA

0   75   150km

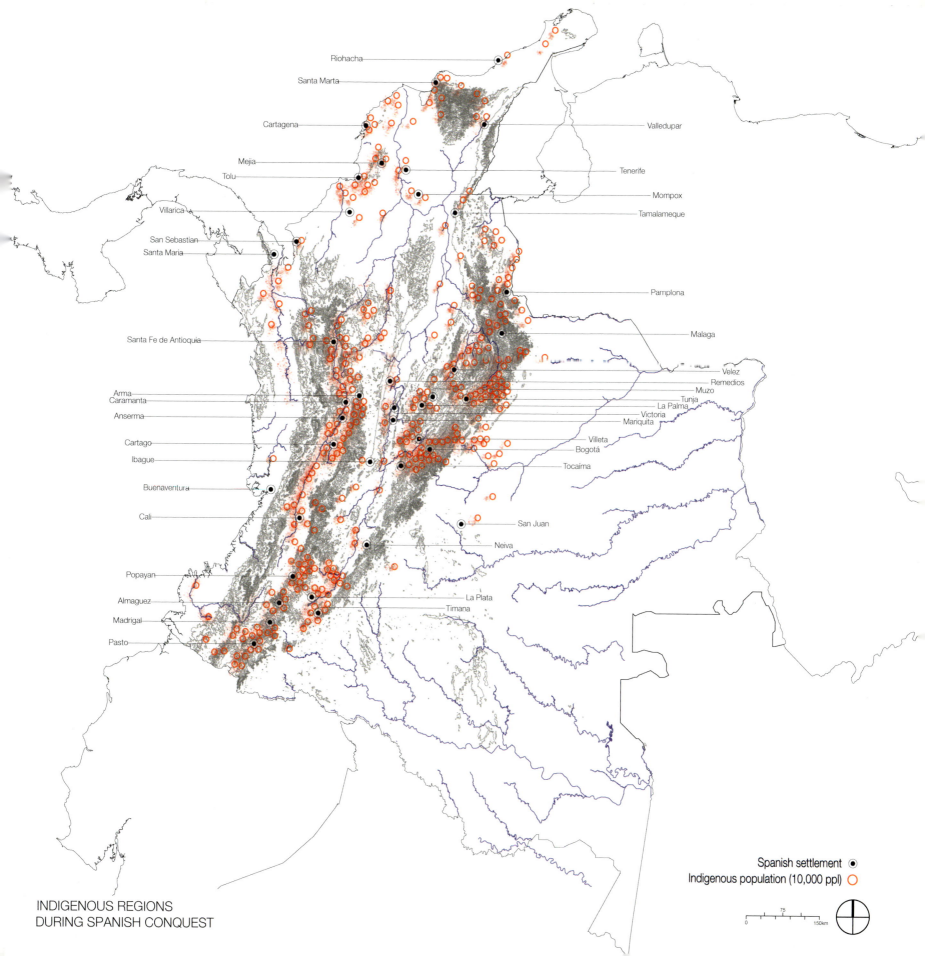

Riohacha

Santa Marta

Cartagena

Valledupar

Mejia

Tolu

Tenerife

Mompox

Tamalameque

Villarica

San Sebastian

Santa Maria

Pamplona

Santa Fe de Antioquia

Malaga

Velez

Arma

Remedios

Caramanta

Muzo

Tunja

Anserma

La Palma

Victoria

Mariquita

Cartago

Villeta

Ibague

Bogotá

Tocaíma

Buenaventura

Cali

San Juan

Neiva

Popayan

Almaguez

La Plata

Timana

Madrigal

Pasto

Spanish settlement

Indigenous population (10,000 ppl)

INDIGENOUS REGIONS
DURING SPANISH CONQUEST

75

0

150km

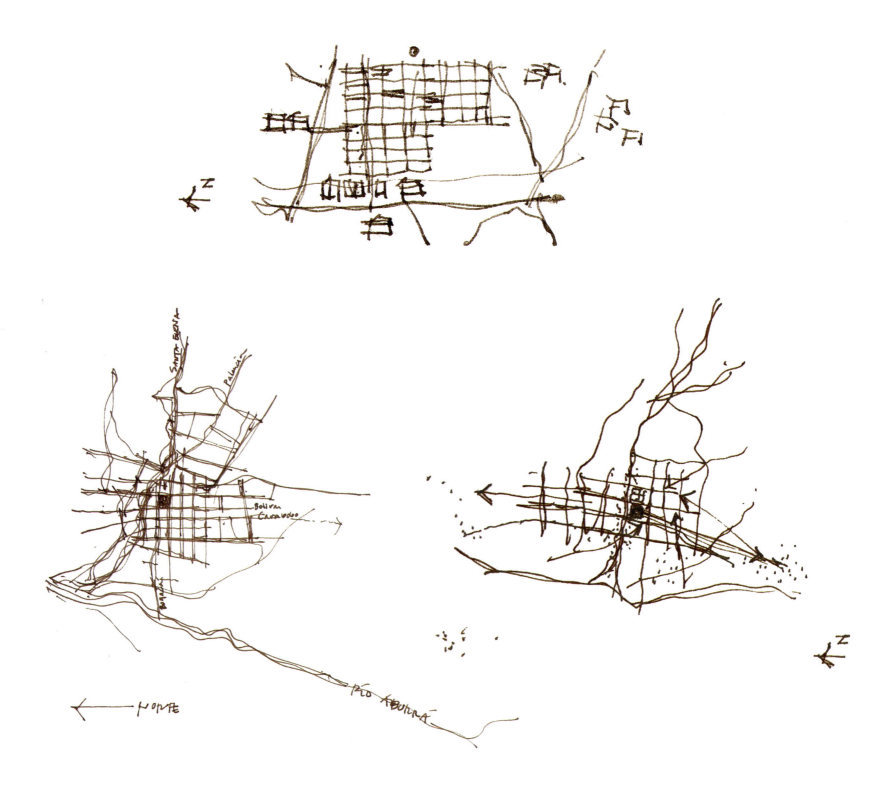

Above: Sketches, evolution of Medellín's urban grid, *María Bellalta*.

Right: Study of Medellín's indigenous settlements and colonial growth, *María Bellalta*.

City COLONIAL CITY
lunging against Sta. Elena quebrada, which limits its
urban growth there. 1791... has □ model, imposed
by Spanish bureaucratic order
                                    Spanish grid model

was created in area where there were already
a few dozen houses/dwellings around a church ✝,
and spread in a random order. consequently CHURCHES

Near 1670, the valley had 'other' small urban
nuclei, separated by a few kms.
                                        Barbosa

this is important b/c as   Girardota
Aná accumulates 60 families (excluding slaves),   Hatillo
families (excluding slaves),   Ancón
develops hierarchy, soon   Copacabana
commence + is able to   (Tasajera)
accelerate faster than   Bello
other groups! These latter   Fortidueño
become dependent on   ANÁ
aná, further enhancing   Sa. Vicente   Gorge of Sta. Elena
it as the major force   Puente
as well as propelling   Nueva
the overall growth of   Bolívar   Bridges
the area.   Covarrubias
From here, other   San Lorenzo
routes extend   La Estrella   Palencia   Eleun
out, or expanding   Hatoviejo
the footprint of   San   Envigado La Culata (San Cristóbal)
the city   Antonio   Guayabal
                              Itagüí   Río Negro
                        San Lorenzo de Aburrá
              Caldas   El Poblado

        → routes and 'camellones'/WARU-WARU
           ... excavated canals for cultivation
                    connected

NUESTRA SEÑORA DE LA CANDELARIA DE ANÁ AND THE PUBLIC SQUARE

The Law of the Indies in 1646[d] marks another poignant moment in the history of the Aburrae people. With the original intent to protect the indigenous families in the area, the Law dictated that they be moved to El Poblado de San Lorenzo and be separated from the mestizo and Spanish gathered there. The affluent, aristocratic Spaniards relocated just north, along the confluence of the Quebrada Santa Elena, from where many Aburrae had originated, then named Quebrada Aná. Derived from and reminiscent of the native landscape, "Aná" is an indigenous word fittingly synonymous with water. The Spaniards designated the first public square here in Aná, where today's Parque Berrio in the center of the City of Medellín is located, as the place where only the rich were free to convene and cajole. While the Law of the Indies had intended to safeguard the indigenous, it had also prescribed the physical order and administrative power of the city as stemming from the square. Displaced Aburrae were excluded from this civic space, in essence marking the ground with symbolic notions of spatial and social segregation. The first Roman Catholic Church, moreover, Nuestra Señora de la Candelaria, was built adjacent to the public square only a few years later. Due to the central location of Aná, situated between new gold mines to the northeast, and with Santa Fe de Antioquia to the northwest, the Valle de Aburrá became an ideal agricultural farmstead to fuel the exploited mining slaves, with Aná as a strategically located commercial center. From what had been the natives' land for cultivating varied grains, fruits, and vegetables as part of their innate agrarian traditions, was then supplanted by a foreign mixture of aristocracy, piety, and commercial thirst. As a result, the valley was reconfigured into an expansive, efficient agricultural field, where delineated plots functioned, devoid of the undulating profile of the landscape or its dendritic streams. Finally, in 1674, named after the church presiding over the public plaza, Nuestra Señora de la Candelaria de Aná, or Villa de la Candelaria, was officially decreed the new town in the Valle de Aburrá, with 600 Spanish inhabitants, and another 3,000 across the valley.[20] By contrast, as it had occurred with natives living in the greater region of Antioquia, of the near 2,500 indigenous living throughout the Valley de Aburrá, none remained there by the turn of the 17th-century.[21]

REGIONAL AND RACIAL INFLUENCES

The layout of the square and the expansion of the grid went on, farther out, imposing straight lines over the landscape, as extensions of unwavering Spanish rule. Nuestra Señora de la Candelaria expanded along the Quebrada Aná, and later, westbound toward the Medellín River, with a rectilinear pattern of streets to connect the colonial buildings that were erected. These were joined by an incremental addition of ecclesiastical buildings and public squares that filled in the rectangular voids of a rigid framework over the lower valley's eastern slope. Main streets and "camellones,"[22] as excavated canals used for cultivation and connectivity, further fragmented the landscape, as the center of La Candelaria continued to spread. The surrounding plots of land, by now operating under Spanish control, relied on the centrality of La Candelaria for their ongoing development, for merchandise, as well as for her role as a commercial depot, facilitating local commerce, which by then included sugar, coffee, as well as cotton.

Within a regional context, as La Candelaria grew, the physical layout and socio-cultural customs across broader Antioquia further influenced the development of the valley in distinct, if not enigmatic ways. From the geographical characteristics of the province, its mixed profiles, the mountainous physique, the qualities of the coastal rims, as well as its prolific hydrological system, derived an influx of migrant cultures. The psycho-social relationship each of these native and migrating settlers brought with them, be they Indigenous, European, Afro races, or the mestizo, created a multidimensional people, over a singularly and mis-constructed ruling class.[23] Antioquia today represents a sample of the broader range of social norms that exist across Colombia.

---

d   The Law of the Indies was officially drawn up in 1542 by King Charles V of Spain; these laws sought to protect indigenous populations by removing the encomienda system in the colonies, abolishing slavery, and requiring indigenous tributes to the crown in goods, versus labor. https://www.crf-usa.org/bill-of-rights-in-action/bria-15-4-c-laws-of-the-indies-spain-and-the-native-peoples-of-the-new-world

Right: Study of Medellin's footprint over time, *María Bellalta*.

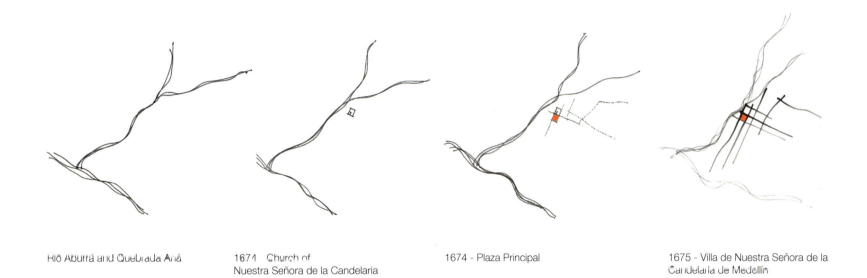

Río Aburrá and Quebrada Aná

1674 - Church of
Nuestra Señora de la Candelaria

1674 - Plaza Principal

1675 - Villa de Nuestra Señora de la
Candelaria de Medellín

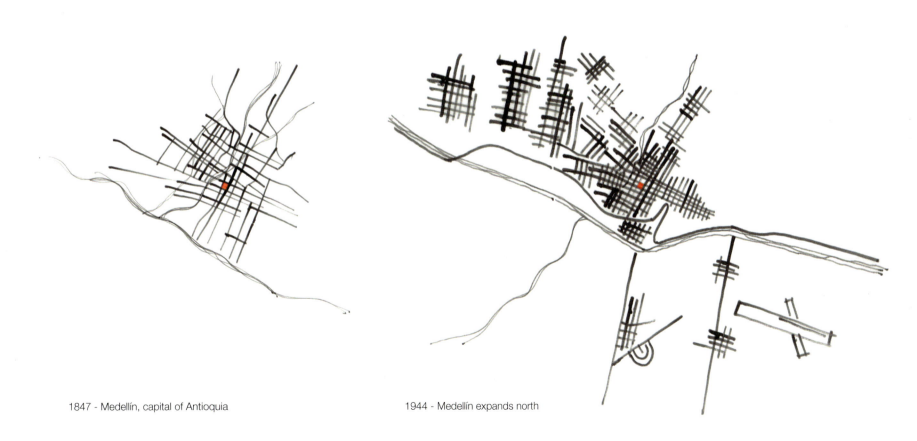

1847 - Medellín, capital of Antioquia

1944 - Medellín expands north

EVOLUTION OF MEDELLÍN AND THE PUBLIC SQUARE
1674 - 1944

MINING AND THE EMERGENCE OF TRADE
Mid-17th to late 18th Centuries

Mining in Antioquia in 1599 had resulted in the extraction of 1,700,000 pesos of 22 karat gold.[e] By 1674, only 100,000 pesos were extracted, causing the encomenderos, or mining "lords," to turn toward commercial trading. Given the Law of the Indies, as referenced earlier, indigenous labor in the mines diminished, requiring work to be substituted by imported Afro, and later, Afro-descendant slaves from the coastal regions. The practice permitted the continuation of large-scale mining, but also led to the emergence of independent miners, known as "Mazamorreros,"[24] who were composed of mestizos, mulatos, and free blacks. In order to enhance their livelihoods, the Mazamorreros, in part, spurred merchant trading to obtain supplies from sources not readily available within the valley. They also engaged in subsistence farming, with small plots of land to produce essential food products. The increase in these smaller-scale mining practices required viable transport routes to support the exchange of gold and broader commerce throughout the area.

TRADE ROUTES
The 18th Century

The voyage into Antioquia involved traversing a complex terrain, steep and slippery, with most of the courses outlined as precarious mule tracks, often impassible during the reoccurring rainy seasons. The three key points of entry into the valley occurred via El Camino del Espíritu Santo, from the north; El Camino de Nare, from the east; and the route through Popayán, from the south. By the late 17th-century, the Valle de Aburrá became such a prominent commercial hub, that the ancient Espíritu Santo route was later abandoned, and instead the principal thoroughfare became Nare, linking Nuestra Señora de la Candelaria to Puerto Berrio on the Magdalena River. This newly recognized passage solidified the Aburrá Valley as an established agricultural center. "Medellín was a crossroads: those who went north, those who went to the capital and those who went east, all passed somehow through these lands, which made this site a must for travelers and commerce."[25] The years that followed saw a more democratic society in Antioquia, formed by the prevalence of varied population groups and customs, smaller scale, independent production, along with multiple entrepreneurial spirits.

While the continued migration to the valley offered prosperity, it also placed a heavy burden on the land, compromising the capacity of agricultural plots that could sustain the economic affluence of the area. Governor of Antioquia, Juan Antonio Mon y Velarde, went on to lay out a plan for social and economic reform by increasing agricultural production and promoting livestock grazing, intensifying the exploitation of the landscape for purely economic motives.

Mon y Velarde's census of 1786 reveals a population in La Candelaria of 14,507 inhabitants.[26] In an attempt to evacuate the valley by opening it up for endless agricultural, and therefore lucrative purposes, Mon y Velarde encouraged migration elsewhere, to nearby areas in the region, reducing settlement and lessening congestion in the alluvial plain, as a means of protecting financial interests in his valley.

COLONIZATION OF ANTIOQUIA
The 19th Century

As the region expanded via its agricultural productivity, new developing nodes in the area surfaced. These required direct relations to the Valle de Aburrá, with evident dependencies for their economic, social, and political viability. The trade routes passing through from Caldas, Risaralda, Quindio, and Rio Negro, to the south and southeast, among settlements in Ebéjico, Angosturra, and Valdivia, to the north and northeast, moreover, became compounded by extensive agricultural land use in the valley, only adding to the density of the inhabited area. The concentration of towns across the Department of Antioquia strengthened the central region, with this surge in population during these early decades of the 19th-century, marking a recognizable boom early on. Nonetheless, gold mining dwindled, with forced labor or independent mining unable to accommodate Antioquia or appease the inhabitants of the Valle. Marked by the commotion in the public square of Nuestra Señora de la Candelaria, the expanding footprint of the notorious town commanded yet greater commerce to satisfy the increasing numbers that made up the emerging upper class. Merchants traveled to incorporate businesses in Kingston, Jamaica, as the mid-point between Europe, initially importing precious garments and ornaments to pronounce those who strolled through the town in high dress. In this way, the merchants' quests relieved the miners', their *aurum*, malleable mineral, festive glitter, and gift of the glorious earth, as intended for the people of its sacred origins, if only for a time.

---

e   In 2017, Antioquia produced approximately 634,655 ounces of gold, a value of roughly $670-million U.S. dollars.

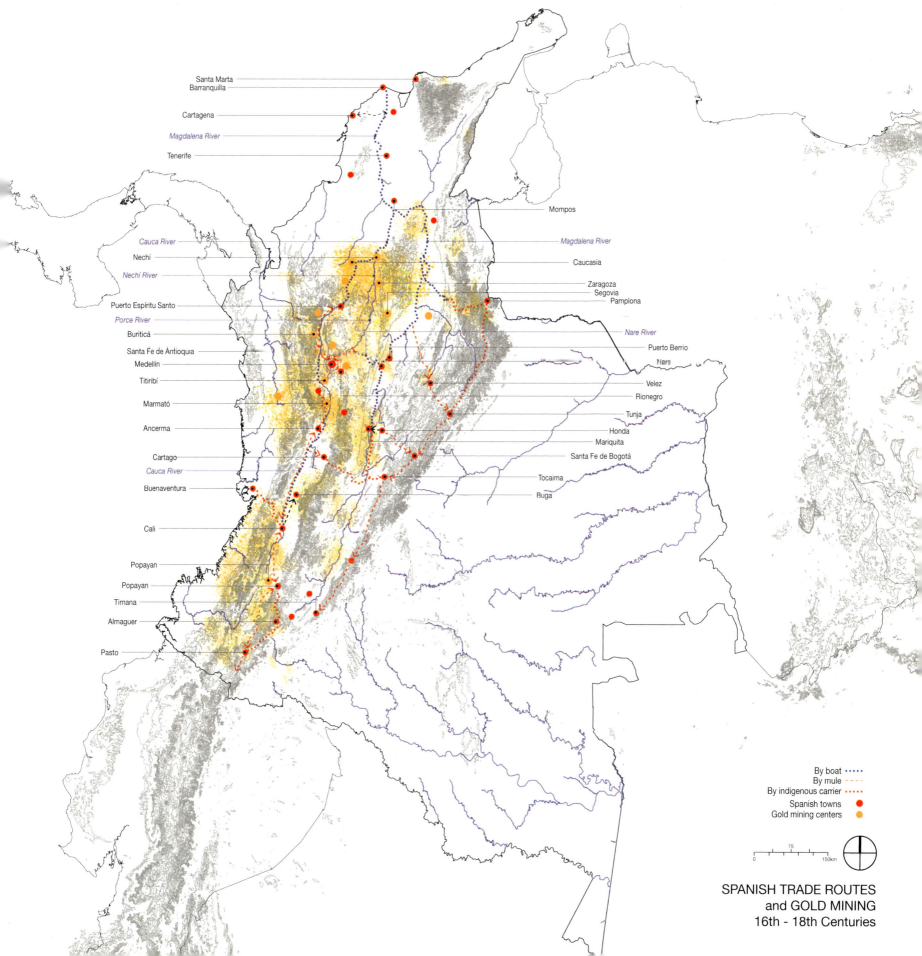

Santa Marta
Barranquilla

Cartagena

Magdalena River

Tenerife

Mompos

Cauca River

Nechí

Magdalena River

Caucasia

Nechí River

Zaragoza
Segovia
Pamplona

Puerto Espíritu Santo

Porce River

Nare River

Buriticá

Puerto Berrio

Santa Fe de Antioquia

Nare

Medellín

Velez

Titiribí

Rionegro

Marmató

Tunja

Ancerma

Honda
Mariquita

Cartago

Santa Fe de Bogotá

Cauca River

Tocaima

Buenaventura

Buga

Cali

Popayan

Popayan

Timana

Almaguer

Pasto

By boat ·······
By mule ·······
By indigenous carrier ·······
Spanish towns ●
Gold mining centers ●

75

0   150km

SPANISH TRADE ROUTES
and GOLD MINING
16th - 18th Centuries

GRAN COLOMBIA, THE REPUBLIC, AND MEDELLÍN

While these shifts took place at a regional scale, at the federal level, 1818 was marked by independence from the New Kingdom of Nueva Granada and the Spanish vice-royalty. Simón Bolivar had created a consolidated Republic of Gran Colombia, with Colombia then still joined with Panamá, Venezuela, and Ecuador, which only lasted 13 years. Given the distances between these territories, communication and proper administration were difficult. The War of Independence had devastated the area, with production and commerce declining significantly. The centrality of Bogotá, moreover, and its role as capital of Nueva Granada dating back to 1718 was, in the end, challenged.

The City of Medellín was named and inaugurated as the capital of the Department of Antioquia in 1828, where a "New Society"[27] filled with international relations was promoted. Tobacco, and later coffee production between 1840 and 1880, followed by the inauguration of the Escuela Nacional de Minas e Ingenería in 1886, increased economic success, promoting eliteness, morale, and even religious righteousness, as indicators of a "superior race."[28] The city had grown to 80,000 inhabitants, where Medellín enjoyed its full social and economic debut, as a period of enlightenment, flaunting its status with the Junín Theatre and the adornment of new architecture, as well as by educating its community with the founding of the Universidad de Antioquia in 1901. The San Juan de Dios Hospital was soon constructed to serve the community. The first liberal, anti-Jesuit newspaper, *El Amigo del País,*[29] circulated to inform the public, just as added plazas and gardens for strolling enhanced the cultural opportunities of the citizens. The Plaza became indicative of the higher status, where administrative factions, prominent residences, and fancy shops were located, as physical imprints continued to reinforce a leading social class. Disputes between the clergy and the government, however, given the idealization of the Kingdom of Christ contrasting with the perceived disruptions created by social and economic progress in the nation, suggest a clear moment where conservative and liberal positions diverge. In the center of Medellín, the plaza, or square, bordered by distinguished buildings representing not only the Crown, but also the Church,[f] are symbolic of the power evoked by this physical space and its occupation, a syndrome that lingers.

Antioqueños, as belonging to the Department of Antioquia, have been described as being a strong race, founded on family and religious principles with diverse lineages including indigenous, European, and African origins, as the geography and the migration have so defined.[30] The binding relationships they have held with the landscape have been the impetus for gravitating toward Aná and the valley, as an innate magnetic pull from which this community has radiated. Over time, the valley's mountains, streams, and the products of its soil have extended the prosperity of the region, providing the natural elements as agents of development. Only as the augmentation to the initial location and role of Aná, as a preexisting geographical nucleus having already been identified early on by native Aburrae, did the eminence of Nuestra Señora de la Candelaria become accentuated later as Medellín. This was three hundred years after the colonists first discovered the Aburrae had already been settled, for millennia, along the fertile Quebrada Aná and Río Aburrá, in the center-most point of an extraordinary mountainous valley.

A CENTRALIZED GOVERNMENT
Liberals vs. Conservatives

In 1831, Colombia and Panama dissolved from the Republic of Gran Colombia, becoming a separate state, also named Nueva Granada. The existing and largely autonomous provinces of the region were re-instituted as departments and administered by an appointed governor. The president, Francisco de Paula Santander, directly selected the governors, devoid of a popular vote. Conservative and liberal parties were formalized in 1849, and 1853 saw a shift toward liberalism, with the abolition of slavery, introduction of the popular vote, and election of governors and congressmen, together with the separation of Church and State. Nueva Granada became the Republic of Colombia in 1886 with president, Rafael Nuñez, ratifying a new constitution that centralized the governance of the country, reversing many of the earlier liberal positions.[31] Finally, in 1899, the Thousand Day War between conservative and liberal parties ended with the independence of Panama, no longer a part of Nueva Granada.

---

f   In the mid-1800s, local Medellín priest José María Botero publicly complained against Colombian President Santander, viewing independence from Spain and the installation of a Republican government as a precursor to heretic and impious behaviors.

MEDELLIN.

PLAZA PRINCIPAL

(lado de oriente)

Above: Plaza Principal, circa 1860, Simon Eladio Salom, Museum of Antioquia. 105

1717 Viceroyalty of Nueva Granada

1739 Viceroyalty of Nueva Granada

1717 Viceroyalty of Nueva Granada

1810 Viceroyalty of Santa Fe

1819 Republic of Colombia

1824-1831 Gran Colombia

1831-1858 Republic of Nueva Granada

1858-1863 Confederacion Granadina

1863-1886 United States of Colombia

1886-1903 Republic of Colombia

1903-1910 Republic of Colombia

1966 Republic of Colombia

EVOLUTION OF COLOMBIA FROM 1717 TO 1966

1990 REPUBLIC OF COLOMBIA

Antioquia

0   75   150km

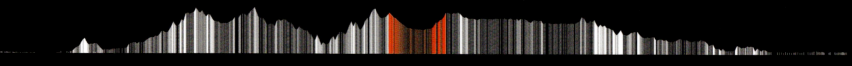

EL CHOCÓ & RIO ATRATO   WESTERN CORDILLERA   RIO CAUCA   VALLE DE ABURRÁ   CENTRAL CORDILLERA

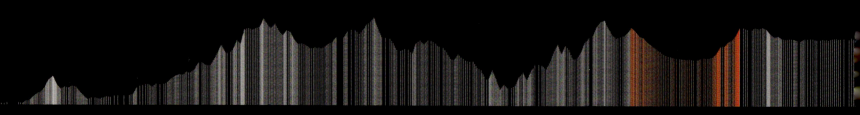

WESTERN CORDILLERA   VALLE DE ABURRÁ

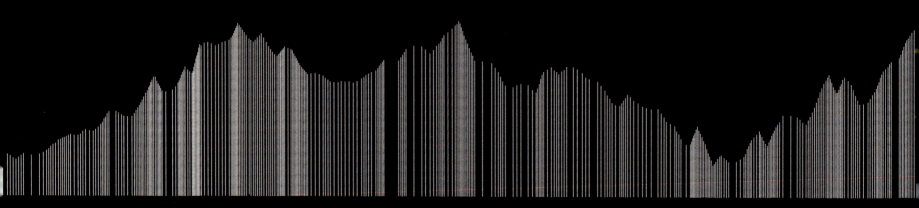

WESTERN CORDILLERA

VALLE DE ABURRÁ

CENTRAL CORDILLERA

0   5   10km

WESTERN REGION OF CHOCÓ TO EASTERN LLANOS, THROUGH VALLE DE ABURRÁ

A RIGID IMPRINT

Earlier footprints of Aná and Nuestra Señora de la Candelaria illustrate how the town settlement had adhered to an east-west orientation, along the Quebrada Aná, later Quebrada Santa Elena, bounded by the geography and the natural course of the stream. The original orientation of the Aburrae settlement, long ago, had also aligned with the Quebrada Aná, descending down to the Aburrá River, with reverence to the stoic mountains of the Cordillera Occidental. Although this layout became the nexus for the development of Nuestra Señora de La Candelaria during colonial times, its growth and orientation was abruptly redirected north, compressing, rather than embracing the expansive and magnificent landscape that lay beyond. Later references illustrate the extension of the city according to principal, rectilinear thoroughfares: Calle Palacé, laid in 1811, running south-north between the church and the square; Calle Boyacá, laid in 1819, running east-west along the Santa Elena stream, and intersecting with right angles at the public square with Calle Bolivar, reaching north-south. These were succeeded by a series of parallel extensions. Calle Carabobo, in 1821, followed in line, as the northbound route, which much later arrived to El Poblado in the south after crossing the first bridge, El Puente Guayaquil, over the Medellín River.[32] This rigid network of routes continued to expand, resulting in a framework that created a solid order over the organic forms of the landscape.

The orthogonal imprint was handed down from Spanish legislation and marks the beginning of urbanization for many Latin American cities. This can easily be detected by the gross similarities of one city to another, though far away and in completely disparate regional landscapes. The expansion of the grid, subdivided into singular lots with varying uses, had no real connection to the earth, rather, the order was purely a method of codifying plots with a mathematical value. The scribed land closer to the dominant square in the grid, as being the first one to be laid down, was worth more; those that were farther out, less. Associations to the proximity to the water's edge or to the undulating topography, to highest views or orientation toward the sun, for instance, were ignored, and the imposition of an artificial pattern instead dominated. It seems counter-intuitive to have crossed the streams of such a prolific hydrological landscape by protruding straight, formal lines in order to simply control more. Puente de la Toma, built in 1857, crossing the Santa Elena stream, was considered a gateway to the growing city despite the fact that this was the mouth of the aqueduct. The force of the stream

eventually destroyed the original bridge in 1871. As a continuation to these mundane maneuvers, the naming of streets also appeared banal, with earlier connotations symbolic of the lovely botanical species or celestial skies adored by the indigenous, later replaced by strict Cartesian coordinates instead.[33] By the early 1900s, Medellín's city limits were marked by the Santa Elena stream to the north, the Medellín River to the west, the existing San José street to the south, and the Buenos Aires neighborhood along the east side.

THE RECONFIGURATION OF THE CITY
The 20th Century

The turn of the century marked an influx of migrants seeking employment and the desire to partake in civic enjoyment. The demands of industry pulsated. Looms were imported, followed by textile machines, with Coltejer founded in 1907 as the major textile company, marking the industrialization of Medellín. Coal and hydro-electric plants propelled production, and the first tram line in the city in 1921 along Buenos Aires accelerated the urbanization of the eastern slopes. The Antioquia Railway, initiated in 1874 in Puerto Berrío, reached Medellín in 1914, ending the Cisneros Station. The line was finalized in 1927 with stations further westward. The railroad sped freight and passenger travel with transportation routes reaching the Magdalena River, south to Caldas and the Cauca Valley, as well as to the Caribbean, Europe, and eventually the north, extending industrialization and international business enterprises in Antioquia.

As the open space in the colonial city became constricted by the increasing numbers who arrived, a linear promenade planted with ceiba trees (Ceiba pentandra) along the refreshing Santa Elena stream replaced the public square for a time, again populated by affluent families who built prestigious homes and gathered in greater form. Over time, however, the growing waste-water resulting from the increasing population, together with the intensity of the textile industry and its heavy chemicals were dumped into the basin, severely polluting the water and air quality, marring the public realm and the essence of urban life. The area concentrated around Junín Street and Parque Bolivar later known as La Toma was designated as a red-light district, where artisans, musicians, laborers, and the lower income classes were relegated. La Toma was a public

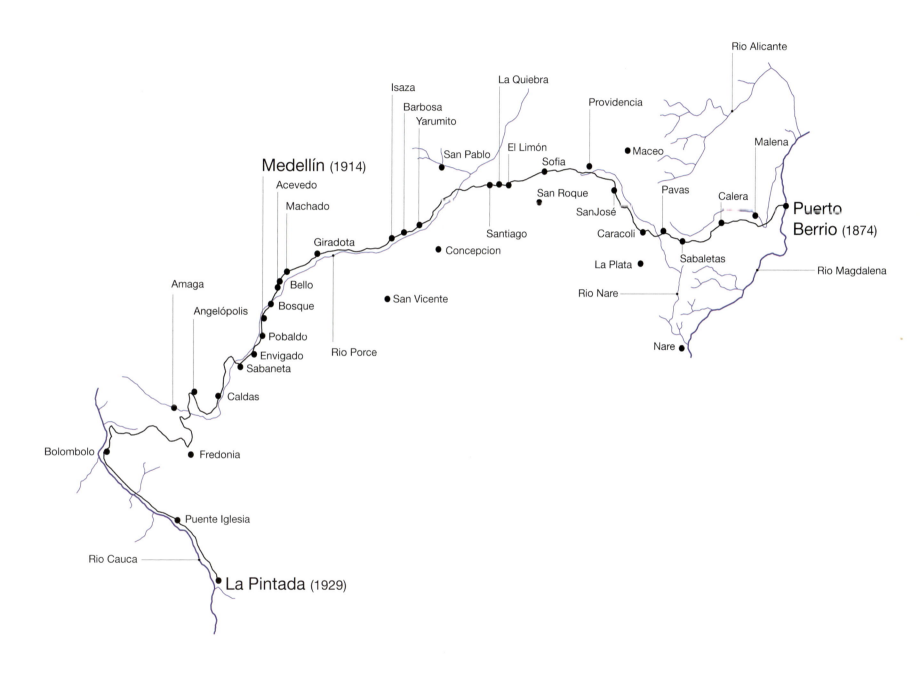

Rio Alicante

Isaza

La Quiebra

Barbosa

Providencia

Yarumito

Malena

Medellín (1914)

San Pablo

El Limón

Maceo

Sofia

Acevedo

San Roque

Machado

SanJosé

Pavas

Calera

Puerto
Berrio (1874)

Giradota

Santiago

Caracoli

Bello

Concepcion

Amaga

Bosque

La Plata

Sabaletas

Rio Magdalena

Angelópolis

Pobaldo

San Vicente

Rio Nare

Envigado

Sabaneta

Rio Porce

Caldas

Nare

Bolombolo

Fredonia

Puente Iglesia

Rio Cauca

La Pintada (1929)

ANTIOQUIA RAILWAY ROUTE
1874 - 1963

75

0   150km

works project initiated by community demand and funded by both the administration and private property tax revenue.[34] The Santa Elena was eventually channelized and covered by a paved street, La Playa, "the beach", named for the memory of the playful character of the water and enjoyment that had run through, but rid of the fetid smells and diseases that it later carried. Several bridges crossing the Quebrada from north to south were eliminated as well, as were many of the memorable Ceiba trees that had aligned this green-blue corridor in the landscape, further disconnecting the city from its natural origins. By 1932, the inhabited footprint of the city had doubled in size from1900, with new working-class neighborhoods expanding north beyond the pre-existing Santa Elena, and east, including Manrique, Aranjuez, and Berlin, with El Prado reserved for the emerging bourgeoisie who sought greener, fresher areas. Although the city had extended to the north, northeast, and to the east, the west-most point continued to be delineated by the Aburrá or Medellín River until Palacé and Carabobo streets were elongated in 1938 toward the basin. Here the natural curve of the river was later rectified toward the south of the valley, where the Puente Guayaquil served as the first bridge to cross the Medellín River. Once crossing to the west, new industrial development and the incorporation of villages such as La America and Belén provided housing for workers who exited the countryside as they served the process of industrialization in the growing city. The footprint continued with the incorporation of additional villages, such as Robledo and San Cristóbal, Itagüí, Bello, Sabaneta, and El Poblado to the southeast, in the area of old San Lorenzo del Poblado, each with a church and a public square with principle roads that aligned them, similar to the earlier layout of Aná.

The industrial revolution of Medellín was represented by urban gestures that reflect the social and economic dynamics of the era, which are still prevalent today. Quebrada Santa Elena, at La Toma, had been transformed from a natural element and open space to an industrial residual stream and malignant urban corridor. The railroad that had transported people and commerce had, in the end, bifurcated the city and its inhabitants from their engagement with the Medellín River. As the central spine of the Aburrá Valley, the river had not been deemed as the garden for the city. Instead, the city had only offered its back, with the river aligned with growing numbers of commercial and industrial buildings that carried the city's waste. Similarly, the market that moved the commodities throughout the city was predominately a private space for the wealthy, as were the "public" squares, and latter promenade, minimizing the community's rightful access to the public realm.

THE CITY OF THE FUTURE

El Plano de Medellín Futuro, Medellín Future Plan in 1913, had marked the first formal management plan that addressed the growth of the city and the need for viable public space for its community. The Plan, derived from a competition, sought to create tools that could assist the municipal agencies in guiding the development of the city. It included green public spaces, while identifying the necessity for wider roads and avenues to further articulate the train, tram, and the car. A few social services, such as the San Vicente Hospital, schools, a theatre, and the Palacio de Bellas Artes, were built as a result, and the demand for public services, such as electricity, telephone, water, and some minimal levels of sewer systems were recognized by the EPM, Empresas Públicas de Medellín, established in 1918.[35] Slight deviations to the orthogonal form of the city were constructed in Los Laureles, designed by architect Pedro Nel Gómez of Universidad Pontificia Bolivariana in the mid-1940s on the center-west side, where perfect concentric curves shaped the buildings' layout, aligned by rectilinear tree-lined streets crossing through.[36] This motif broke with the traditional colonial order, albeit formal, possibly representing a shift toward the city beautiful movement and modern city planning qualities, with a closer response to the natural character of the terrain, to the dominance of the trees, and which addressed the need to provide attributes for enhancing the social well-being of urban residents. Karl Brunner, Austrian urbanist, visited in 1934 and offered his expertise on how to control the increasing development through planning codes and permits.[37] How much these regulations or the Future Plan envisioned the city's growth as a comprehensive framework or spatial vision, with projected zoning districts, built and open space programming, circulation, and their interconnections, is unclear.

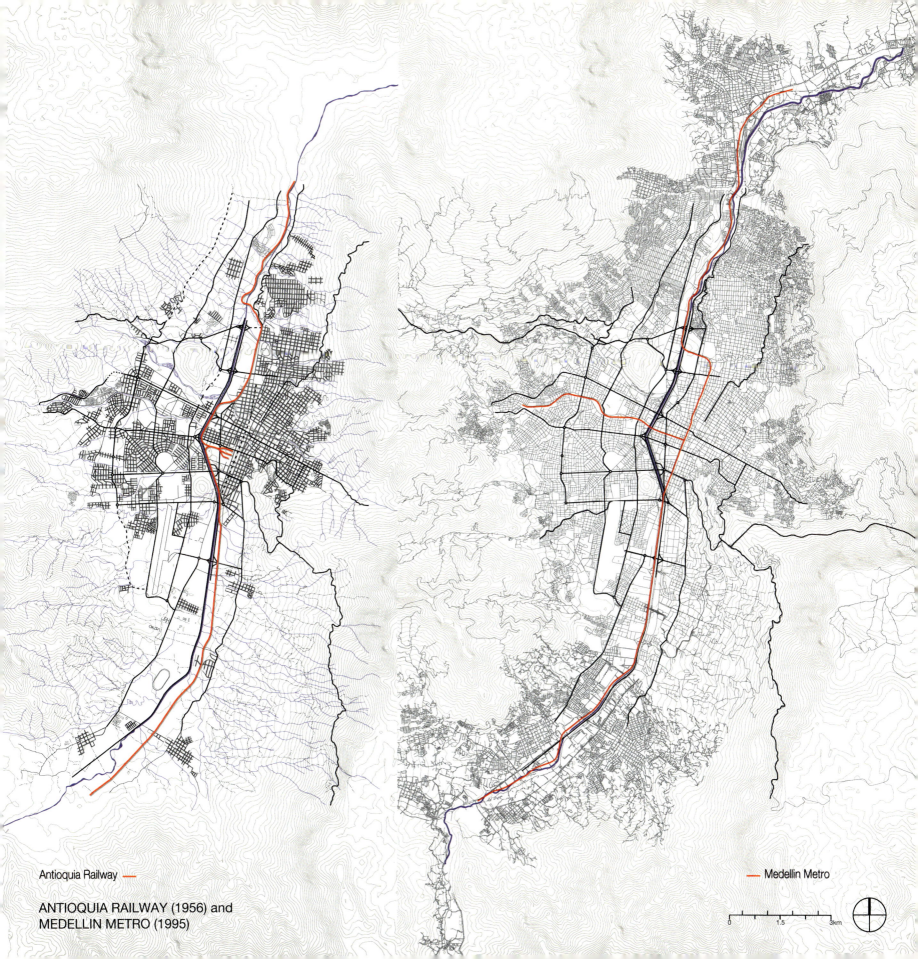

Antioquia Railway ─

ANTIOQUIA RAILWAY (1956) and
MEDELLIN METRO (1995)

─ Medellin Metro

0   1.5   3km

PLAN PILOTO

The city had experienced a 6% growth rate between 1938 and 1951, increasing from approximately 160,000 people to nearly 360,000 during a 13-year period,[38] instigating new plans that offered solutions for tackling urbanization through the idealization of a modern city. The influences of Le Corbusier (Charles-Édouard Jeanneret), renowned Swiss architect and city planner, functionalist and modernist of the era, are evident by his recommendations for a master plan for structuring the city. Le Corbusier was left perplexed by his visit to Medellín in 1948, unable to understand the order of Medellín, unsurprisingly given the random mountains and organic character of the region. Of note is his earlier work in São Paulo in the 1920s with plans for a city that debunked nature, bisecting it with viaducts crossing over the landscape in superior and unyielding fashion, paving the way for the "age of the machine."[39] Studies for the Plan Piloto ensued, designed by Josep Lluís Sert, a Le Corbusier descendant, Spanish architect, and city planner whose work included the master plan for the City of Barcelona (1933–35), and acting as dean of Harvard's Graduate School of Design (1953–69), together with German born Paul L. Wiener, award winner of the International Paris Exposition.[40] Through their office, Town Planning Associates, together with local engineering and architectural support, the Plan Piloto offered a radical new approach to planning through a city-wide extension and renewed version of "imported order." The Plan promoted international scholars and practitioners whose interest in the "form" of the Latin American city had peaked. Considered through a more deliberate city center filled with intense cultural programs protruding as far as Alpujarra on the west side where administrative and governance functions were sited, the Plan envisioned a greenbelt at the top perimeter of the city, an element that contradicted the known limitations of populating the higher, riskier slopes. It also projected the development of the valley's southern zone with industrial uses, with the intention of protecting the air quality from contamination, not to mention the detrimental channelization of the Medellín River.[41] While these ideas had conceptually informed how to organize the future program for the city's expansion, in the end the Plan was abandoned.

Alongside turbulent political and economic times that followed, to be discussed later on, the Plan had overlooked the influx of projected migrants to the slopes, to the higher perimeter, where public investments had not been calculated, therefore extending the lines of the drawing or the illusion of the city beyond the budgetary realities or tangible extents of the region.

Notwithstanding, effective or confining, certain of the Plan Piloto's elements can be detected in the city today. The spine of the valley has been reinforced by following the linear profile of the river, aligned with past and existing train tracks and the planned parallel motorways that have intensified this linear condition over time. This is symptomatic of the industrialization of the landscape, the quest for modernity, resulting in the forced and rapid movement of trucks and vehicles traversing from south to north, or vice versa, that have dominated, creating a deep cut through the heart of Medellín, limiting accessibility to or connections across the river. The decentralization of the downtown area, furthermore, has occurred as the aftermath of the machine supplanting pedestrians, encroaching on the value of communal public space and leaving the city wary and ironically barren in many ways, despite its earlier planned commerce and administrative area in Alpujarra, or even its lively congestion.

As the years progressed, so did the migration to the city, as the indigenous settlers and rural farm owners were displaced from the countryside, fleeing social and economic hardships of extraordinary magnitude created by a push-pull of industrialization and perpetual international dependencies. The footprint of the city continued during the mid-to late-20th-century, bounding the ability of the Aburrá Valley to physically provide viable space for more inhabitants to take part, and accelerating a political crisis that has continuously compromised the physical and social evolution of the city and the community. Let us not forget that the landscape is fundamental to the cultural values that originally sustained the Aburrae and other peaceful tribes in the region, and that this sacred space, and everything else here, have been disrupted.

Right, top: Plan Piloto, *Josep Lluis Sert and Paul Lester Wiener,* 1950.

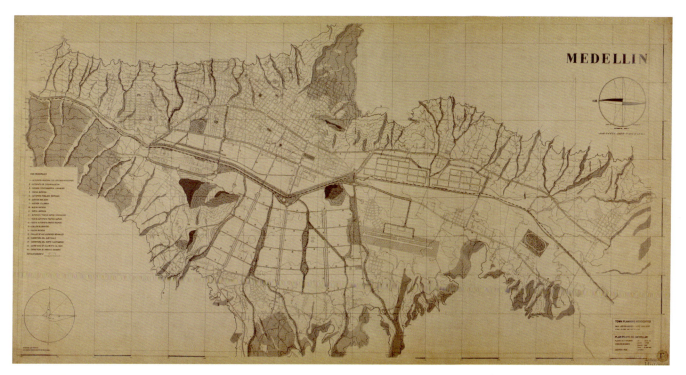

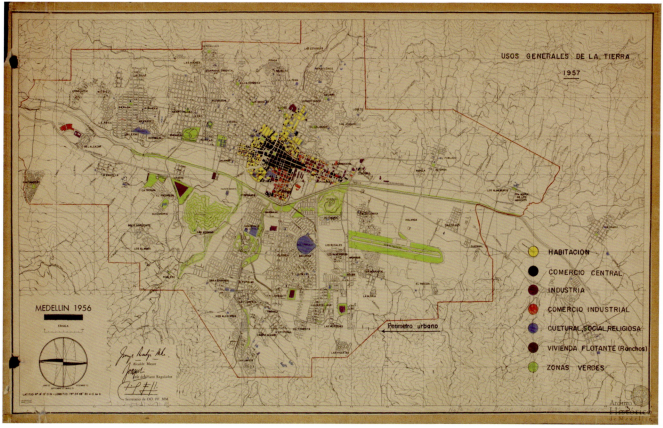

USOS GENERALES DE LA TIERRA

1957

MEDELLIN 1956

ESCALA

Perimetro urbano

● HABITACION

● COMERCIO CENTRAL

● INDUSTRIA

● COMERCIO INDUSTRIAL

● CULTURAL SOCIAL RELIGIOSA

● VIVIENDA FLOTANTE (Ranchos)

● ZONAS VERDES

Above: Plan Piloto, General Land Use Plans, *Josep Lluis Sert and Paul Lester Wiener*, 1956. 115

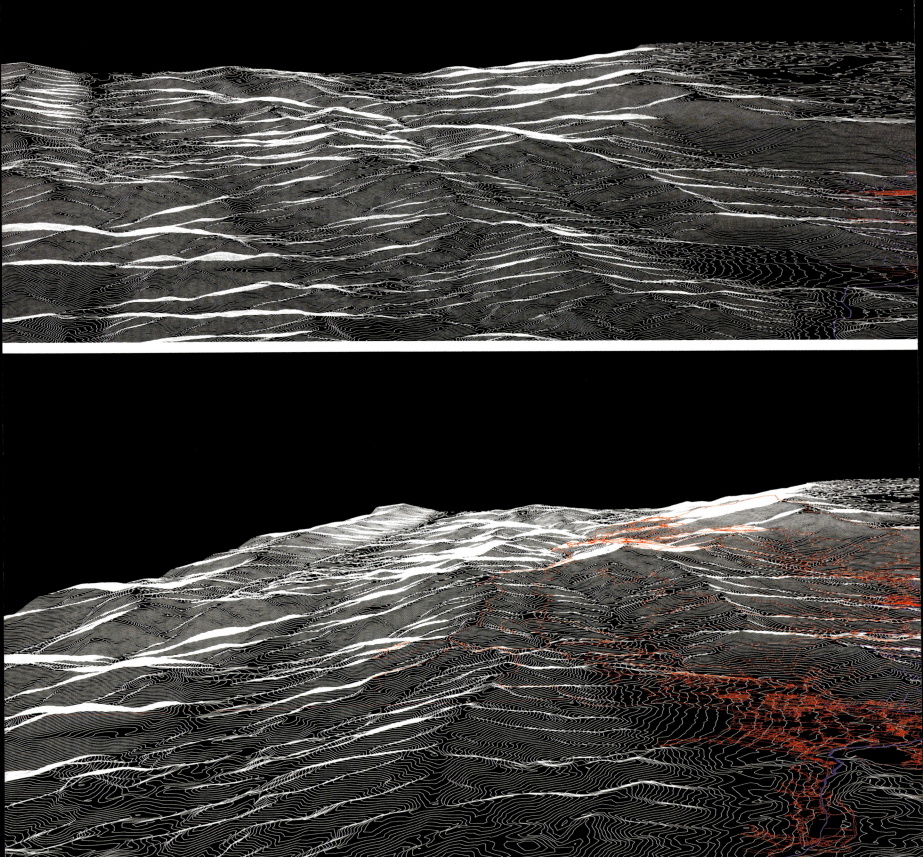

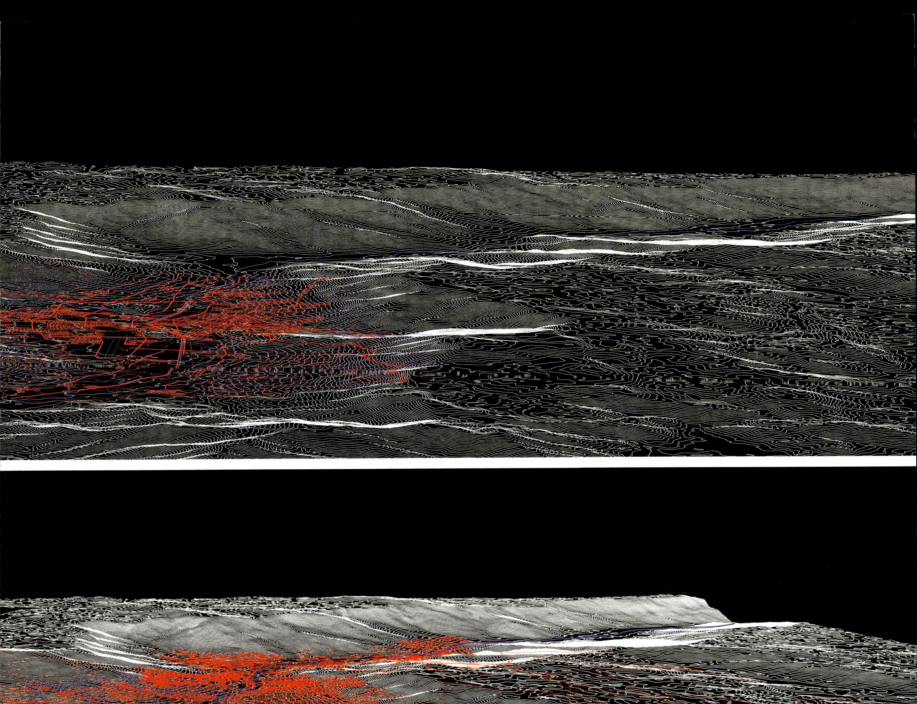
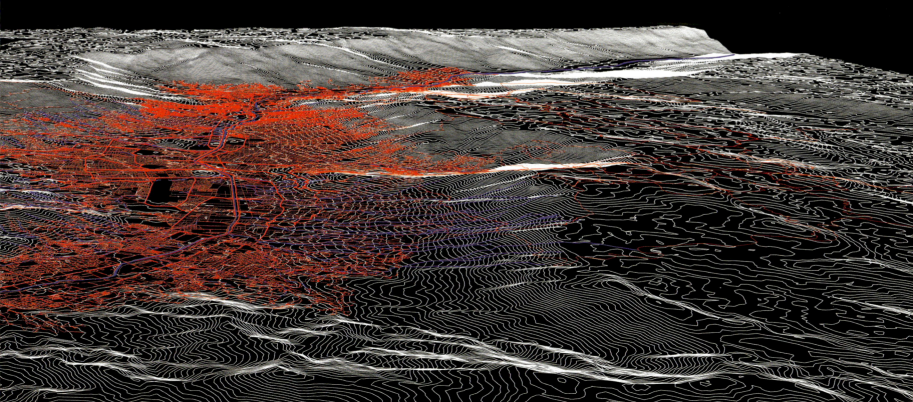

NOTES

1   Camilo Londoño, Antoine Cleef, and Santiago Madriñan, "Angiosperm flora and biogeography of the páramo region of Colombia, Northern Andes,"
      Flora - Morphology, Distribution, Functional Ecology of Plants, 209, no. 2 (2014): 81–87, https://www.sciencedirect.com/science/article/pii/
      S0367253014000024.

2   "Colombian Geography," Colombia - SA, accessed September 6, 2019, https://www.colombia-sa.com/geografia/geografia-in.html.

3   "How does the political and administrative organization work in Colombia?" ProColombia, last modified January 18, 2017, https://www.colombia.co/en/co
      lombia-country/colombia-facts/how-the-colombian-state-is-composed/.

4   Lilliam Eugenia Gomez Alvarez, "La Historia de la Agricultura y de la Tenecia de Tierras en el Valle de Aburra," *Repertorio Histórico de la Academia Antioqueña
      de Historia,* 108, no. 26 (2014): 47.

5   Juan Camilo Escobar Villegas, "La historia de Antioquia, entre lo real y lo imaginario. Un acercamiento a la versión de las élites intelectuales del siglo XIX,"
      EAFIT University Magazine 40, no.134 (2012): 60, http://publicaciones.eafit.edu.co/index.php/revista-universidad-eafit/article/view/879.

6   Gomez Alvarez, "La Historia," 48.

7   Ibid., 46.

8   "The Bromeliads," University of California, Berkeley, accessed October 10, 2019, https://ucmp.berkeley.edu/monocots/bromeliflorae.html.

9   Gomez Alvarez, "La Historia," 48.

10   "The Cretaceous Period," University of California, Berkeley, accessed October 13, 2019, https://ucmp.berkeley.edu/mesozoic/cretaceous/cretaceous.php.

11   Luis Fernando Muñera Lopez, "Historia de Medellín a cuentagotas 1," *El Mundo*, June 9, 2019, https://www.elmundo.com/noticia/Historia-de-Medel
      lin-a-cuentagotas-1/376794.

12   "Encomienda," Encyclopedia Britannica, last modified 2019, https://www.britannica.com/topic/encomienda.

13   Ibid.

14   Axel I. Mundigo and Dora P. Crouch, "The Laws of The Indies," in "The City Planning Ordinances of the Laws of the Indies Revisited, Part I: Their Philosophy
      and Implications," *The Town Planning Review*, 48, no. 3, (1977): 247–68. Translation of ordinances 92,102–7 by Ramon Trias.

15   "Encomienda," https://www.britannica.com/topic/encomienda.

16   Marcelo Jaramillo Ramirez, "El Desarrollo Económico En Antioquia Entre 1760 Y 1830: La Formación De Una Ciudad Como Centro Económico Y Como
      Capital" (Monografia de grado Economia, Universidad EAFIT, 2005), 9.

17   Gomez Alvarez, "La Historia," 51.

18   Ibid.

19   Ibid.

20   Jorge Orlando Melo, "Espacio e Historia en Medellín," Colombia es un Tema, last modified October 2016, http://www.jorgeorlandomelo.org/
      espaciomedellín.htm.

21   Ibid.

22   Ibid., 30.

23   Escobar Villegas, "La historia de Antioquia," 62.

24   Ramirez, "El Desarrollo Económico," 7.

25   Ibid., 13.

26   Ibid., 19.

27   Escobar Villegas, "La Historia de Antioquia," 59.

28   Juan Camilo Escobar Villegas, "La historia de Antioquia, entre lo real y lo imaginario. Un acercamiento a la versión de las élites intelectuales del siglo XIX,"
      EAFIT University Magazine 40, no.134 (2012): 62, http://publicaciones.eafit.edu.co/index.php/revista-universidad-eafit/article/view/879.

29   Ibid., 66.

30   Ibid., 62.

31   Hernán Alejandro Olano García, "Historia de la regeneración constitucional de 1886," *Revista IUS*, 13, no. 43 (2019), https://www.redalyc.org/jatsRe
      po/2932/293259573009/html/index.html.

32   Melo, "Espacio."

33   Ibid.

34   Vanessa Restrepo, "Cuando Medellín tenía una playa para nadar." *El Colombiano,* August 10, 2019, https://www.elcolombiano.com/antioquia/que-habia-an
      tes-en-la-avenida-la-playa-canalizacion-de-quebrada-santa-elena-IL11389414.

35   Pablo Rodriguez Jimenez, "Medellín: La Ciudad y su Gente," Banrepcultural, 2017. https://www.banrepcultural.org/biblioteca-virtual/credencial-historia/nume
      ro-230/medellín-la-ciudad-y-su-gente.

36   Melo, "Espacio."

37   Rodriguez Jimenez, "Medellín: La Ciudad," 7.

38   Melo, "Espacio."

39   G. Pianca, "Le Corbusier and Sao Paulo - 1929: Architecture and Landscape." Paper presented at Le Corbusier, 50 years later, Valencia, November 2015,
      http://ocs.editorial.upv.es/index.php/LC2015/LC2015/paper/viewFile/937/1337.

40   Juan Jose Cuervo Calle, " El Centro Cívico para Medellín:del Plan Piloto de Wiener y Sert al Centro Administrativo La Alpujarra," *Iconofacto*, 13, no.20 (2017):
      208–10, https://revistas.upb.edu.co/index.php/iconofacto/article/view/7859/7175.

41   Rodriguez Jimenez, "Medellín: La Ciudad."

Right: Resident in Barrio Santo Domingo, in Medellín's urban periphery.

on SOCIAL URBANISM

An Overview

3

ON SOCIAL URBANISM
An Overview

As part of human nature, our inseparable affinity to the landscape has ironically led to a paradigm that has misguided the manner by which urban development has occurred throughout history. The reciprocal relationship between space and culture form the basis for behavior and the quality of life, as two interconnected parameters that must be reconciled in order to engage in constructive ideologies over the physical and social conditions for developing cities of the Global South. The pre-Columbian rituals and traditions discussed earlier frame a geographical landscape that has shaped the cultural norms and traditions of native people, which, when broken, have resulted in the spatial and social disruption of the community.

During his Nobel Peace Prize acceptance in December, 1982, Gabriel Garcia Marquez[a] shared the following,

> Latin America neither wants, nor has any reason, to be a pawn without a will of its own; nor is it merely wishful thinking that its quest for independence and originality should become a Western aspiration. However, the navigational advances that have narrowed such distances between our Americas and Europe seem, conversely, to have accentuated our cultural remoteness. Why is the originality so readily granted us in literature so mistrustfully denied us in our difficult attempts at social change? Why think that the social justice sought by progressive Europeans for their own countries cannot also be a goal for Latin America, with different methods for dissimilar conditions?[1]

These tendencies are evidenced in Medellín, Colombia through the physical evolution of a stolen city, layered over a productive, yet delicate landscape, in which a social strata has been cast unto its inhabitants, ranked according to international interests and far away influences, over local and autonomous virtues. As the aftermath of a gravely imbalanced schema, the rapid growth of Medellín is demarcated by its progression as a commercial depot in central Antioquia since its colonial discovery in the 15th-century onwards, until reaching its fulcrum, unable to mitigate the demands between habitable space and social equity. Many developing cities struggle from similar syndromes, steeped in economic dependen-

cies that prevent the realization of planning visions that could otherwise engender sustainable growth, as integral to the landscape in which the local communities have naturally existed and where there is great potential to thrive. Medellín has endured tremendous political hardships over its evolution, and over the past several decades in particular, driven by external, and later, internal conflict, compounding the detriment of an unsupported and disregarded community, conflating into a chaotic state bearing close attention. As the tipping point between despair and renewed hope, the emergence of social urbanism, as an inclusive socio-political and practical approach to the urbanization of Medellín, offers renewed perspectives for ably nourishing the future growth of this unique city.

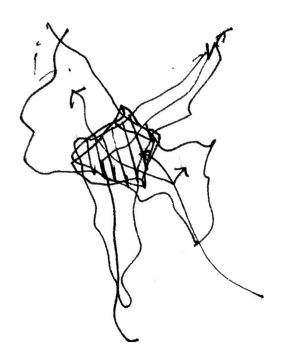

a   Gabriel Garcia Marquez was a Colombian novelist and journalist, best known for his works of *magic realism*, such as *One Hundred Years of Solitude*.

Above: Sketch Studies of the Valle de Aburrá, *María Bellalta*.
Right: Medellín, Colombia figure/ground with topography.

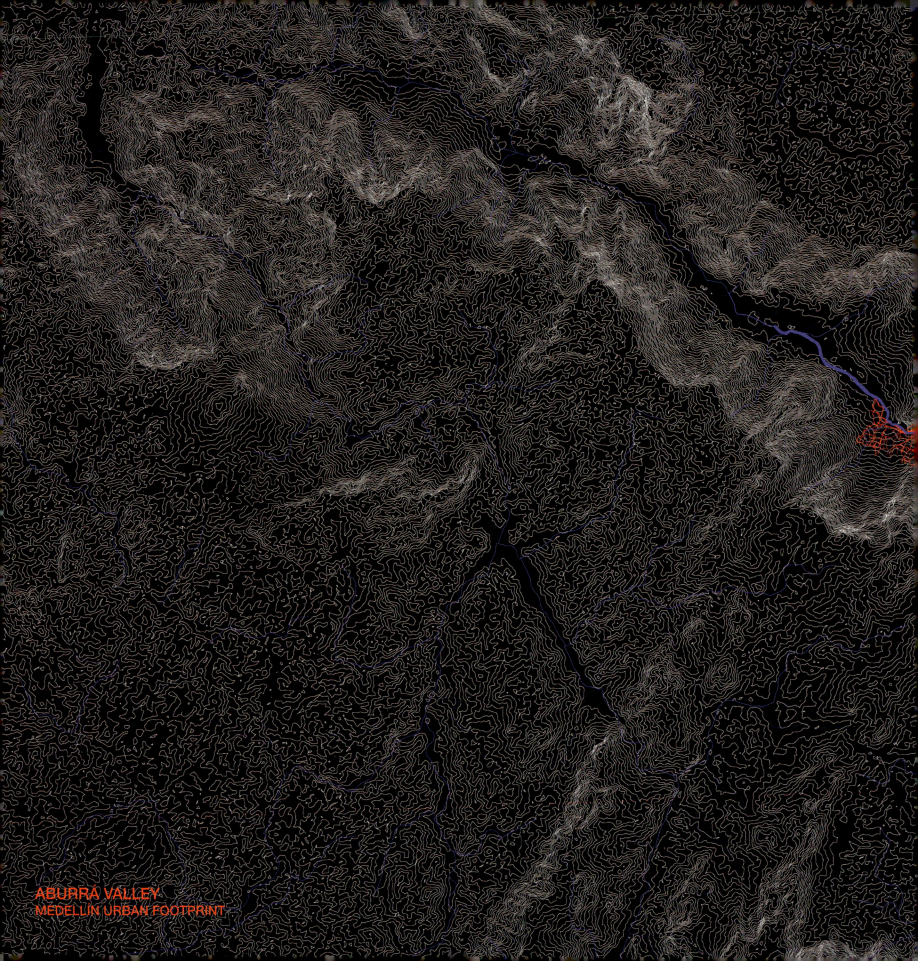

ABURRÁ VALLEY
MEDELLÍN URBAN FOOTPRINT

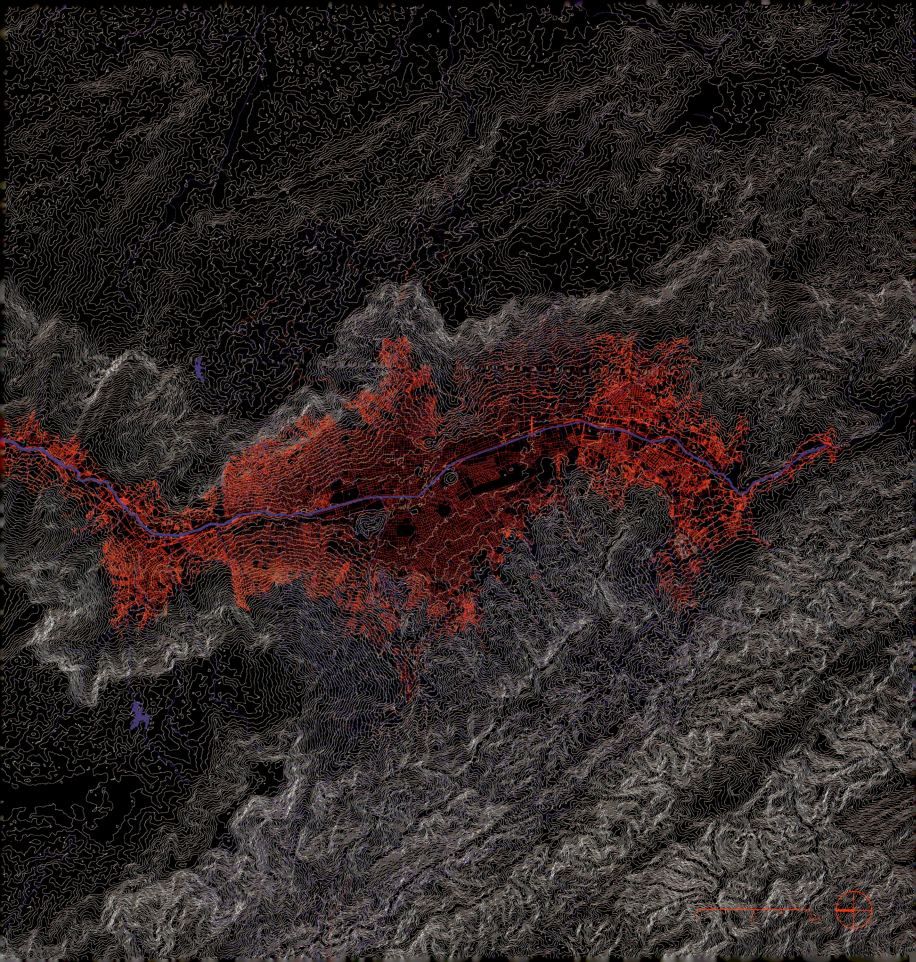

THE ORIGINS OF POWER AND VIOLENCE

The commercial prominence of Medellín continued through the mid-20th-century, until tensions escalated between church and state, the upper and working classes, and among the viewpoints of liberal and conservative parties, shaking the political climate and provoking the onset of frantic rural migration. Between 1951 and 1975, the city's population spiked from 360,000 to 1.1 million inhabitants [1,2], a 32% rate of growth over a 24-year period. This increase took place all while contending with the limitations of a sloped playing field, with steep 35% gradients, and a central cut in the middle of the basin, created by the Medellín River running through and dividing the city from east to west. The encircling aspect of the surrounding mountains added to the containment of the valley, preventing the footprint of the city from spilling over to accommodate more inhabitants. The increased population during this period was the result of power struggles, of one class over another, stemming from a social structure fashioned by the land value as part of the landscape itself. The profile of central Antioquia, its peaks and valleys, promoted territoriality from one side of the mountains to the other, which together with the desire to appropriate the most advantageous slopes for cultivation, set up inherent disputes over the agrarian region. Coffee exports paved the way for transportation and further urbanization, and eventually to the service industry, though through a drastically disproportionate distribution of wealth. The latifundio land reform practices, mentioned earlier, proliferated during this period of Medellín's development, having by now established an international dependence through the increased production for multinational consumption, practices that provided lucrative profits for the latifundistas, in relative terms, while for the working class, the struggle was dire: a forced loss of land tied to a compulsory move to the city in search of shelter and any work that could be attained. Much like before, the history of the indigenous tribes repeated itself through the expulsion of farmers from their land, though this time not only made to evacuate their farmsteads, but in doing so, intensifying the rapid, unplanned growth of the city. These are the evident struggles between the inhabitants and the nuances of the agrarian landscape, tied to the natural resources and to land ownership, dating back to the pre-colonial era, which continue today, forming a culture of conflict and displacement that have shaped the city of Medellín.

The migration to the city and the inflated population in Medellín dramatically impacted the economy, with increasing demands for employment, which, coupled with the country's political division, was manifested through prolific violence, social inequality, and exploitation, resulting in a five-decade civil conflict. During his second presidential campaign in 1948, liberal politician Jorge Eliécer Gaitán was assassinated, provoking the onset of a tragic and violent war in Colombia, La Violencia, between the two main political forces that had dominated the country for over a century— the conservative party and the Colombian liberal party.[3] An estimated 250,000 lives were lost and 5.7 million displaced throughout the country as a consequence of these struggles.[4] La Violencia ended in 1958, with many liberal party supporters demobilizing, while others continued to operate in the rural areas, leading to further conflicts and to what eventually became a civil war in the 1960s. Amidst these conflicts, the sale of the Antioquia Railroad in Medellín to the National Railroad in 1961 severed mobility and the city's commercial prosperity.

Not long after, Las Fuerzas Armadas Revolucionarias de Colombia, FARC, became an officially organized left-wing guerrilla group in 1966 led by Pedro Antonio Marín. FARC was disillusioned and against the liberal party's leadership, and subsequently turned to a form of governance identified by the Global North as communism. The main goal set out by FARC had been, and in many ways continues to be, the redistribution of land to benefit the rural farmers, although its implementation often deviated from this mission. Their work has included protection and social services for poor families living in the countryside at the expense of a "gramaje", or farm tax.[5] FARC has also operated through kidnappings and extortion, the exchange of captives for their jailed guerrillas, and has benefited from over $600 million dollars in drug trade annually.[6] A parallel guerrilla group emerged shortly after, intensifying the revolutionary force in Colombia, with El Ejercito de Liberacion Nacional, ELN, a highly political unit composed of students, Catholic radicals, and left-wing intellectuals inspired by the Cuban revolution and Marxist ideology.[7] The ELN, likewise, engaged in kidnappings and ransom, alongside mechanisms that paralyzed communities by destroying and collapsing the infrastructure throughout the region, making the area impassible and disconnecting the cities. Both FARC and the ELN represented marginalized groups, those evicted from their agricultural plots, the poor and destitute, against the Colombian wealthy classes. Together they opposed the United State's influence in Colombia, the privatization of natural resources, multinational corporations, and rightist violence.

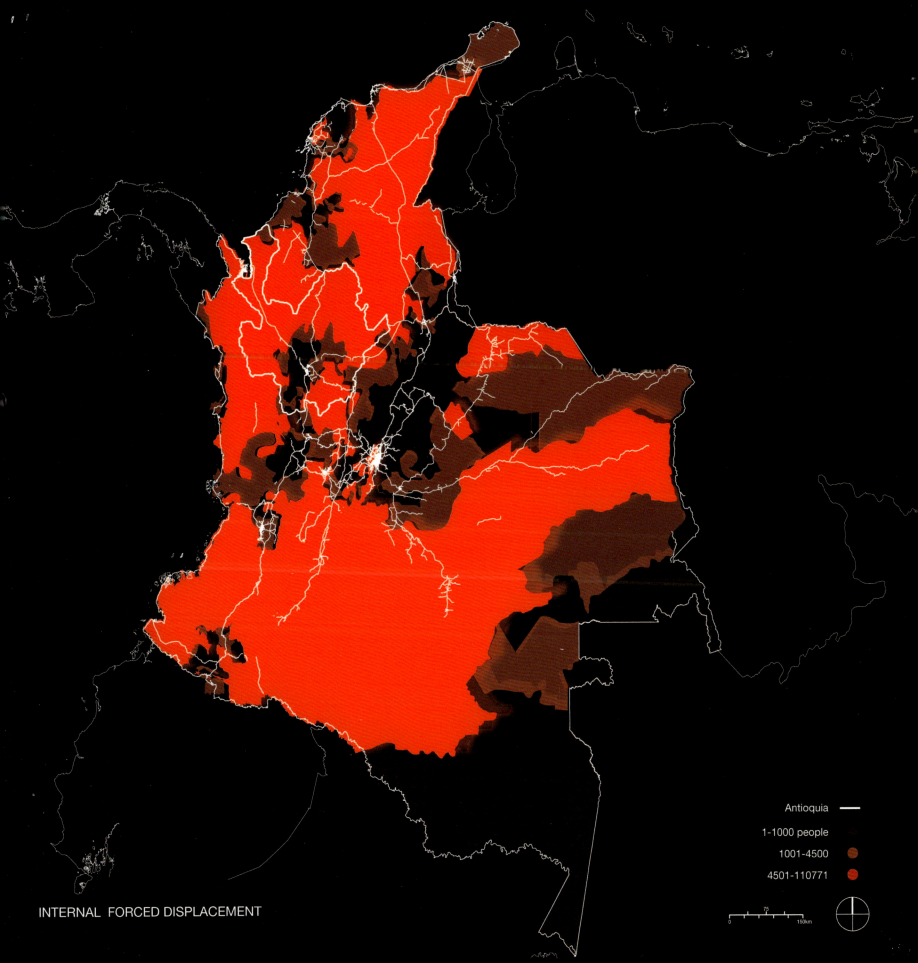

INTERNAL FORCED DISPLACEMENT

Antioquia ⎯⎯

1-1000 people

1001-4500

4501-110771

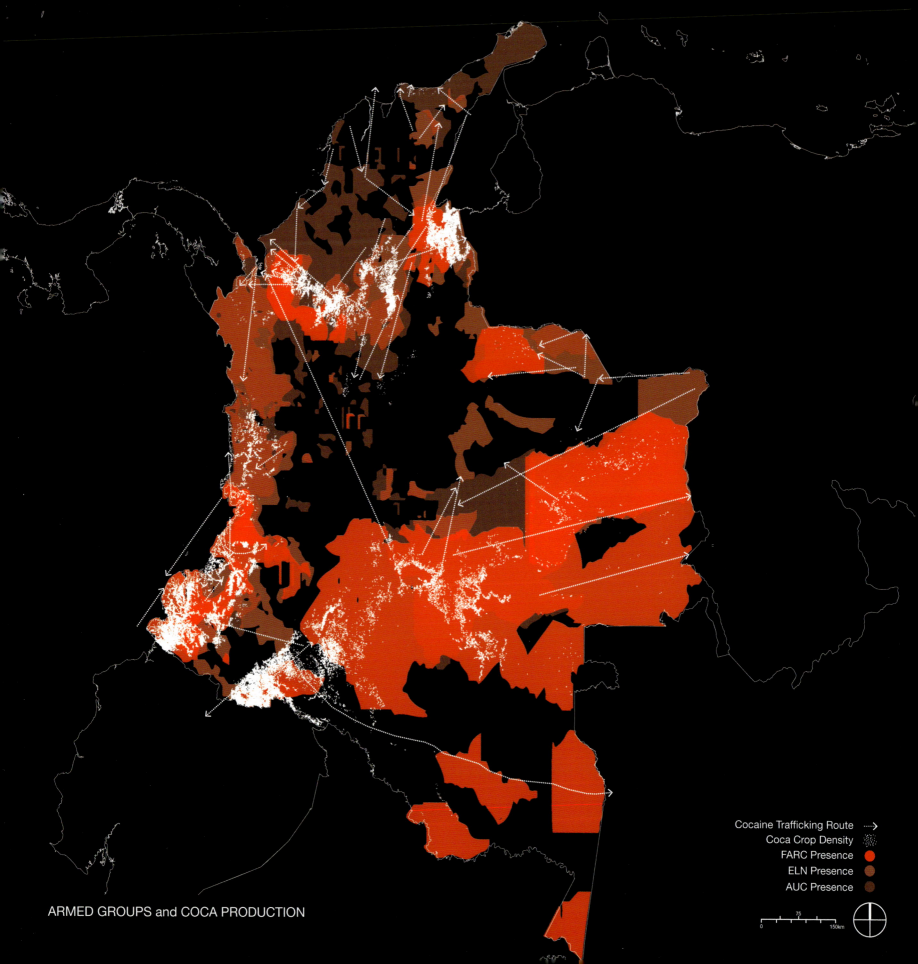

ARMED GROUPS and COCA PRODUCTION

Cocaine Trafficking Route ┈┈➤
Coca Crop Density
FARC Presence
ELN Presence
AUC Presence

75
0   150km

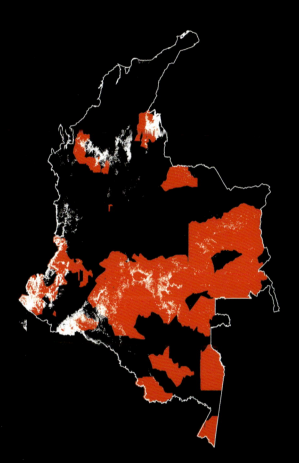

FARC
Fuerzas Armadas Revolucionarias de Colombia
Revolutionary Armed Forces of Colombia

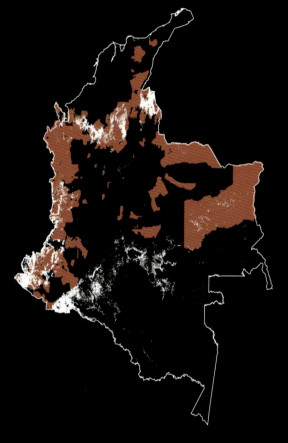

ELN
Ejército de Liberación Nacional
National Liberation Army

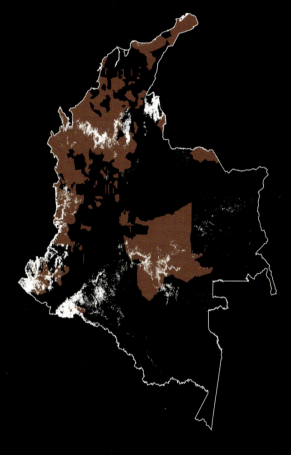

AUC
Autodefensas Unidas de Colombia
United Self-Defense Forces

Coca Crop Density
FARC Presence
ELN Presence
AUC Presence

ARMED GROUPS and COCA PRODUCTION

150
0   300km

In response to this leftist movement, several right-wing paramilitary groups developed, with the Auto Defensas Unidas de Colombia, the AUC, eventually becoming the principal "umbrella" organization to combat FARC and the ELN.[8] Wealthy elites and drug traffickers supported this armed organization, and rather than defending the oppressed, this group instead secured the economic interests and safety of the upper class. The Colombian State was clearly absent. The consolidation of these revolutionary groups, left-wing guerrilla and right-wing paramilitary, competing for territorial power and wealth through force and oppression, rendered the Colombian State a weak figurehead.   An additional type of insurgence arose as smaller, violent barrio gangs in periphery neighborhoods around Medellín, in the "comunas,"[b] typically led by disenfranchised and excluded young men, usually unemployed, who often ended as murder victims. Gangs and gang leaders, given the ineffectiveness of the State and its inability to protect the political space of these marginalized communities, took matters into their own hands. In the end, through the complexity of the geographical region, the political land disputes of Colombia in general, and the central Antioquia region and Medellín in particular, the evolution of various tiers of power has been perpetuated, from global to local scales.

As the country's internal political conflicts intensified through the mid-1970s, the world economy simultaneously experienced a critical recession, with oil prices skyrocketing and coffee plummeting, unemployment and inflation rising, and the Latin American debt crisis prohibiting development or foreign investment.[9]

---

b   Comunas, or comunes, are administrative borders that divide Medellín into 16 spatial units, each with a high level of socio-economic heterogeneity; their average size is 6.30 km^2 x 2.86 km^2.

During this period, the international demand for psycho-actives was at an all-time high, and while Cuba and Panama had been targeted for their cocaine exportation to the U.S., Medellín, tucked away in the Valle de Aburrá, was an ideal hideaway. Not only was this the logical location for coca production, with an optimal climate for cultivation, it was also the place with a complete breakdown in social order. Colombia produced 80% of the global cocaine market at the time, with $5.7 million U.S. consumers.[10]

Here lies the geographical and socio-political context that predisposed Medellín as a derelict city, that only later facilitated Pablo Escobar with the ability to destroy civil society and seize a global empire on drug trafficking. Escobar was born to peasant farmers and endured the trials of extreme poverty and inequality. He crawled out, and up, as a thief, by 1982 regarded as a renowned drug-lord earning $70 million dollars a day through his Medellín Cartel.[11]

With his demand for "plata o plomo,"[12] silver or lead, Escobar, supported by his own people through gang violence, terrorized the State's elite, the police force and military, escalating the murder rate in Medellín. While the State attempted to regain control with support from the United State's military, the U.S. had its own agenda of fighting communism and maintaining access to Colombian resources.

Ever since, Medellín has been blasphemed as a narcotics laboratory, as the cartel empire of Pablo Escobar, stigmatized as the city otherwise known as the "Murder Capital of the World."[13] In 1991, the homicide rate in Medellín reached 375 murders per 100,000, a figure 37.5 times higher than the World Health Organization's average figure of 10 per 100,000.[14] By comparison, New York City's homicide rate was nearly ten times less, at 35 per 100,000.[15]

In the end, there are several elements, broken and violated, that have contributed to the onslaught of extreme violence in Medellín. Defined as the complete disruption of a social order, violence occurred in the city due to a series of compounded factors, including: rural and intra-urban displacement of the poor, both from the agrarian regions and from urban areas within the city; the fast rate of population growth; the extreme levels of unemployment, poverty, and inequality; the exclusivity of the rich; and as the result of a male dominated society. Violence, more simply put, is the result of the prevailing historical and political geography of the region, and to the manner in which power has been produced and dispersed, which, through force, has been imposed throughout the city.[16] If mediated by social rules and norms, and situated within an economic and political context of a community, then violence becomes part of the social structure itself, thereby rendered not only as a dreadful catalyst of abused power, but of a deadlocked and harmful cultural syndrome.[c] The World Bank Gini coefficient used to represent the statistical dispersion of income or wealth distribution has, in fact, classified Medellín as one of the most unequal cities in Latin America.[17,d] The result, as evidenced in Medellín, has been a politicized landscape ruled by this abuse of power, where both physical and community fabrics are fractured. The emergence of Pablo Escobar and his criminal empire are a product of power, displaced through violence, where Escobar was able to shatter all social codes, epitomizing the symptoms of the oppression endured in Medellín. It is important to note, however, that Escobar offers nothing more than a synthesis, as a veiled episode of a catastrophe that has been personified and disguised, over a crisis that stems from much further afield, from atrocious acts of colonialism and northern oppression spread over an entire culture and society.

These scenarios drastically deviate from traditional programmatic elements and from how we typically decipher the criteria for informing planning models. These problems call for a much broader understanding of the conditions, not only of landscapes less familiar to northern geographies, but of the social systems that have derived from these unique natural conditions and regions as well. We have to dig much deeper, to unravel the history of an agrarian community, in this instance, to comprehend how it has been beaten by tiers of power, of colonial conquerors, international envoys, or local echelons; how the community has been unfairly aggravated and assaulted over its very own productive landscape through centuries of displacement. It is crucial that violence and corruption be understood in relation to the "higher" world's greed for these regions, and to the disregard for the natural resources these provide to the inhabitants, which if left undisturbed, could better serve the development of the local community. Only then can one re-contextualize the criminal and narcotrafficking empires, get past these preludes, to then reorient the spatial and social dilemma that Medellín exhibits as an emerging city. As part of a prolific agricultural region in Antioquia, with external allure and internal demands marked by its rapid growth, Medellín must be repositioned as viable, rather than purely as a quintessentially "dangerous" part of the developing world. Here we are summoned to extraordinary levels of scrutiny as spatial thinkers, planners, and as 21st-century agents.

---

c   I do not mean to suggest that Medellín, Colombia, or Latin America, are alone is this matter of violence. The current political landscape is the U.S. is revealing a system that is well ruled by the abuse of power, and less so by the honor of a democracy by a civilized society.

d   The World Bank Gini coefficient is used to represent the statistical dispersion of income or wealth distribution, and has classified Medellín as one of the most unequal cities in Latin America. https://data.colombiareports.com/medellin-economy-statistics/. (Accessed May 14, 2017).

Urban centers ●
Coca cultivation ◉
Medellin Cartel routes ──
Cocaine trafficking routes ──

COCAINE NARCOTRAFFICKING
IN LATIN AMERICA

500
0   1000km

A SHIFTING POLITICAL ARENA

Latin American countries have each sought their independence, yet most continue to struggle with a class structure that is the result of colonialism, capitalism, and what little remains of the indigenous people. As mentioned earlier, the lasting impressions marked by the landscape of these regions have been the enticing draw for intruders, as they have also been the sustenance and basis forming Latin American values. The mining and agrarian labor are directly correlated to the geomorphology and climate of the central region, and the entrepreneurial drive of Antioqueños has coincided with the prime location of Medellín and its progress. The bright colors of Colombia's national flag, yellow, blue and red, also symbolize connections to the region, with Colombia's rich soil, gold, agriculture, and the sun expressed by a wide yellow band; the blue oceans that surround the country, the multiple rivers, and the eternal sky represented by a middle blue stripe; and red, the bottom band, representative of the bloodshed Colombians have endured as they have fought for independence and symbolizes the struggle and perseverance of the Colombian community.[18,e]

The political poles in Colombia, and the deriving levels of inherent power, are indicative of the various geographical influences, which have swung back and forth, from conservative, with ideals of a centralized ruling state, to liberal, with visions for more autonomous governances, as represented by individual states, cities, and municipalities. Given the distinctions among the five continuous ecological regions that make up Colombia, it's important to recognize that each has an intricate set of natural systems and assets, and therefore of cultural habits and attitudes that are formed. The distinct physical and social dynamics of individual regions have been contradicted by the notion of a single ruling state and may help to understand the root of many of Colombia's internal conflicts, which when coupled with external forces and oversights, have devastated the country for many decades. With Bogotá at the helm dominating the executive branch of the nation, and Medellín as a subsidiary in spite of its central location in the country–with significant economic and commercial power– for example, alone poses political challenges. This is compounded by Medellín's mixed culture, made up of Afro races, European, and mestizo,

from coastal, montane, or plateau landscapes, and conflated by the surge of forced migration from all over Colombia as a result of industrialization and political force.

In Medellín, this migration was challenged by the fluctuating demands and lack of employment, insufficient habitable space, and an increasing divide between income levels, resulting in a city ruled by violence and corruption. The oligarchy and the upper class, over the agrarian landscape and the civil rights of the community, infected the political stream to a near degree of normalcy. The assassination of presidential candidate Luis Carlos Galán in 1998, moreover, and the dread left by the attempted murder of César Gaviria Trujillo (1990–1994), Galán's successor, loomed over the city. One hundred men, women, and children were murdered aboard the aircraft that would have carried Gaviria, shattering Medellín with terror and despair. The Colombian administration, as a result, initiated a significant political shift that de-centralized the executive branch, marking a poignant moment in the country's conscious quest for social change. Under Gavíria's presidency Colombia's new constitution of 1991 was instituted, which sought to build human rights, partly through the ability for political parties to be represented and by promoting the emergence of local governance through an electoral process. The constitution aimed to redistribute the lost powers of the legislature and judiciary and to invite more diverse citizens into the political sphere; it expanded a bipartisan model by incorporating seats among three, not the usual two, political parties: the Liberal, the Conservative, and the Social Conservative Parties.[19] These entities were envisioned as holding political, economic, and social agendas granting a level of autonomy to departments and to their regional municipalities. It would follow that these more localized governances would be in closer touch with the realities of the region than the distant capital state had ever managed to be, therefore strengthening the ability to ameliorate the political, economic, and social crisis of individual cities in the country, and in this case, of Medellín. These political changes, by and large, helped to maintain the country's partisan gridlock by providing an inherent system of checks and balances—something the U.S., despite touting its great democracy and modernism, risks losing, setting the

---

e   The typical interpretation over the colors of the flag that I have come across while traveling in Colombia are similar to the popular Colombian children's song that states: "Yellow is our gold, blue is our vast seas (oceans), and red is the blood that gave us our freedom (from Spain), S.C., December 6, 2000. The following two interpretations are also offered: 1. The yellow symbolizes sovereignty and justice; the blue nobility, loyalty, and vigilance; and the red valor, honor, generosity, and victory achieved at the high cost of bloodshed. 2. The yellow symbolizes universal liberty; blue the equality of all races and social classes before God and the law; and red fraternity. Source: Alfred Znamierowski's World Encyclopedia of Flags, 1999. Phil Nelson, February 28, 2000; https://www.crwflags.com/fotw/flags/co.html#first

country far behind as a world leader. The danger is a society that is no longer represented by an even distribution of its members, but rather, by one supreme, corrupt regime.

Although beyond the purview of this book, it is interesting to note the patterns of governance that have been in effect in Colombia over the past two centuries. From a singular oligarchy in the early 19th-century, to two recognizable forces between liberal and conservative parties with alternating administrations, until the murder of liberal party candidate Jorge Gaitán in 1948, having potentially extended the conservative Party rule. A decade later, following La Violencia, the National Front emerged during 1958 and 1974, as a period where conservative and liberal parties alternated, united against the potential for Gustavo Rojas Pinilla's military dictatorship of 1953 to 1957 to take further hold.[20] Subsequently, the nation again returned to a fairly balanced period between liberal and conservative parties, until liberals led between 1986 and 1998, marking a 14-year liberal party rule. The new constitution goals for encouraging alternative parties is not evident until 2002, with the presidency of Álvaro Uribe Vélez and the Colombia First Party. Despite appearing as a diverse new party, however, Uribe continued to steer the country to the far right, without the rural communities and agrarian families originating here in mind. He strategically expended U.S. aid under the Plan Colombia, intended to combat the War on Drugs, and instead fueled Colombia's military strength to fight off FARC and the ELN.

Even while the numbers of leftist guerrillas dropped significantly, the fact that his popular ratings were high and foreign investment, in some respects, had returned to the country, Uribe has also represented the epitome of Colombia's political corruption. The Agro Ingreso Seguro Fund, for example, was promoted as creating funds to stimulate small-scale farming and labor, yet instead were embezzled, passing into the hands of the upper class.[21] Uribe has also been tied to the AUC, Colombia's right-wing paramilitary coalition, which has violated human rights, even beyond those inflicted by FARC and the ELN; he has been an apparent ally to the U.S., although in 1991 a U.S. intelligence report deflected this claim by linking Uribe to the Medellín drug cartel.[22] In 2016, President Juan Manuel Santos, representing the new National Unity Party, by contrast, received the Nobel Peace Prize "for his resolute efforts to bring the country's more than 50-year-long civil war to an end,"[23] a move strongly opposed by Uribe, who has argued that offering impunity to insurgents from crime or

extradition, has essentially condoned acts of violence by FARC and the ELN.[24]

The election of Iván Duque Márquez in 2018, ultra-conservative, guised as the new Democratic Center, with 54% of the popular vote,[25] points back to Uribe's years of the far right. A common anecdote is that Duque is an Uribe puppet, trained to follow in his footsteps, with false promises, corruption, and elites' interests. On the other hand, the two opposing presidential candidates of the 2018 campaign offered much fresher points of view. The election included former Bogotá Mayor Gustavo Petro, a progressive candidate defamed for his liberal views on abortion and same-sex marriage, and defeated through usual political bribes, cronyism, and even violence toward supporters in non-conflict areas where the popular vote was more easily swayed. In the north of the country, in Santander and the metropolitan area of Cúcuta near the Venezuelan border, for example, Petro was portrayed as a Chavista and a friend of Maduro, a whole topic of deep debate in itself, as we do not really know which came first, the internal regime or the external oppression of Venezuela. Sergio Fajardo Valderrama, the third presidential candidate, only took 24% of the vote during the final round with the Green Alliance, a center-left party.[26] Notwithstanding, as former mayor of Medellín from 2004–2007, and governor of Antioquia from 2012–2016, Fajardo's work continues to be recognized worldwide, for his strategic and inclusive approach, and for restoring community hope as a valuable impetus and symbolic shift paving the way for Medellín's future.

PRESIDENTS OF COLOMBIA 1819-1974

Simon Bolivar y Palacios 1819-1830

Joaquin de Mosquera 1830
Rafael Urdaneta 1830-1831
Francisco de Paula Santander 1832-1837

Jose Ignacio de Marquez Barreto 1837-1841

Pedro Alcantara Herran Martinez 1841-1845

Tomás Cipriano de Mosquera 1845-1849

Jose Hilario Lopez Valdez 1849-1853

Jose Maria Obando del Campo 1853-1854
Jose Maria Melo y Ortiz 1854
Mariano Ospina Rodriguez 1857-1861

Bartolome Calvo Diaz 1861
Tomás Cipriano de Mosquera 1861-1864

Manuel Murrillo Toro 1864-1866

Santos Acosta Castillo 1867-1868
Santo Guiterrez Prieto 1868-1870

Eustorgio Salgar Moreno 1870-1872

Manuel Murrillo Toro 1872-1874

Santiago Perez de Manosalbas 1874-1876

Aquileo Parra Gomez 1876-1878

Julian Trujillo Largacha 1878-1880

Rafael Nunez Moledo 1880-1882

Francisco Javier Zaldua 1882
Jose Eusebio Otalora Martinez 1882-1884

Rafael Nunez Moledo 1884-1894

Miguel Antonio Caro Tobar 1894-1898

Manuel Antonio Sanclemente 1898-1900

Jose Manuel Marroquin Ricuarte 1900-1904

Rafael Reyes Prieto 1904-1909

Ramon Gonzales Valencia 1909-1910
Carlos Eugenio Restrepo 1910-1914

Jose Vicente Concha Ferreira 1914-1918

Marco Fidel Suarez 1918-1921

Jorge Holguin Mallarino 1921-1922
Pedro Nel Ospina Vazquez 1922-1926

Miguel Abadia Mendez 1926-1930

Enrique Olaya Herrera 1930-1934

Alfonso Lopez Pumarejo 1934-1938

Eduardo Santos Montejo 1938-1942

Alfonso Lopez Pumarejo 1942-1946

Mariano Ospina Perez 1946-1950

Candidate, Jorge Gaitan, assassinated 1948
Laureano Gomez Castro 1950-1953

Gustavo Rojas Pinilla 1953-1957

Alberto Lleras Camargo 1958-1962

Guillermo Leon Valencia Munoz 1962-1966

Carlos Lleras Restrepo 1966-1970

Misael Pastrana Borrero 1970-1974

POLITICAL PARTIES IN COLOMBIA

One Year   No Party   Military

1974-2019 (Presidents of Colombia)

- Alfonso Lopez Michelsen 1974-1978
- Julio Cesar Turbay Ayala 1978-1982
- Belisario Betancur Cuartas 1982-1986
- Virgilio Barco Vargas 1986-1990
- César Gaviria Trujillo 1990-1994
- Ernesto Samper Pizano 1994-1998
- Andres Pastrana Arango 1998-2002
- Alvaro Uribe Velez 2002-2010
- Juan Manuel Santos Calderon 2010-2018
- Ivan Duque Marquez 2018-

GOVERNORS OF ANTIOQUIA 1975-2019

- Oscar Montoya Montoya 1975-1976
- Jaime Sierra García 1976-1978
- Rodrigo Uribe Echavarría 1978-1980
- Álvaro Villegas Moreno 1980-1981
- Iván Duque Escobar 1981-1982
- Álvaro Villegas Moreno 1982-1983
- Nicanor Restrepo Santamaría 1983-1984
- Alberto Vásquez Restrepo 1984-1986
- Bernardo Guerra Serna 1986-1986
- Antonio Yepes Parra 1986-1987
- Fernando Panesso Serna 1987-1988
- Antonio Roldán Betancur, assassinated 1989
- Helena Herrán de Montoya 1989-1990
- Gilberto Echeverri Mejia, assassinated 1992
- Juan Gómez Martínez 1992-1994
- Álvaro Uribe Vélez 1994-1998
- Alberto Builes Ortega 1998-2000
- Guillermo Gaviria Correa, assassinated 2004
- Aníbal Gaviria Correa 2004-2008
- Luis Alfredo Ramos Botero 2008-2012
- Sergio Fajardo 2012-2016
- Luis Pérez Gutiérrez 2016-2019

MAYORS OF MEDELLIN 1975-2019

- Victor Cádenas Jaramillo 1975-1976
- Sofía Medina de López 1976-1977
- Guillermo Hincapié Orozco 1977-1978
- Jorge Valencia Jaramillo 1978-1979
- Bernardo Guerra Serna 1979-1981
- José Jaime Nicholls 1981-1982
- Álvaro Uribe Velez 1982-1983
- Juan Gaviria Gutiérrez 1983-1984
- Pablo Peláez González 1984-1986 assasinated 1989
- William Jaramillo Gómez 1986-1988
- Juan Gómez Martínez 1988-1990
- Omar Flórez Vélez 1990-1992
- Luis Alfredo Ramos 1992-1995
- Sergio Naranjo 1995-1998
- Juan Gómez Martínez 1998-2001
- Luis Pérez Gutiérrez 2001-2004
- Sergio Fajardo 2004-2008
- Alonso Salazar 2008-2012
- Aníbal Gaviria 2012-2016
- Federico Gutiérrez 2016-2019

Legend:

- ● Partido Conservador Colombiano
- ● Partido Liberal Colombiano
- ● GSC Independientes
- ● Daniel Quintero Calle 2020-

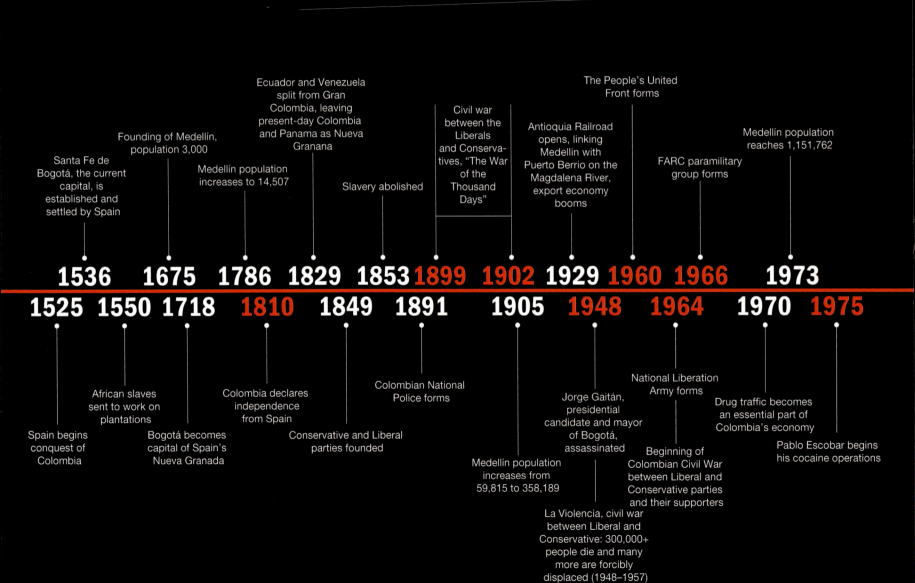

Ecuador and Venezuela
split from Gran
Colombia, leaving
present-day Colombia
and Panama as Nueva
Granana

The People's United
Front forms

Founding of Medellín,
population 3,000

Civil war
between the
Liberals
and Conserva-
tives, "The War
of the
Thousand
Days"

Antioquia Railroad
opens, linking
Medellin with
Puerto Berrio on the
Magdalena River,
export economy
booms

Medellín population
reaches 1,151,762

Santa Fe de
Bogotá, the current
capital, is
established and
settled by Spain

Medellín population
increases to 14,507

Slavery abolished

FARC paramilitary
group forms

1536   1675   1786   1829   1853 1899   1902   1929 1960   1966   1973

1525 1550 1718 1810   1849   1891   1905   1948   1964   1970   1975

African slaves
sent to work on
plantations

Colombia declares
independence
from Spain

Colombian National
Police forms

National Liberation
Army forms

Jorge Gaitán,
presidential
candidate and mayor
of Bogotá,
assassinated

Drug traffic becomes
an essential part of
Colombia's economy

Spain begins
conquest of
Colombia

Bogotá becomes
capital of Spain's
Nueva Granada

Conservative and Liberal
parties founded

Beginning of
Colombian Civil War
between Liberal and
Conservative parties
and their supporters

Pablo Escobar begins
his cocaine operations

Medellín population
increases from
59,815 to 358,189

La Violencia, civil war
between Liberal and
Conservative: 300,000+
people die and many
more are forcibly
displaced (1948–1957)

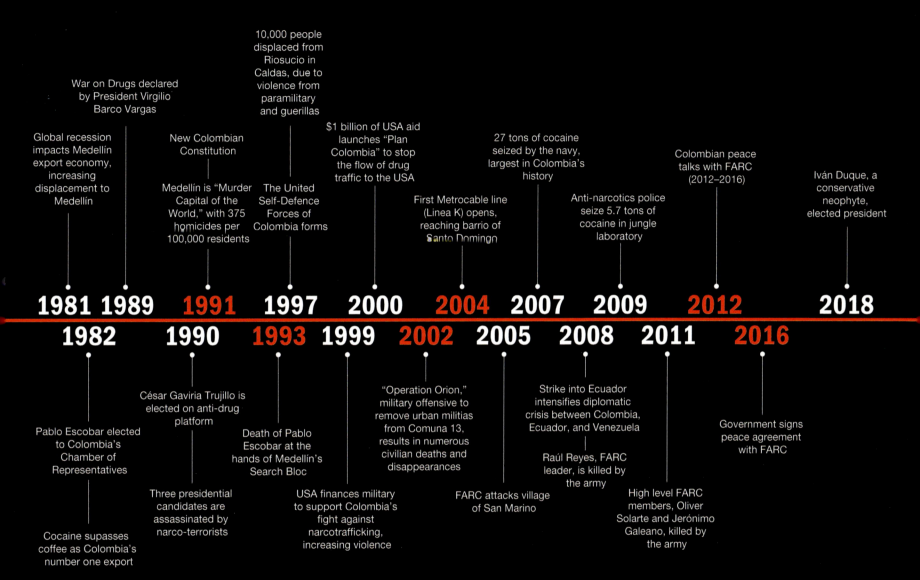

1981
Global recession impacts Medellín export economy, increasing displacement to Medellín

1989
War on Drugs declared by President Virgilio Barco Vargas

1991
New Colombian Constitution

Medellín is "Murder Capital of the World," with 375 homicides per 100,000 residents

1997
The United Self-Defence Forces of Colombia forms

10,000 people displaced from Riosucio in Caldas, due to violence from paramilitary and guerillas

2000
$1 billion of USA aid launches "Plan Colombia" to stop the flow of drug traffic to the USA

2004
First Metrocable line (Linea K) opens, reaching barrio of Santo Domingo

2007
27 tons of cocaine seized by the navy, largest in Colombia's history

2009
Anti-narcotics police seize 5.7 tons of cocaine in jungle laboratory

2012
Colombian peace talks with FARC (2012–2016)

2018
Iván Duque, a conservative neophyte, elected president

1982
Pablo Escobar elected to Colombia's Chamber of Representatives

Cocaine supasses coffee as Colombia's number one export

1990
César Gaviria Trujillo is elected on anti-drug platform

Three presidential candidates are assassinated by narco-terrorists

1993
Death of Pablo Escobar at the hands of Medellín's Search Bloc

1999
USA finances military to support Colombia's fight against narcotrafficking, increasing violence

2002
"Operation Orion," military offensive to remove urban militias from Comuna 13, results in numerous civilian deaths and disappearances

2005
FARC attacks village of San Marino

2008
Strike into Ecuador intensifies diplomatic crisis between Colombia, Ecuador, and Venezuela

Raúl Reyes, FARC leader, is killed by the army

2011
High level FARC members, Oliver Solarte and Jerónimo Galeano, killed by the army

2016
Government signs peace agreement with FARC

COLOMBIA TIMELINE
1525 - 2018

PARADISE

The breathtaking views from the Valle de Aburrá are intoxicating. Deep and oblong, crossed by the Medellín River, and enveloped by the Andes Mountains reaching over 3,000 meters (nearly 10,000 feet), Medellín sits amidst the center of the valley as part of a multifaceted landscape, with profuse emerald hues from the lush tropics and a warm terracotta glow radiating from the mountains. Medellín is often remarked upon as the city of "eternal spring", as part of Colombia's rich biosphere, the second most abundant after Brazil. The city celebrates its reign as the world flower market, with over $1.35 billion[27] in annual exports, and the "Desfile de Silleteros", a colorful flower festival that has been celebrated every August since 1957. During the festivities, "Silleteros,"[f] the local farmers, descend from the misty mountains with their harvested blooms to parade and dance to local music, adorned with flower displays carried on their backs.

Medellín occupies 380.64 km^2, (roughly 147 mi^2), with a metropolitan area alone of approximately 166 km^2 (64 mi^2).[28] The central, urban area of Medellín is organized into six zones: north, east and west; central, east and west; and south, east and west. Within these, there are 16 comunas, varying in strata,[g] where peripheral, denser comunas, with lower quality of housing and lack of open space typically correspond to a lower stratum. The city's elevation ranges from 1,900 meters at the southern end, to 1,300 at the north, with an average elevation of 1,450 meters (4,757 feet) above sea level. Medellín's municipal boundaries span roughly 13 kilometers in length, south to north, and seven to eight kilometers from east to west at its widest point in the center of the city. Beyond Medellín's urban zone, there are five "corregimientos"[h], San Sebastián de Palmitas, San Cristóbal, Altavista, San Antonio de Prado, and Santa Elena, composing the urban-rural, rural, and ecological areas of the municipality of Medellín. The surrounding mountains stretch for 60 kilometers at the perimeter of the valley, opening widely at the southern canyon, and compressing tightly at the northern tip, where the narrow opening is only three kilometers in width.[29] The urban corridor of the Aburrá Valley goes beyond Medellín's political boundaries at the southern and northern tips, and extends throughout its length, spanning in a linear direction, creating a conurbation with the municipalities of Itagüí and Envigado to the south, and Bello, north of the city. The valley today includes a total of 10 municipalities, with a metropolitan area occupying 1,164 km^2, which is six times the exclusively urban area of the Municipality of Medellín alone.

Medellín has continued to grow from the east, though now the settlements are moving upward, toward the mountains, as part of the origins of the city at the Quebrada Santa Elena, at Aná. It has also continued to populate on the west side, along the Quebrada Iguaná, where the second major stream-bed of the valley runs down. United Nations population estimates for Medellín in 2018 were 3,933,652, suggesting a density of 10,351 people living per square kilometer (0.38 mi^2).[30, i] The population is settling in areas beyond the projected limit for planned development, at the periphery, and even beyond the rim of the valley. These areas are characterized by steep slopes within the rural and ecological conservation regions on the east and west sides, classified as "high-risk zones". For the informal settlements relegated to these inclined areas, political agendas or budgets may not always coincide, nor exist. In 1950, 35% of Medellín's inhabitants lived in informal areas; and this number has increased to 78% presently,[31] an indication that the city has exceeded its ability to function for the number of people that inhabit it. Less than 30% of Medellín's citizens are living with adequate housing and services.

The rural migration to a city that sits within a geographical bowl is not a simple proposition. The lack of horizontal and habitable space poses challenging planning strategies that are not easily resolved, and by default, the millions that have run to the city, fleeing displacement and violence, and in search of work, have had no option but to squat with whatever means they have been able to find, clinging for dear life to the slopes. The angles of repose and the clay composition of the soil, combined with the regions intense hydrological character, with gushing steams running down from the high altitudes, predispose all remnants of space to torrential rains and flooding, and ultimately to disastrous landslides that can wipe out entire communities in a matter of seconds[j].

---

f   "Silleteros" stems from the Spanish word "silla," or chair, indicative of a time when local peasant men strapped wooden chairs on their backs to carry their crops, children or noblemen. I was told in Medellín that silleteros had traditionally carried their elderly or sick on a chair on their back, down from the mountainsides to the city to reach medical services. See https://www.colombia.co/en/colombia-culture/folklore/everything-need-know-silleteros-medellins-flower-festival/

g   Strata levels in Medellín are associated with housing grades, as evaluated by the exterior of a property, the conditions of the roads where the properties are sited, and the proximity to public services, health, education, and employment. Strata 6 is the highest and 1 is the lowest. Strata levels coincide with the provision of public subsidies. Distribution of strata are mapped on page 169. See https://medellinguru.com/colombia-estratos

h   "Corregimiento" is a term in Colombia defnining the internal portion of a departament, and is a zone typically less populated than a municipality.

i   By comparison, New York City has a population of 100,000, with 10,194 people per km^2. (26,403 per mi^2), similar to Medellín's density, yet which despite its own hardships, is sited on a flat footprint where accessibility and services are within reach

j   A catastrophic landslide occurred in Medellín on September 27, 1987 in Villa Tina, an informal settlement on the east. Five hundred people were killed, 1,300 wounded, and 120 houses destroyed.

Right: Coffee region, La Palma, Medellín, Colombia.

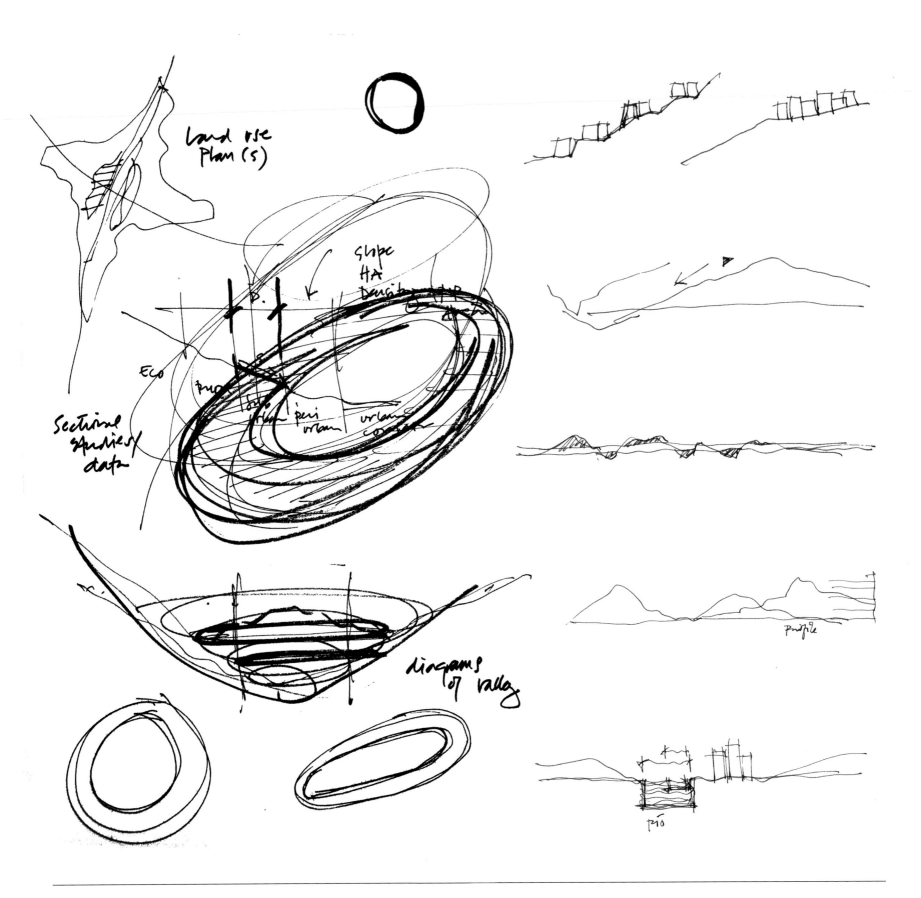

Land use
Plan (s)

slope
HA
Density

ECO

Sectional
studies/
data

diagrams of valley

profile

rio

Right: Sketch studies of Medellín's comunas along the Valle de Aburrá, *María Bellalta.*

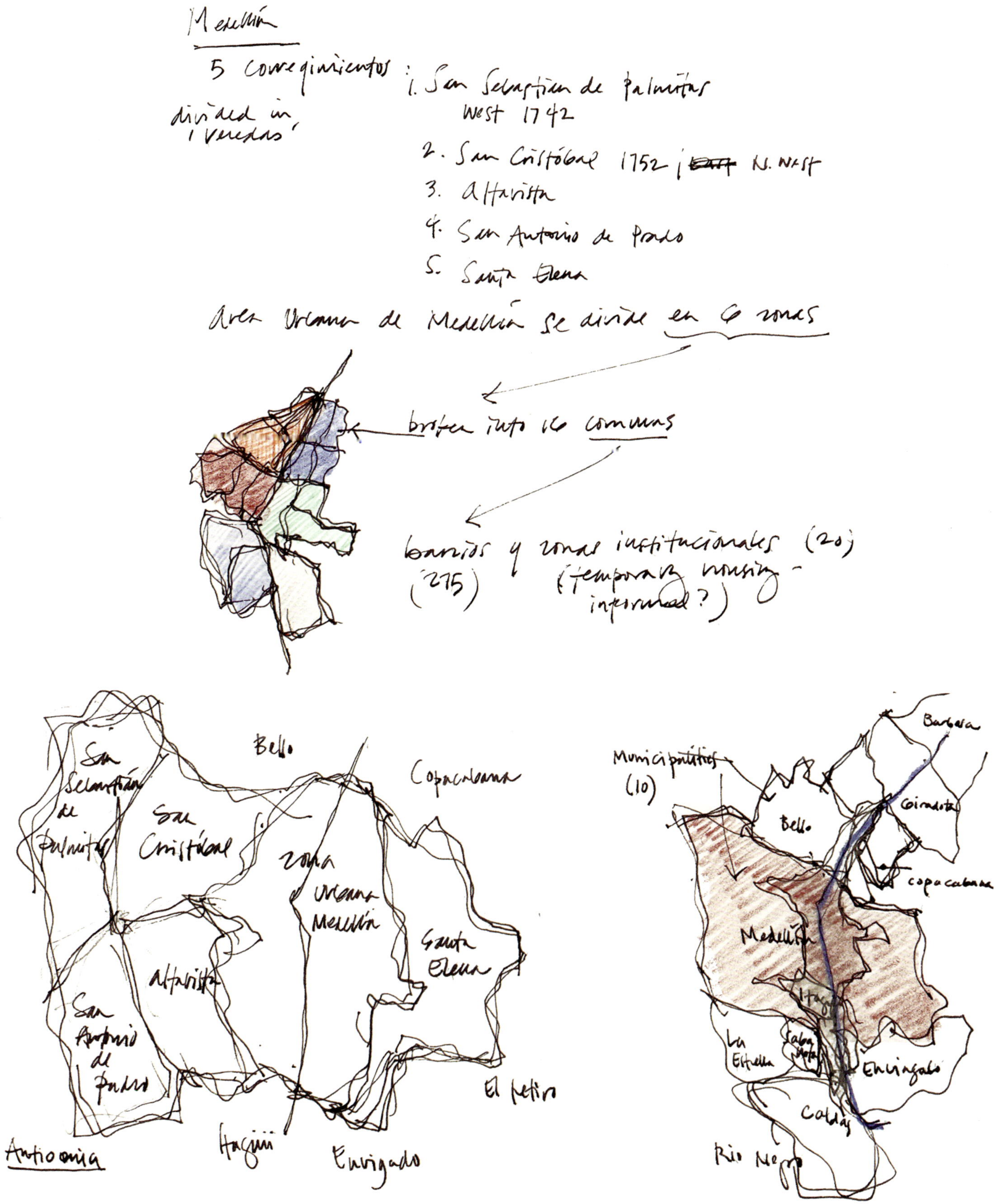

Medellín

5 corregimientos : 1. San Sebastián de Palmitas
                             West 1742
divided in,
i veredas'   2. San Cristóbal 1752 ~~2M~~ N. West
                   3. Altavista
                   4. San Antonio de Prado
                   5. Santa ~~Elena~~ Elena

Área Urbana de Medellín se divide en 6 zonas

broken into 16 comunas

barrios y zonas institucionales (20)
(275)   (temporary housing -
                     informal?)

San Sebastián de Palmitas
Bello
Copacabana
San Cristóbal
Zona Urbana Medellín
Santa Elena
Altavista
San Antonio del Prado
El Retiro
Antioquia
Itagüí
Envigado

Municipalities (10)
Barbosa
Bello
Girardota
Copacabana
Medellín
Itagüí
La Estrella
Sabaneta
Envigado
Caldas
Río Negro

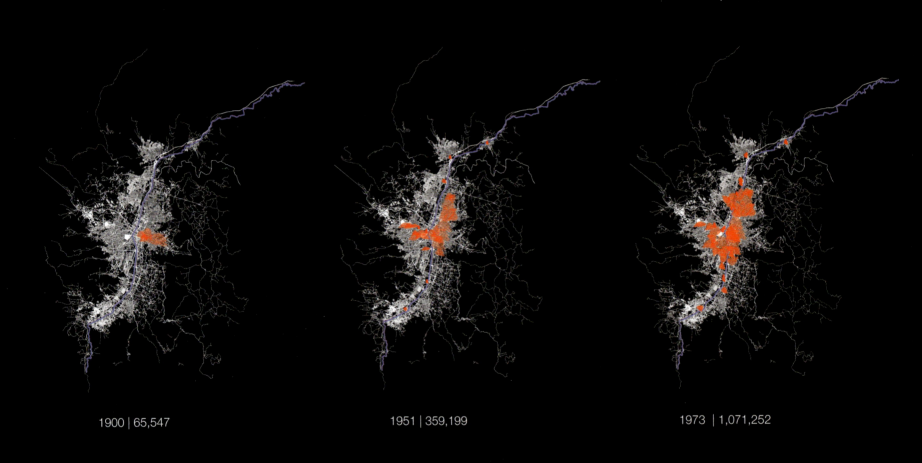

1900 | 65,547   1951 | 359,199   1973 | 1,071,252

MEDELLÍN
URBAN GROWTH

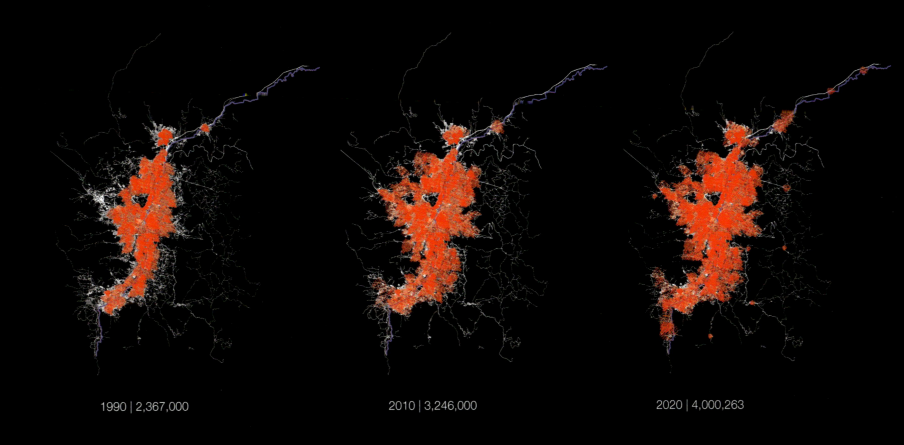

1990 | 2,367,000   2010 | 3,246,000   2020 | 4,000,263

7,5

0   15km

Following pages: Medellín's footprint and sectional studies along the Valle de Aburrá.

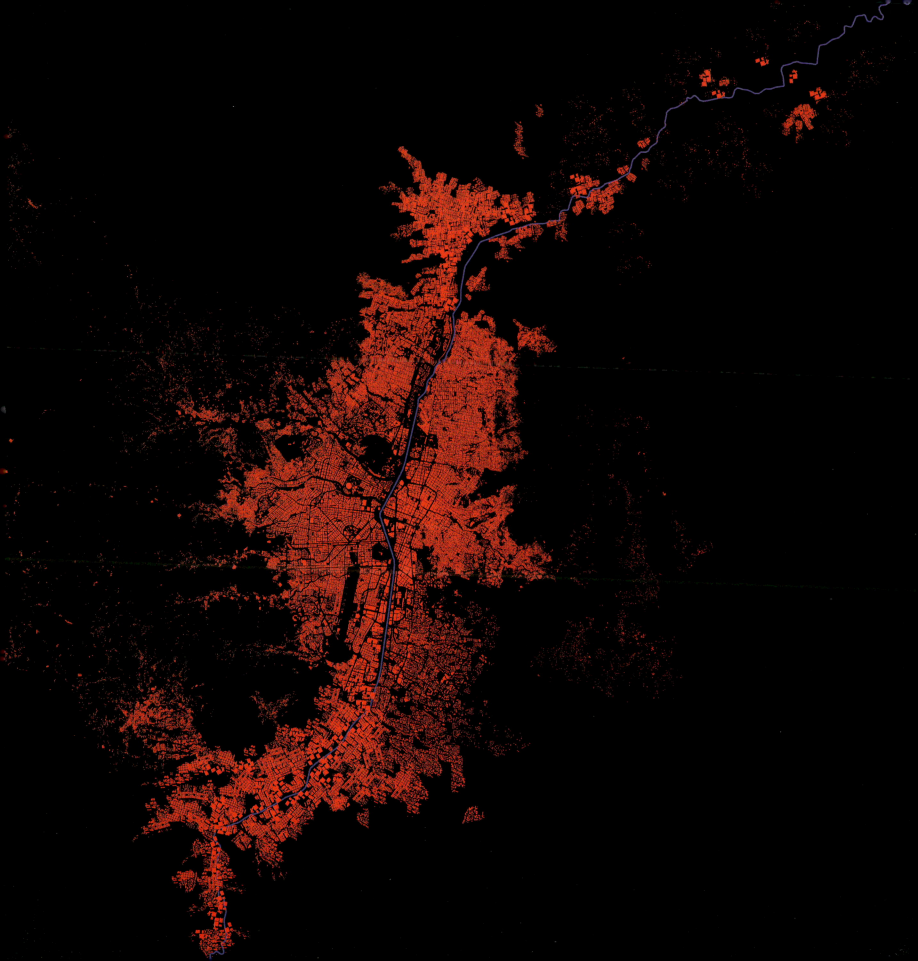

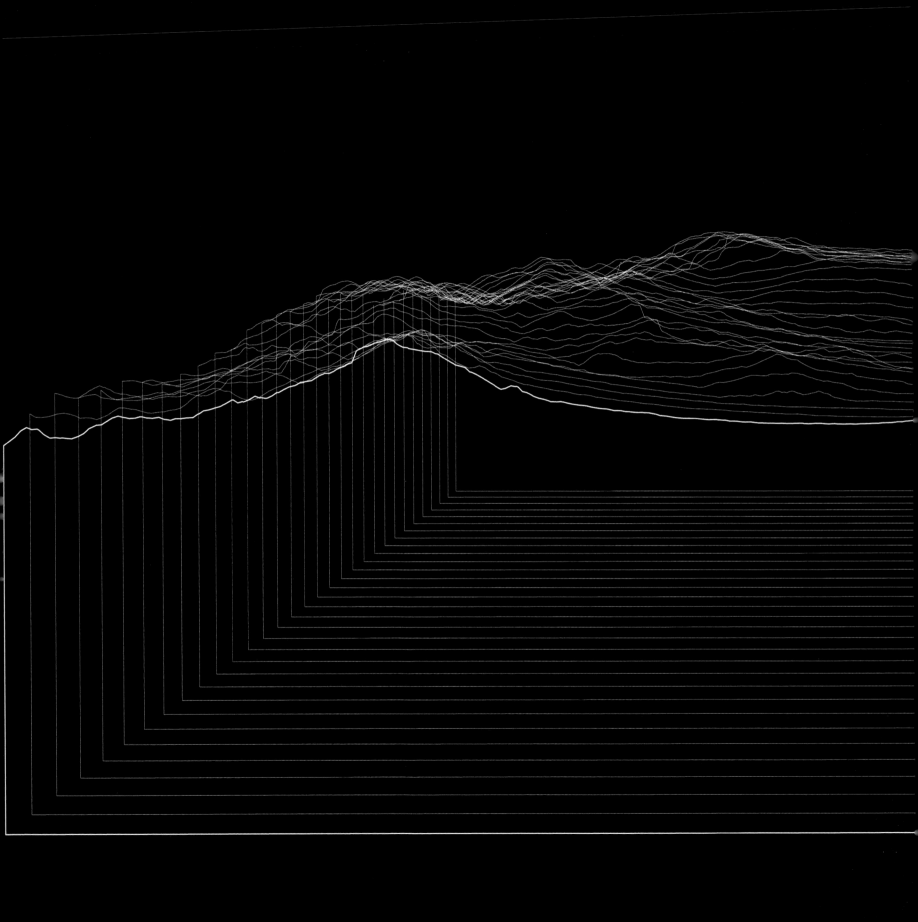

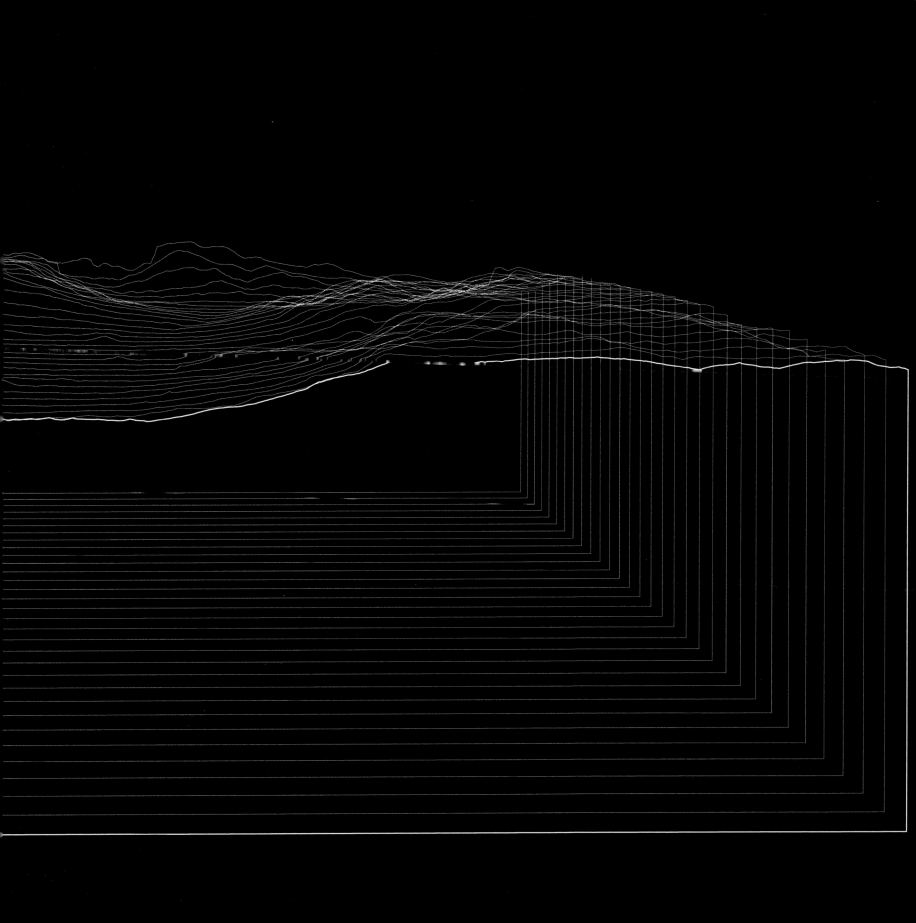

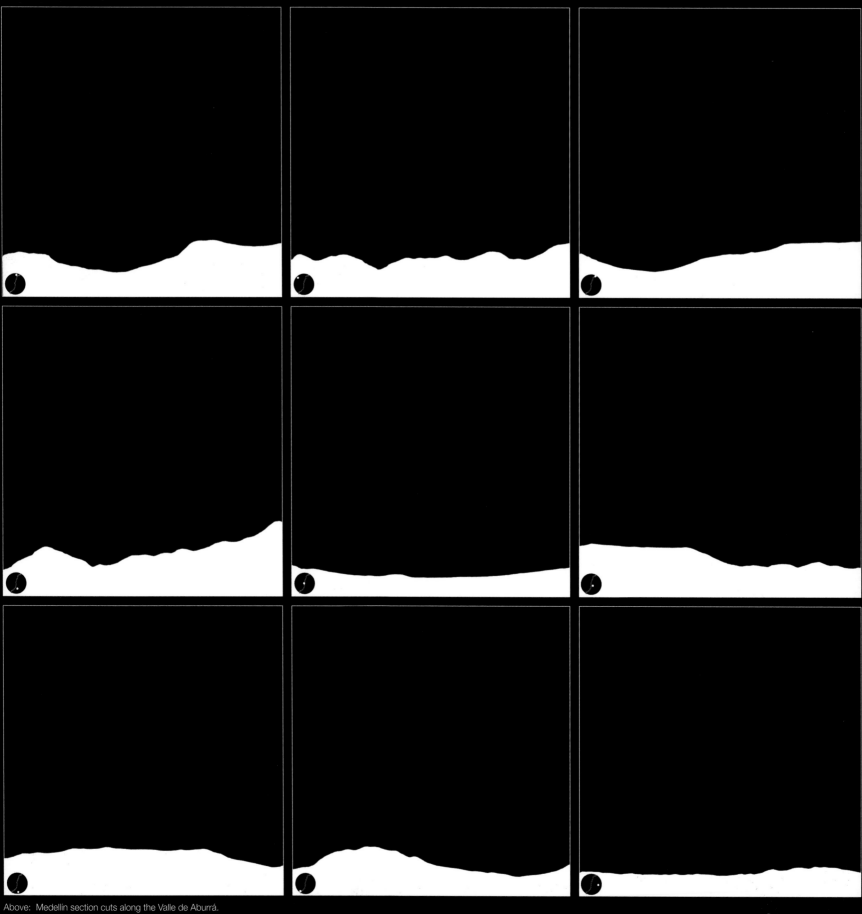

Above: Medellín section cuts along the Valle de Aburrá.

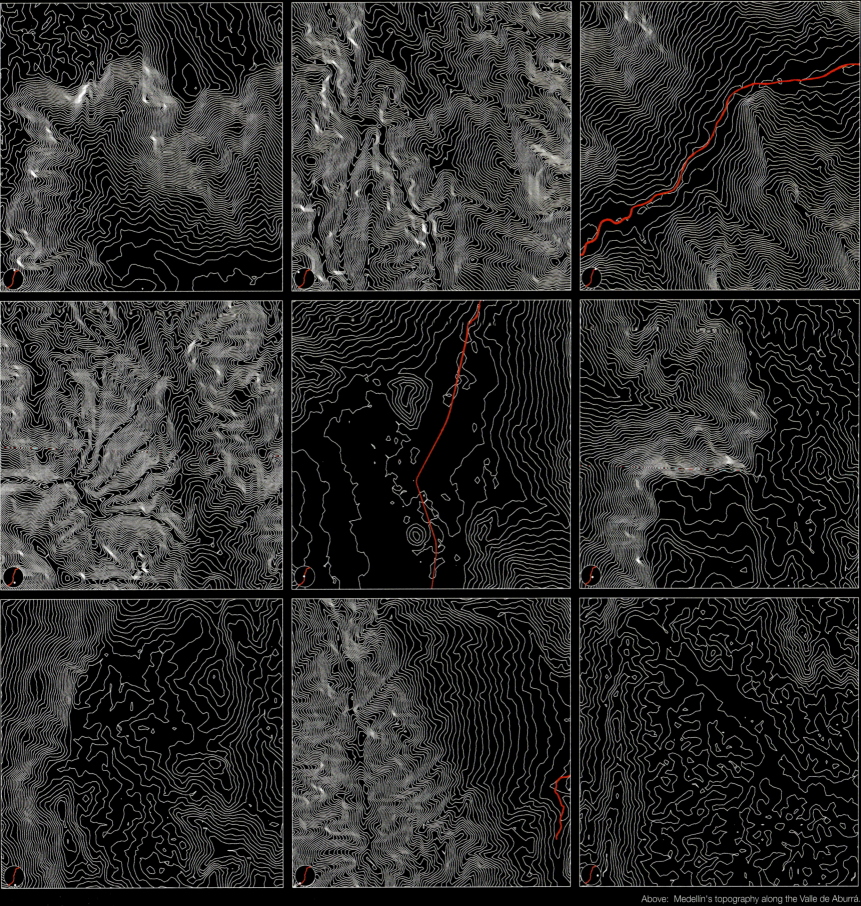

Above: Medellín's topography along the Valle de Aburrá.

- Moravia/ Comuna 4
- El Pajarito/ Comuna 7
- Laureles/ Comuna 11

- San Javier/ Comuna 13
- El Poblado/ Comuna 14
- Popular/ Comuna 1

- La Candelaria/ Comuna 10
- Villa Hermosa/ Comuna 8
- La Candelaria/ Comuna 10

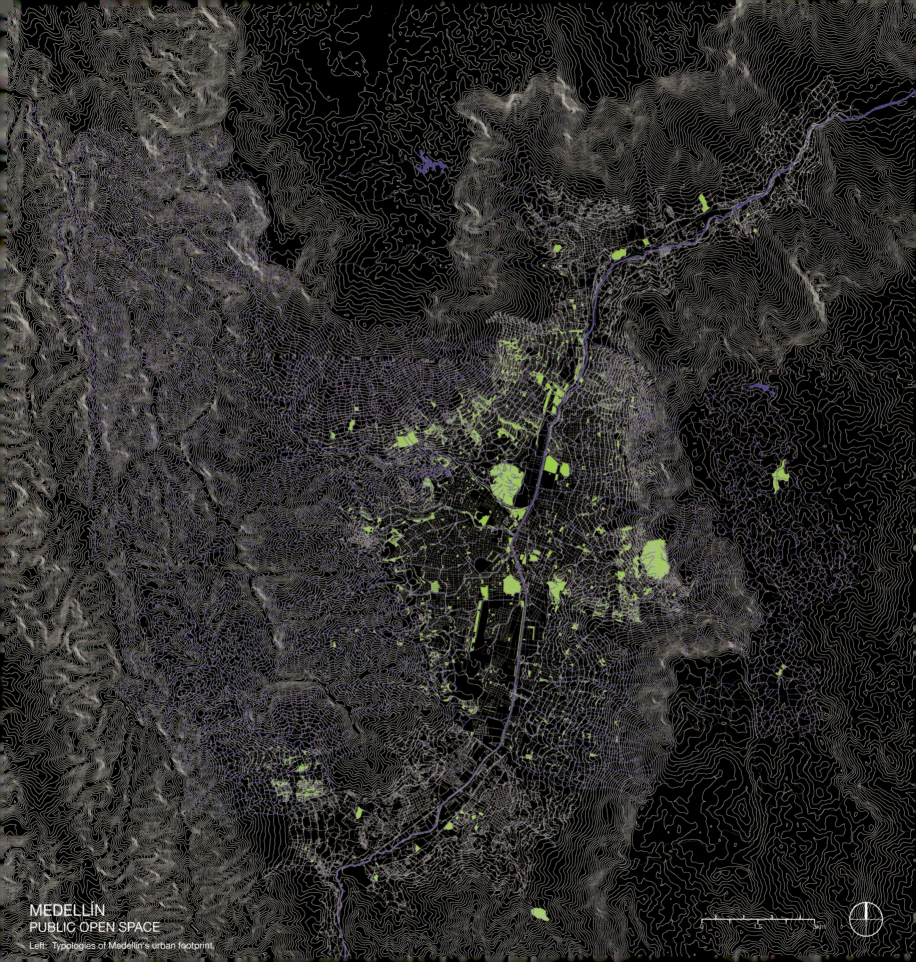

MEDELLÍN
PUBLIC OPEN SPACE
Left: Typologies of Medellín's urban footprint.

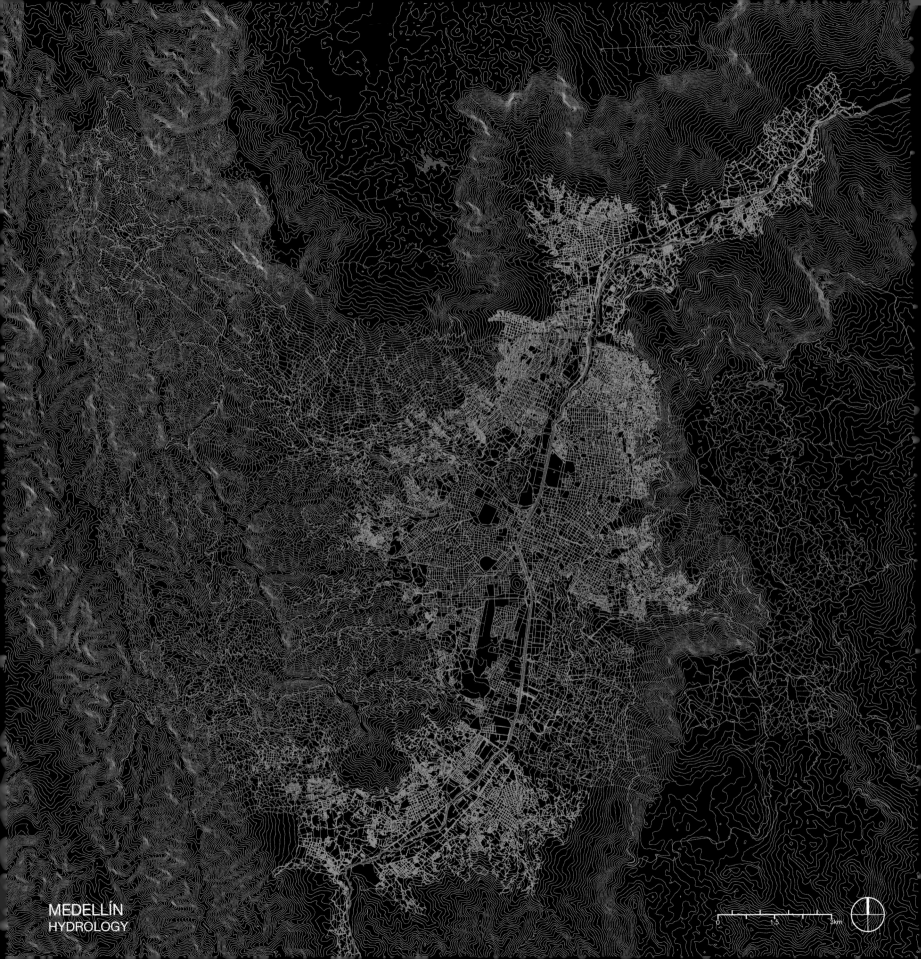

MEDELLÍN
HYDROLOGY

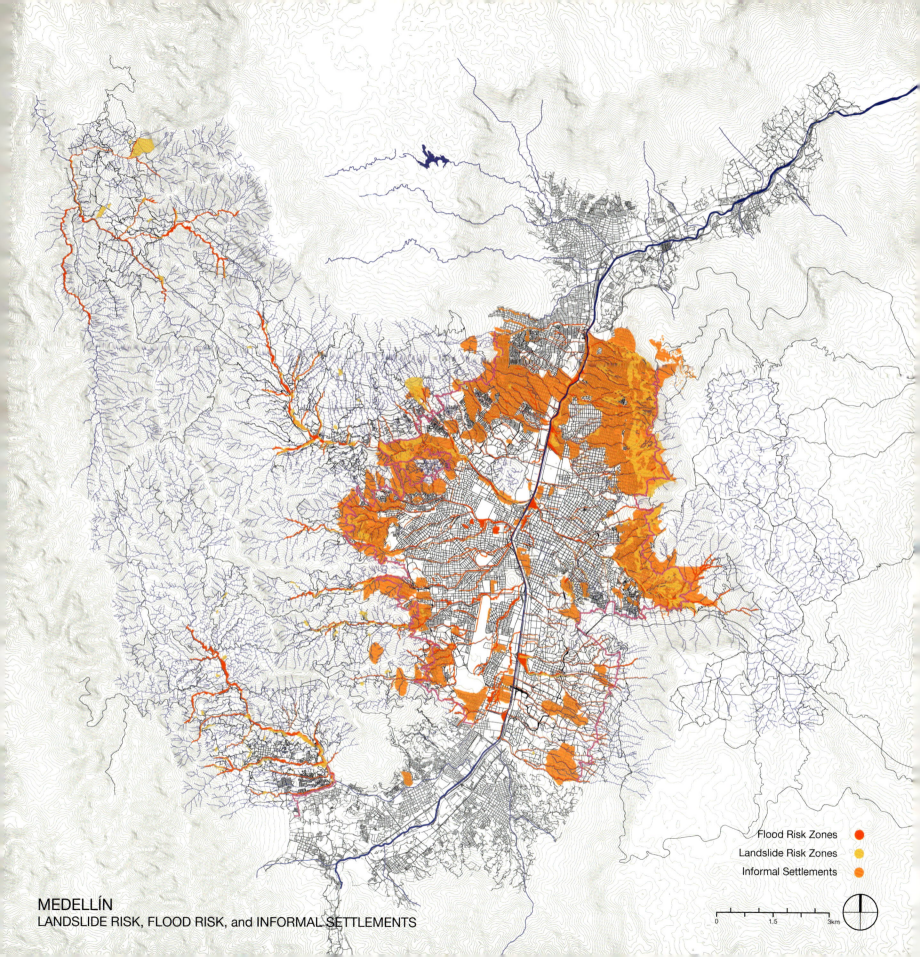

MEDELLÍN
LANDSLIDE RISK, FLOOD RISK, and INFORMAL SETTLEMENTS

Flood Risk Zones
Landslide Risk Zones
Informal Settlements

0   1.5   3km

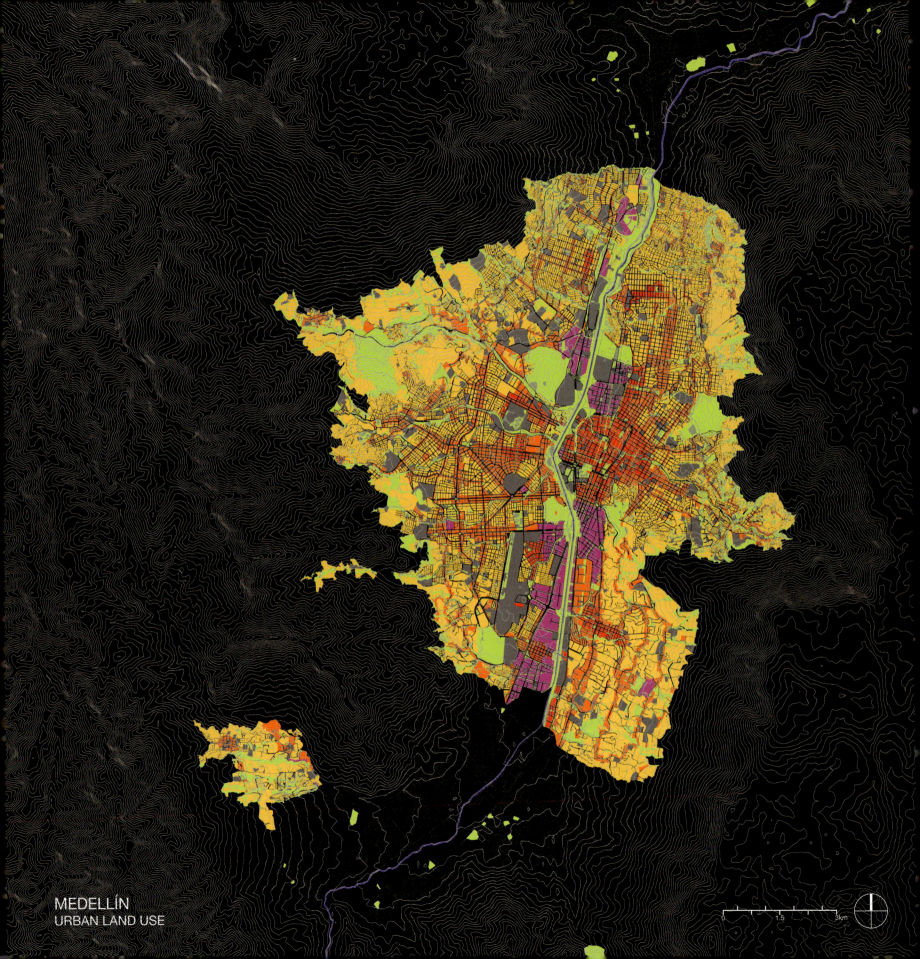

MEDELLÍN
URBAN LAND USE

0   1.5   3km

● Residential

● Institutional

● Medium Mixed Use Commercial

● Industrial

● High Mixed Use Commercial

● Existing Open Space

Above: Land Use Diagrams, not to scale.

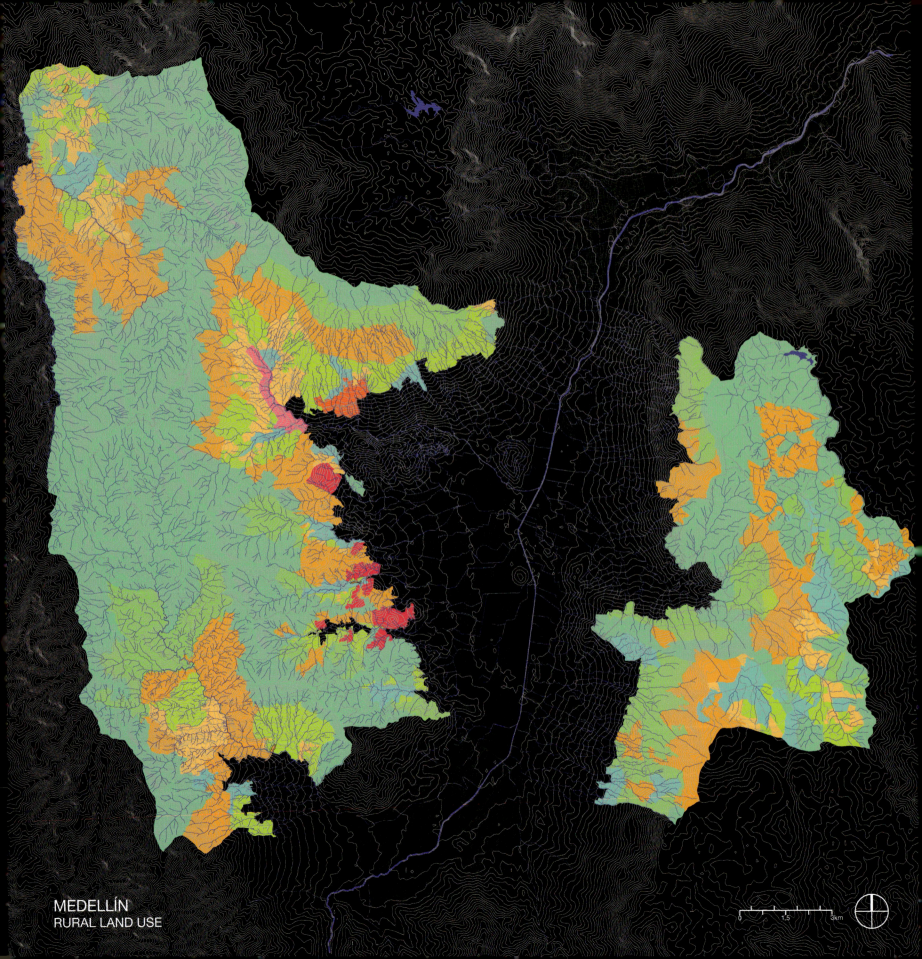

MEDELLÍN
RURAL LAND USE

0   1.5   3km

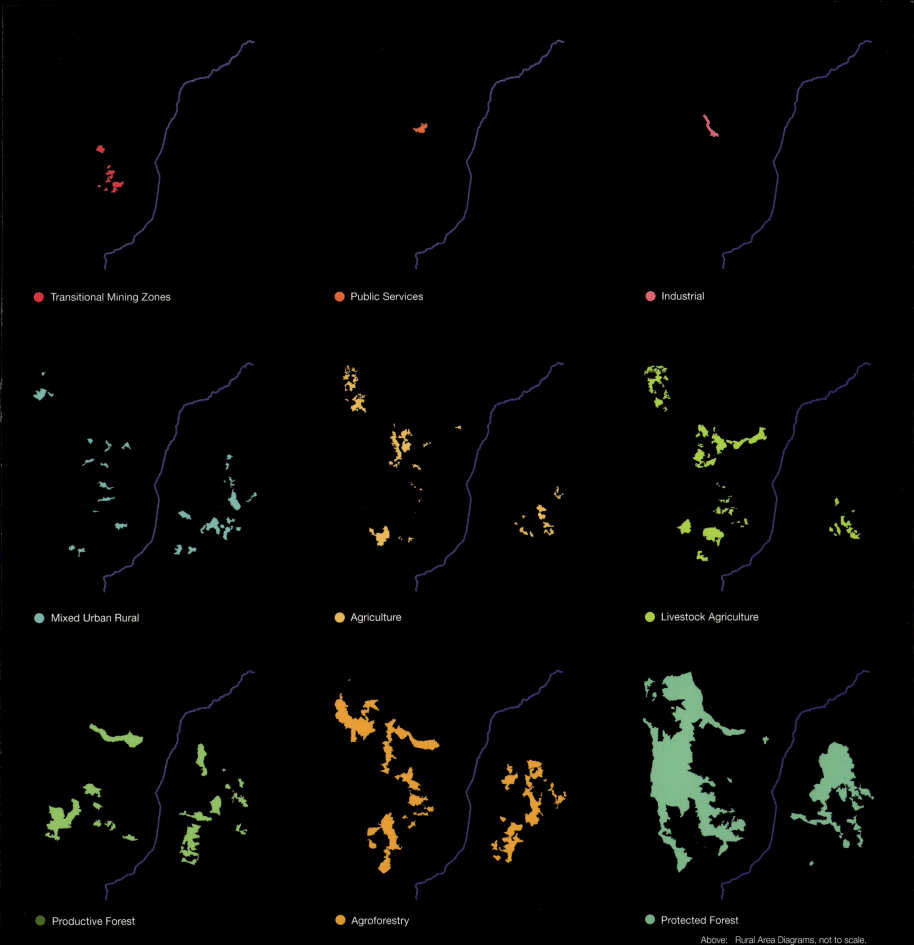

Transitional Mining Zones

Public Services

Industrial

Mixed Urban Rural

Agriculture

Livestock Agriculture

Productive Forest

Agroforestry

Protected Forest

Above: Rural Area Diagrams, not to scale.

CONSEJERIA PRESIDENCIAL, UNESCO AND PRIMED

In a context of corruption and endless migration, the ability for Medellín to operate and be responsive to the growth of the city continues to be challenged. Its recovery has depended on a complete new order and a long-range plan that has required the commitment of many constituents, including the transformation of political agendas, the participation of the community, and the collaborations among academic institutions—public agencies and active groups geared toward the management and administration of the urban city—as part of a collective system.[32] The 1991 new constitution offered the potential for increased autonomy and the reinstatement of frozen budgets within the Department of Antioquia and the Municipality of Medellín, permitting the emergence of the city's political entity in unison with the community as a force for change. President Gaviria went on to establish the Consejería Presidencial para Medellín (1990–1994; later the Consejería de Medellín)[33] as an advisory council and public forum geared toward intercepting the violence experienced throughout the city and to re-establishing a civil accord between the national government and citizens. The Consejería promoted community participation, young leadership, discussions, and working groups, tactics that led to a more constructive dialogue. Pablo Escobar was finally captured and killed during this period, emitting some measure of relief throughout the city.

The UNESCO General Conference was held during this period in Paris (1993), where the emphasis was the creation of an integrated approach to urban development that could provide models for mitigating the chaos of rapidly urbanizing areas. The UNESCO agenda resolutions addressed the increasing problems of population growth, in tandem with a greater regard for the environment, while considering quality of life, social justice, and peace for all citizens.[34] Mayor of Medellín, Sergio Naranjo Perez (1995–1998), later applied these principles to the creation of a pilot project through the Programa Integral de Mejoramiento de Barrios Subnormales, Integrated Program for the Improvement of Subnormal Barrios, or PRIMED.[k] Through PRIMED the following parameters were outlined: building of a safe city that could promote coexistence; mitigating negative impacts of production into real opportunities for the people of Medellín; and building of a modern city with a focus on collective public spaces that could offer optimal social engagement for the community.

The PRIMED development plan, implemented from 1992–1997, focused on 15 hillside barrios, and encompassed roughly 28% of the peripheral districts of Medellín.[35]

EPM, EDU, and POT - 1999

Empresas Públicas de Medellín (EPM) was established in 1958, an entity similar to the Department of Public Works (DPW), and provided the financial backing for much of the work that lay ahead. In addition to implementing engineering and public improvement services, EPM's annual margin of profit was in the vicinity of one-billion pesos,[36] a significant amount that helped propel public enterprises in Medellín, including the Metro, the Empresa de Desarrollo Urbano (EDU), and Empresa de Seguridad Urbana (ESU), agencies for planning and urban development, and public safety, respectively, among many other improvement entities.[37, l] This system contradicts the typical models of public privatization, and instead utilizes public services as an industry benefiting the development of the city and the community it also employs. This is a radical shift from what is currently happening in Santiago, Chile where the privatization of services precisely represents a hold on democracy and social stability.

Newly elected mayors were charged with formulating a strategic plan for development (Plan de Desarrollo, 1995–1997), derived through a community process to properly identify the priorities of citizens, and which requires the approval of Medellín's City Council.[38] Additionally, law 388 in 1997 introduced the requirement for mayors to coordinate their strategic plans with a Territorial Ordering Plan (Plan de Ordenamiento Territorial, POT) as an urban development framework and matrix for planned growth. The POT has served at a municipal scale, and was as much a process as an instrument for promoting a culture of urbanization in Colombia. The law intended to recover the public functions of the city, while designating responsibility to the municipalities. Executed by the Planning Department, the POT included public and private agencies, and defined the existing and potential programmatic norms in order to formulate a model for occupation for a compact and sustainable city.[39] As part of the Consejeria de Medellín, the first POT was adopted in 1999, with a focus on zoning, over

---

l   Between 2001–2011, EPM contributed 50% of its profits, roughly $877 million U.S. dollars, 27% of EPM's investment profits. In 2010, EPM was a 10-billion-dollar enterprise.

---

k   Barrios, or neighborhoods in Medellín, are a small administrative unit; the city has 243 barrios with an average size of 0.38 km² x 0.21 km²; this number continues to grow.

a broader vision for the future, spatial quality of the city. The POT priori-
tized transportation, programmatic areas and public spaces, and
demarcated concentric zones that organized the city. Beginning with its
central spine, the river was framed as a high density, recovered corridor,
aligned by metro infrastructure to alleviate vehicular congestion, while
at the same time somehow engaging with the natural environment, the
hydrology and the topography of the region. The connectivity to the
river seems contradicted at the onset, given that the major transit routes
continue to impede its accessibility, a continual dynamic since the earlier
Plan Piloto and the initial location of industrial programs over public open
space. Beyond the river, the POT defined distinct zones encircling the
city and ascending up the mountainsides: an urbanized zone, as an area
of development; a rural-urban zone, as a peri-urban transitional zone and
urban containment area; and a rural zone for agricultural and ecological
uses.[40] Additionally, the two smaller valleys crossing diagonally, formed
by La Iguaná and the Santa Elena stream-beds, denoted the center of the
city with an east-west, secondary axis.[m]

The Área Metropolitana del Valle de Aburrá (AMVA), and the AMVA Council,[41] created by the Assembly of Antioquia in 1980, is a coalition of the
municipalities that make up the greater metropolitan area, of which there
are 10 today, including Medellín. The AMVA and Municipality of Medellín
Planning Department are responsible for reviewing the POT's goals, where
regional as well as municipal aspects are considered; the regional over-
laps among the 10 municipalities, however, have not been evenly funded
or executed. As an extension to the Plan de Desarrollo and the POT,
Medellín has also engaged in the Municipal Planning System, from which
local development plans and the participatory budgets have emerged
(Plan de Desarrollo Local and Presupuesto Participativo, respectively).[42]
These have permitted the development of plans and agendas that more
closely follow the intricacies of various neighborhoods and their communities, in addition to a municipal view.

m   The first version of the POT was developed in 1999, with a first review taking place in 2004.
Its second review occurred in 2014, with an intended review cycle every twelve years. Governors and
Mayors operate on a four-year cycle, where POT goals remain fixed according to the POT review sched-
ule.

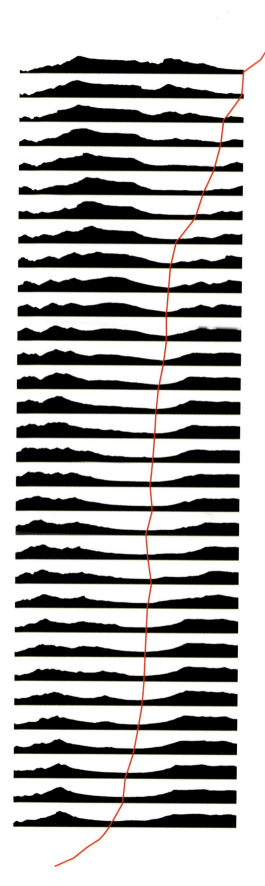

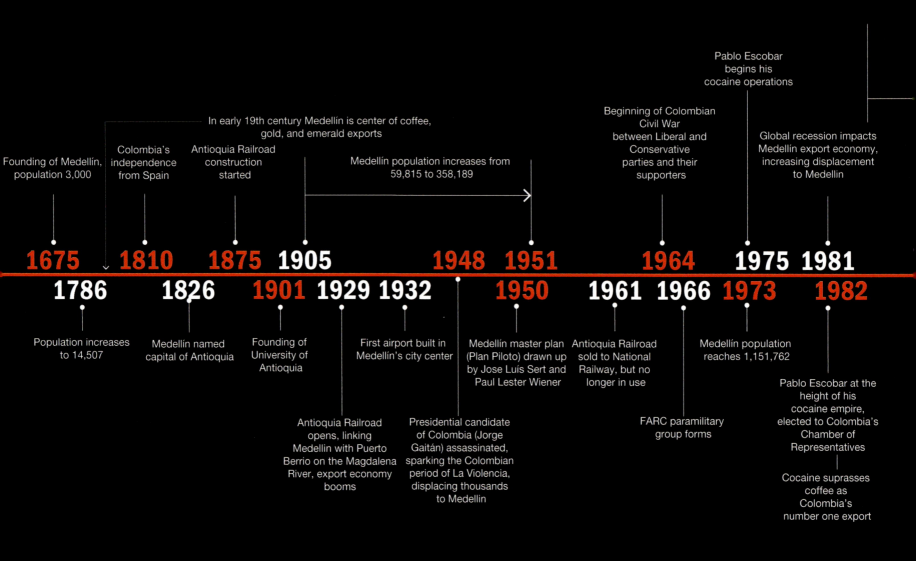

Pablo Escobar begins his cocaine operations

In early 19th century Medellín is center of coffee, gold, and emerald exports

Beginning of Colombian Civil War between Liberal and Conservative parties and their supporters

Global recession impacts Medellín export economy, increasing displacement to Medellin

Founding of Medellín, population 3,000

Colombia's independence from Spain

Antioquia Railroad construction started

Medellín population increases from 59,815 to 358,189

1675   1810   1875   1905   1948   1951   1964   1975   1981

1786   1826   1901   1929 1932   1950   1961   1966   1973   1982

Population increases to 14,507

Medellín named capital of Antioquia

Founding of University of Antioquia

First airport built in Medellín's city center

Medellín master plan (Plan Piloto) drawn up by Jose Luís Sert and Paul Lester Wiener

Antioquia Railroad sold to National Railway, but no longer in use

Medellín population reaches 1,151,762

Pablo Escobar at the height of his cocaine empire, elected to Colombia's Chamber of Representatives

Antioquia Railroad opens, linking Medellin with Puerto Berrio on the Magdalena River, export economy booms

Presidential candidate of Colombia (Jorge Gaitán) assassinated, sparking the Colombian period of La Violencia, displacing thousands to Medellin

FARC paramilitary group forms

Cocaine suprasses coffee as Colombia's number one export

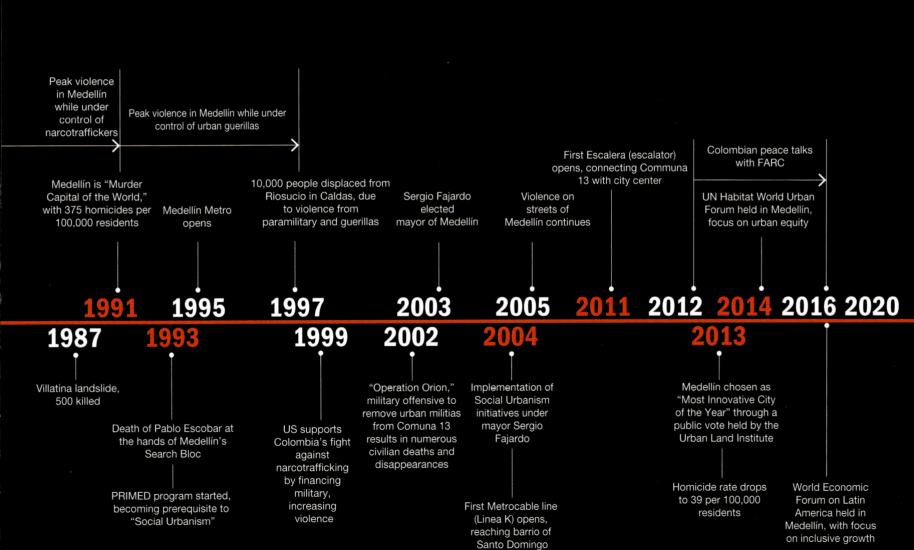

Peak violence in Medellín while under control of narcotraffickers

Peak violence in Medellín while under control of urban guerillas

Medellín is "Murder Capital of the World," with 375 homicides per 100,000 residents

Medellín Metro opens

10,000 people displaced from Riosucio in Caldas, due to violence from paramilitary and guerillas

Sergio Fajardo elected mayor of Medellín

Violence on streets of Medellín continues

First Escalera (escalator) opens, connecting Communa 13 with city center

Colombian peace talks with FARC

UN Habitat World Urban Forum held in Medellín, focus on urban equity

1991 **1995** **1997** **2003** **2005** **2011** **2012** **2014** **2016** **2020**

1987 **1993** **1999** **2002** **2004** **2013**

Villatina landslide, 500 killed

Death of Pablo Escobar at the hands of Medellín's Search Bloc

PRIMED program started, becoming prerequisite to "Social Urbanism"

US supports Colombia's fight against narcotrafficking by financing military, increasing violence

"Operation Orion," military offensive to remove urban militias from Comuna 13 results in numerous civilian deaths and disappearances

Implementation of Social Urbanism initiatives under mayor Sergio Fajardo

First Metrocable line (Linea K) opens, reaching barrio of Santo Domingo

Medellín chosen as "Most Innovative City of the Year" through a public vote held by the Urban Land Institute

Homicide rate drops to 39 per 100,000 residents

World Economic Forum on Latin America held in Medellín, with focus on inclusive growth

COMPROMISO CIUDADANO

In 1999, Sergio Fajardo Valderrama,[n] a teacher and mathematician, gathered colleagues from across disciplines, organizations, and academic institutions to form a distinct political platform in order to formulate an alternative vision for Medellín's society; different means geared toward different outcomes. Through his political campaign as an independent, center party known as Compromiso Ciudadano, he parted from the long-standing clientelism traditions, with the intention of transforming the political sphere, and therefore the comportment of the community and the face of the city. Rather than discounting the thousands of people living in the hillsides, he walked into the discarded barrios of Medellín to meet the citizens and to welcome them into the fold. He invited an open dialogue and listened to the community's despair.[43] He built trust and incentivized participation though an economy based on the regional talents of a rural and diverse culture, akin to agricultural and entrepreneurial "paisa" traditions.[o] Fajardo was elected mayor of Medellín in 2004, energized by the very empowerment he extended to the community, which through the new constitution and the transfer of administrative power, the POT, the various planning strategies, and the financing drawn by the EPM were now plausible. Fajardo's ingenuity and direction capitalized on the potential from these new systems.

Surrounded by an unconventional political group, Fajardo defined the founding principles for guiding the work that would heal Medellín, which, through honesty, a deep understanding over the issues of city life, an unequivocal commitment to the goals set out, and sensibility and respect for every Medellín citizen, began to take shape.[44] He identified the fundamental issues, possible remedies, and, informed by on-the-ground perspectives, invested in tangible solutions. Inequality, as evidenced by the lack of adequate housing and education, and the division and discrimination these created among Medellín's citizens was one central problem. The city's periphery illustrated the severity of this separation, as an area where so many had migrated to escape displacement and violence with the hope of finding a better life, yet where they had been left hanging. These citizens also had rights and responsibilities that needed to be guided. The second issue was the intense narcotrafficking that had occurred during the 1980s and the violence and destruction the inhabitants and their city had endured. Fajardo's Strategic Plan examined the role of police and public safety, reintegration into the community, a pedagogy of coexistence, and a culture of citizenship. Opportunities were included in a framework underscored by education as the catalyst for social transformation.[45]

From 7,081 homicides in Medellín in 1991, with a population of roughly 2,000,000 million;[46] by the end of Fajardo's term in 2007,[47] of a population of 3,250,000 million, the number had dropped to 771. Operación Orión and Operación Mariscal were two military operations that took place in 2002 to tame violence in the San Javier barrio in Comuna 13 on the center-west side, which coincided with the decline of homicides in Medellín. This operation was led by paramilitary interventions who simultaneously assisted the State in taking back control of the city. Orión lasted four days, with approximately 1,000 armed forces who entered by air and land causing mass killings, displacement, and the disappearance of 150–300 people.[48] Many believe that President Alvaro Uribe's (2002–2010) abrupt strategy was necessary in order to pacify the community, to eventually be able to bring the Metrocable,[p] which arrived soon after, in order to brand the city for the global arena. The Bloque Cacique Nutibara, Medellín's toughest paramilitary group, stated "that they had been partly responsible for the fall of homicides in Medellín and that this ensured the necessary climate for investment, particularly foreign, which is fundamental if we did not want to be left behind by the engine of globalization."[49] Either way, Uribe's approach combated inequality and unrest by drawing lines around the city's peripheral neighborhoods, further impoverishing and marginalizing residents through violence, perpetuating a historical syndrome, over the dynamics that Fajardo imparted by inviting the community in the restoration of their city.

---

n   Sergio Fajardo Valderrama, after serving as both mayor of Medellin and governor of Antioquia, became a Colombian presidential candidate in 2018, under his Compromiso Ciudadano party.
o   'Paisas' refers to people from the departments of Antioquia, Caldas, and Risaralda, who share the same linguistic accents, geographical characteristics, and regional borders.

p   The Metrocable in Medellin is a gondola lift system that reaches the city's informal settlements at its periphery. The system started operating in 2004 and currently carries over 30,000 people a day.

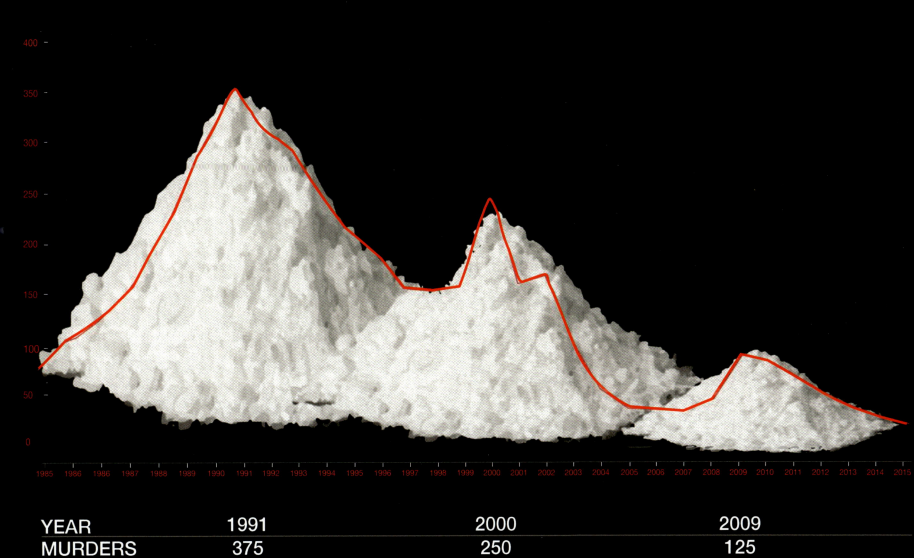

400																															
350																															
300																															
250																															
200																															
150																															
100																															
50																															
0																															

1985 1986 1986 1987 1988 1989 1990 1991 1992 1993 1994 1995 1996 1997 1998 1999 2000 2001 2002 2003 2004 2005 2006 2007 2008 2009 2010 2011 2012 2013 2014 2015

YEAR	1991	2000	2009
MURDERS per 100,000	375	250	125

MEDELLÍN
MURDERS PER 100,000 PEOPLE

SOCIAL URBANISM AND PROYECTOS URBANOS

The PUI Program

Fajardo's work emerged from the foundation laid by the PRIMED program during the 1990s, which he expounded through the development of Proyectos Urbanos Integrales, or the PUI program, and through close collaborations with EDU. As the building blocks of social urbanism, PUI set out to identify the barrios of Medellín that would benefit from urban upgrading projects, where systemic problems readily evidenced at the peripheral communities of the city could be addressed. The PUI program located project sites correlating to the most under-served parts of the city, and included the following three components. First, a social component, recognizing the importance of citizen participation as a methodology for identifying and mitigating community conflicts through a close collaboration with local citizens, with an effort to reverse social segregation and promote coexistence. Second, a spatial component, focused on improving accessibility to and availability of public areas, housing, and public buildings, including health, education, and recreation facilities, while at the same time protecting environmental benefits through the development of new parks and open spaces in remote areas. Third, an institutional component, which identified the importance of security and the State's involvement in protecting and supporting peripheral communities through their presence as these intervention projects got off the ground. Public space became the essential element in various forms through transit, mobility, accessibility, cultural buildings, schools, or plazas. Through "Medellín, un Espacio para el Encuentro Ciudadano" [50, q] the city was considered the forum, or the playground per se, where citizens could re-encounter one another. This extends beyond earlier notions of the public square as an exclusive space, which instead recognizes conviviality as the driving force for urban life.

The northeastern PUI, Juan Bobo, and Moravia are three initial, prominent PUI projects forming part of Medellín's densest, most underserved areas in the city. The northeastern, or Santo Domingo PUI, is sited along the northeastern slope of Medellín, between Comuma One and Two, —also known as Comuna Popular or Santo Domingo, and Comuna Santa Cruz, as respective, preferred names by the residents. The project traverses 158 hectares, includes 11 neighborhoods, with a collective population of 230,000 people, [51] in an area of Medellín that has represented some of the poorest and most violent neighborhoods of the city, with thousands of displaced people settled together—fearful and forced to coexist. Mayor Luis Perez (2001–2003) had introduced a mandate to include cable-cars as a means of connecting outlying communities to the existing Metro system, which had been built in 1995. [52] The northeastern PUI nailed the strategic location, increasing accessibility, while including public spaces that could build community. The Santo Domingo Metrocable (Line K) is a 24-million-dollar project that carves a two-kilometer-long [53] corridor into the fabric of the neighborhood. The transformation created by the mobility of this project has created a positive impact for the community; daily commutes to and fro have gone from taking a few hours to only seven minutes to the Acevedo Metro station, connecting to the rest of the city. The infamous open-air public library, Biblioteca España, [r] at the top of the run, which despite controversy over the building's current condition, has acted as a beacon, from the bottom of the city, looking up, and vice versa, calling out the northeastern neighborhoods of the city, recognizing, rather than omitting them. This type of programming identified the potential for other open-air libraries and public plazas which have been inserted into historically violent areas downtown, Biblioteca Belén (2008), for instance, and La Ladera (2007), on the eastern slopes. These tactics have been employed to "rewire" the social dynamics by providing alternative cultural buildings and spaces for the community, where education, training, and community gathering can take place.

The Juan Bobo PUI, also on the northeastern slopes, is an upgrading project for a neighborhood of 300 families, made up of 1,260 residents, predominantly migrant women, children, and elderly. As a dense settlement, with little habitable space bordering the stream, with 90% of the water contaminated by litter pollution and lack of a sewer system, the residents had also been vulnerable to landslides, with informal houses they had themselves built on unowned land. Through the PUI, this project envisioned how to improve the living conditions, in-situ, over displacing the community, as before, with interventions that included new buildings, along with the improvement of existing dwellings, connections to essential services, the integration of public spaces, and greater accessibility.

---

q   "Espacio para el Encuentro Ciudadano" refers to Fajardo's belief that education is a place of citizen encounter, regardless of the condition that each one of us has; in the public space where we exist, fundamentally, and through education, other links are established.

r   Biblioteca España is an open-air library built in 2005, designed by Giancarlo Mazzanti, architect, and funded by the Royal Spanish government. The library offered educational programs and computer resources and training for the neighborhood residents. The library has been closed over the past few times I have been in Medellín; initially for repairs from a failing facade, possibly from corrupt construction and cost-cutting practices.

Following pages, top left, clockwise: La Aurora, Trece de Noviembre, and Barrio Independencia—informal settlements at Medellín's urban periphery.
Following pages: Left: Biblioteca España, Comuna 1. Right: top left, clockwise: Biblioteca Belén, Comuna 16, and Biblioteca Leon de Grieff, Comuna 8—new library parks.

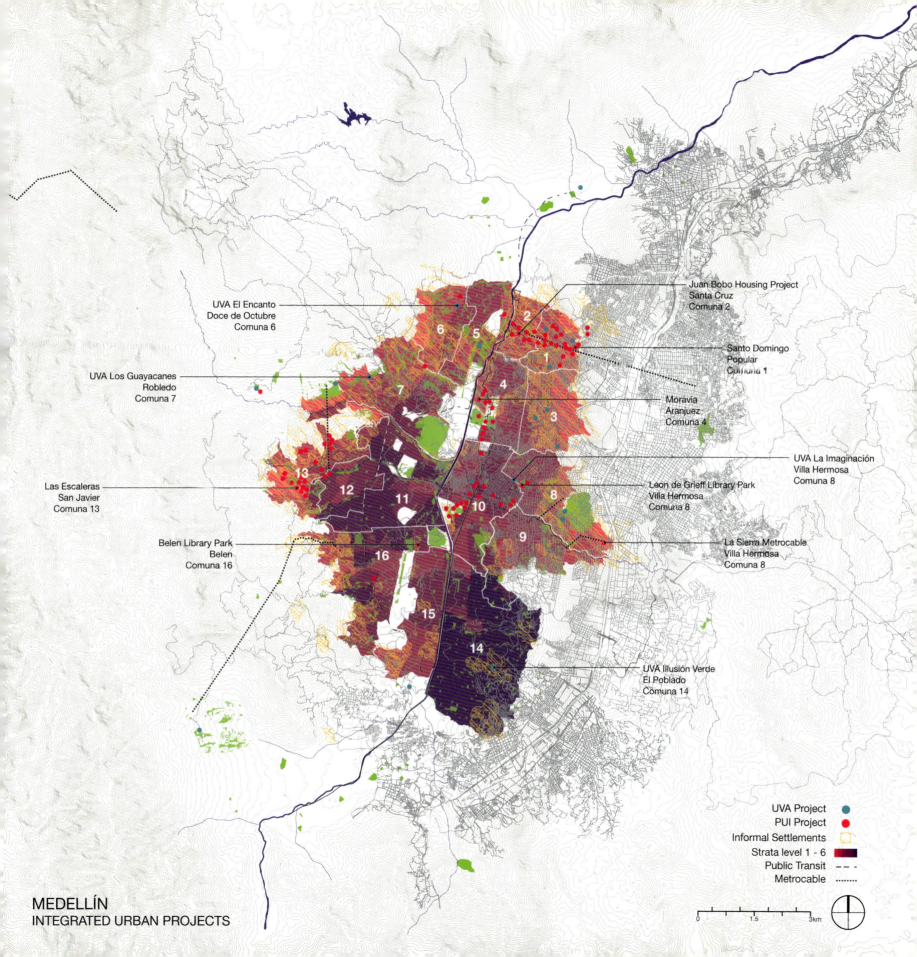

Juan Bobo Housing Project
Santa Cruz
Comuna 2

UVA El Encanto
Doce de Octubre
Comuna 6

Santo Domingo
Popular
Comuna 1

UVA Los Guayacanes
Robledo
Comuna 7

Moravia
Aranjuez
Comuna 4

UVA La Imaginación
Villa Hermosa
Comuna 8

Las Escaleras
San Javier
Comuna 13

León de Grieff Library Park
Villa Hermosa
Comuna 8

Belen Library Park
Belen
Comuna 16

La Sierra Metrocable
Villa Hermosa
Comuna 8

UVA Illusión Verde
El Poblado
Comuna 14

UVA Project
PUI Project
Informal Settlements
Strata level 1 - 6
Public Transit
Metrocable

MEDELLÍN
INTEGRATED URBAN PROJECTS

0   1.5   3km

Strategies for a participatory process of assessment and implementation has yielded stronger social and economic networks over time, creating productive means for the legalization and ownership of viable residential properties.[54]

Situated between Caribe and Universidad Metro stations, Moravia, on the central-eastern bank of the Medellin River, is the site of a dire PUI project. Also displaced by industrialization, and later, violence, migrants first arrived to this prime location in the 1950s, initially due to its proximity to the old rail line, and later as a way of surviving from any remnants found floating along the river. In 1977, the Municipality of Medellín established the city dump in this location, unabashed, it seems, until 1984. As the trash piled up, so did the squatters who found recyclable materials from which to build. Sixty percent of the population was living in non-recoverable risk conditions with precarious structures: 30% of the population were children, with a 67% rate of unemployment, and 98% of the population living with less than one legal minimum salary.[55] Seven years of trash collected from the metropolitan area of Medellin form the profile of the mound that is Moravia. Gloria Ospina, long-time Moravia resident and passionate community leader, mentioned that even though there were wretched odors and carbon monoxide fumes, people found useful things, food, shoes, clothes, and various recyclable materials, which when put to good use enabled them to survive as they formed a cooperative workforce and community. She has lived in Moravia since 1968 and remembers vividly when Fajardo visited the neighborhood in 2004, astounded by the conditions. "Medellín has a historic social debt with Moravia," Fajardo said to her many years ago.[56] Together with the community, government agencies, and the Universidad Nacional, the area was reactivated through the inclusion of cultural and educational buildings, new dwellings, and the transformation of the trash mound into a hillside park. Just south are located Parque Explora, an interactive park and museum adjacent to the Botanical Garden, both built in 2007, which together with the Metro stations, Universidad de Antioquia and Parque de los Deseos (Park of the Wishes), create an urban center and cultural enclave in areas of the city center that had been abandoned or left derelict. Today, the Moravia residents are standing back, fighting eviction as the prospects for gentrification in the central area of the city abound.

SOCIAL URBANISM - A PROCESS

In essence, Fajardo rallied political leaders and provoked the "radicalization of the political class,"[57] leading through and advocating for spatial solutions with a deeper, unconventional vision, in order to resolve the social degradation of the city. He foresaw that the violence, inequality, and rapid densification experienced in Medellín could not be repaired by simply relocating the marginalized masses, but rather, by instilling a new civic culture. By bringing planning and government closer to civil society, through a communal rebuilding process, there had been a radical shift crucial in empowering communities without instilling fear or violence. Through social urbanism and the PUI program, there is a recognition not only of the fact that all citizens deserve dignified and habitable spaces, to both live and gather, but that these are fundamental conditions which they themselves must help to envision and build, creating a sense of ownership while affording an ability to participate in and contribute to the greater progress of the city. In calling on local community leaders across the many comunas to be representatives of these efforts, providing training across many levels and allocating budgets, a more democratic approach to planning emerged. Through top-down activism and organization, and a bottom-up development model of urban renewal, Fajardo affected the underlying principles that initially framed social urbanism, advocating for the value of collective exercises where trust and capital have been proven agents for the transformation of the city and the quality of life for its community.

Alonso Salazar Jaramillo, mayor of Medellín in 2008, together with the many agencies and institutions that had been involved in the reformation of the city during the early years of the 21st-century, continued on with these planning ideals and PUI projects which today characterize the urban fabric of the city. These groups included the Municipality of Medellín and the Planning Department, the EDU, the Universidad Pontificia Bolivariana—Escuela de Arquitectura y Diseño; Universidad National—Centro de Estudios de Hábitat Popular; Universidad de Antioquia—Instituto de Estudio Regionales,[58] among many more. The coalition that had been formed during the early social urbanism years has been acculturated, with continued efforts to refine planning agendas and significant projects that have been built since. These include additional transit routes along the 650-million-dollar Metro system running north-south for eight miles through the city; a bicycle hub-way; the iconic Metrocables now extending up to La Aurora, where the Pajarito neighborhood in Comuna 7 sits on the central-west side; San Javier, in Comuna 13; and the infamous Escaleras Eléctricas, the electric stairs, together with the vivid graffiti that have reconnected residents after the dreadful Orión paramilitary operation. On the center-west side, Metrocable extensions have reached La Sierra, in Comuna 8, an informal neighborhood at 1,900 meters above sea level (6,300 feet), as well as newly inaugurated routes in Trece de Noviembre in Comuna 8, where only a few years ago residents contested eviction.

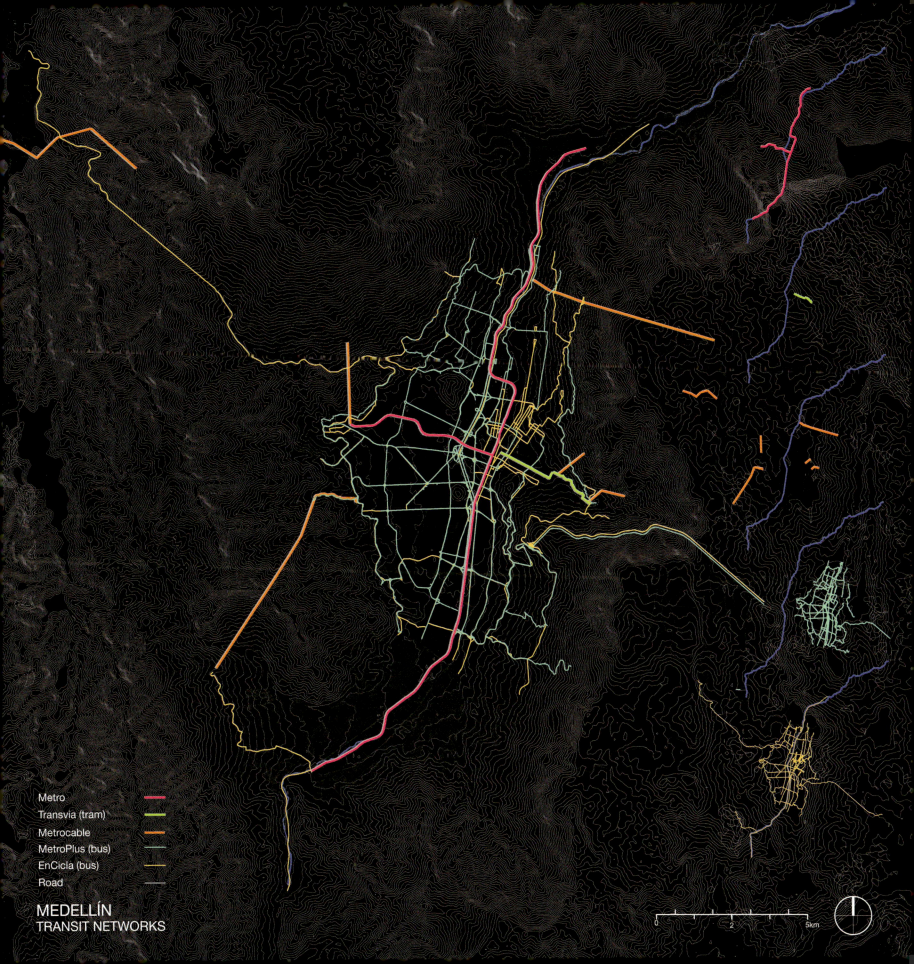

Metro

Transvia (tram)

Metrocable

MetroPlus (bus)

EnCicla (bus)

Road

MEDELLÍN
TRANSIT NETWORKS

0   2   5km

Today the neighborhood has potable water and electricity, and the community has gained valuable skills, a majority of them women, helping to construct the Jardín Circunvalar. Also known as the "Camino de la Vida," or the "Walk of Life", this is a greenbelt and public park encircling the perimeter of the city, intended to deter informal migration beyond this line. The project has commendable goals, in terms of providing incredible views of the city and the Valle de Aburrá, in addition to group building exercises and skill training, yet it envisions a boundary around the city which signals a grave limitation. This "imaginary" delineation, separate from the ecological realities or much else, may once again create an exclusive versus inclusive condition, ongoing topics and dilemmas of urbanization. One way or another, this project has been halted given the new administration, and the prioritization of individual political agendas, and even optics.

UVAs (Unidades de Vida Articulada, Articulated Life Units), managed by EPM, are structures strategically created by repurposing existing water tanks that have formed part of the city's infrastructure and stormwater tanks.[59] UVAs have been transformed to include public meeting spaces, sport, recreational, and cultural programming that facilitate community participation and enhance the quality of life in the comunas. Los Guayacanes, in Robledo, Comuna 7, is an older water tank with a wonderful park with spectacular views; Nuevo Occidente, has been inserted anew, in La Aurora, also Comuna 7, as part of a public housing project. Each one is an iconic architectural building marking a central point, or club, within varying, lower strata neighborhoods. Many buildings, spaces, and programmatic elements are carefully placed throughout the city, the Museo Casa de la Memoria (the Museum of Museum) for instance, as a poignant tribute to those who died and disappeared due to the political violence that dramatically devastated so many in Antioquia and the country at the end of the 20th-century. Downtown, the recent renovation of the Museo de Antioquia, the Metro and green, living walls at Avenida Bolivar, and the quintessential sculptures at Plaza Botero, form part of the old and new city where so many gather today. These public projects are not only public amenities; each one is a purposeful structure and public space, intentionally identified to re-script the urban landscape, opening up the city to all its citizens, allowing them to breathe and behave differently, as part of a cultural renaissance.

BIO 2030

More recently, and beyond the most critical years of Medellín's socio-political crisis, the city has continued to respond to its increasing population

growth and physical expansion. Derived from his collaborations with Fajardo and the goals identified during the social urbanism projects of 2004–2008, as director of both EDU, and Urban and Strategic Projects for the Municipality of Medellín, Alejandro Echeverri Restrepo later founded Centro de Estudios Urbanos y Ambientales (URBAM) as an institutional and urban design think-tank. URBAM, under Echeverri's direction and as part of EAFIT University in Medellín, developed an environmental and urban analysis for the Municipality of Medellín and the AMVA in 2011— BIO 2030 Plan Director de Medellín, Valle de Aburrá— a comprehensive study that examines the metropolitan area and which provides a broader vision for the structuring elements of Medellín and its future development through 2030. Within both a city and regional context, from Barbosa to Caldas, from north to south, the plan considers the natural conditions of the valley, the intense geomorphology, the hydrology of the Medellín River watershed, together with socio-economic and constructed elements as required by increasing urban density and programming. The plan identifies key strategies that could be shared across municipalities that form part of the valley. Social, ecological, and economic opportunities envisioned include: mobility and transit; environmental quality through the inclusion of landscape elements and public spaces; and activity and habitat. BIO 2030 considers how to consolidate urban density to prevent further conurbation into adjacent valleys, the Río Cauca and the San Nicolás valleys, in order to protect the ecological integrity of the region. The plan also integrates the river within the urban fabric as the essential spine of the city, and valley, while simultaneously contending with the linear aspect of the major thoroughfares that currently disengage the river from the natural geography and ecology of the region, as well as from the daily experiences of Medellín's residents. Contamination and deterioration go hand in hand with channelization, as ongoing practices condoned by earlier plans that have overlooked the necessity for connecting with the river. BIO 2030 envisions ways for relieving the river and its border for public access, ecological restoration, and landscape performance as a natural collection point at many levels, while repurposing the transect behind these natural systems for dense housing, institutional, and cultural programming, and as populated transit routes that will no longer encroach on the water. Finally, the plan proposes to return the slopes for agricultural and recreational uses that will protect the environmental quality of the area, while also preventing the unsafe occupation of the mountainsides.[60]

POT 2014

Directed under Jorge Pérez Jaramillo, planning director for the Municipality of Medellín from 2012 to 2015, and former deputy director of the Met-

Preceding pages, top left, clockwise: community engagement in La Sierra, Vill Hermosa, and Moravia. Preceding pages, top left, clockwise: Parque Explora, Metro and Palacio de la Cultura, and the Metrocable of Medellín.

Right: Articulated Life Units (UVAs).

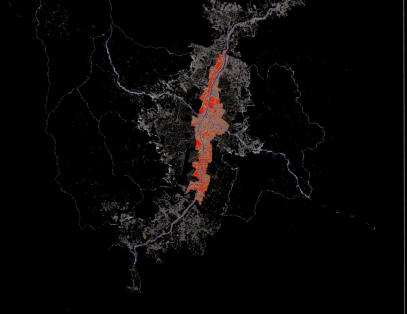

1. Medellín river corridor as public central district and ecological basin

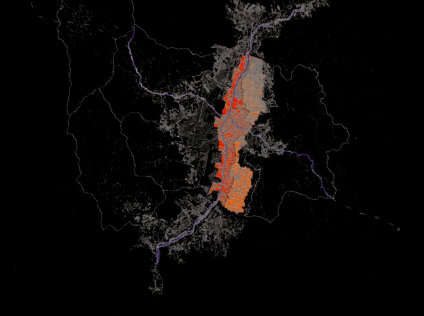

2. High-density residential and mixed-use urban zone as compact core, east Medellín

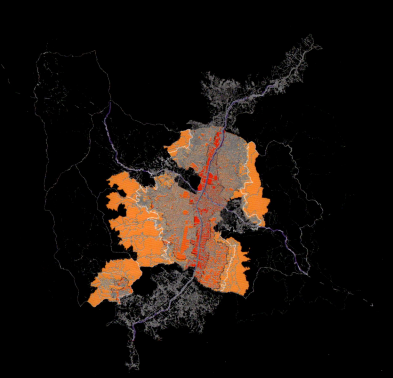

5. Peri-urban border for recreation and agriculture, containing urban expansion, east Medellín

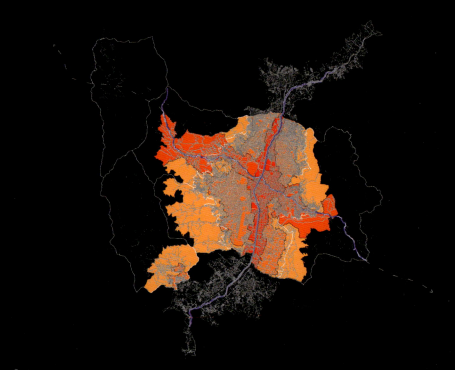

6. East - West transversal, with Quebrada Iguaná and Quebrada Santa Elena connecting to adjacent valleys

MEDELLÍN
PLAN DE ORDENAMIENTO TERRITORIAL - POT / TERRITORIAL ORDERING PLAN, 2014

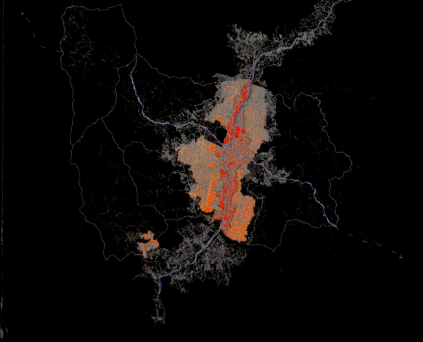

3. High-density residential and mixed-use urban zone as compact core, west Medellín

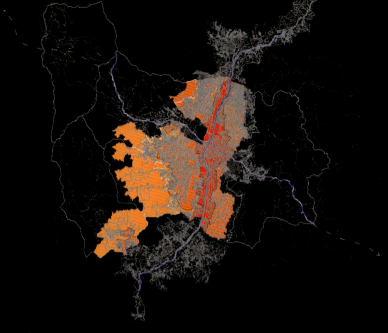

4. Peri-urban border for recreation and agriculture, containing urban expansion, west Medellín

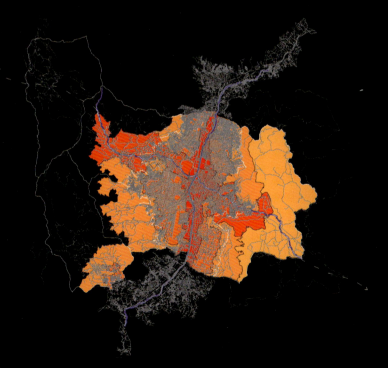

7. Ecological buffer zone encircling the valley, protecting the environmental quality of the Valle de Aburrá, east Medellín

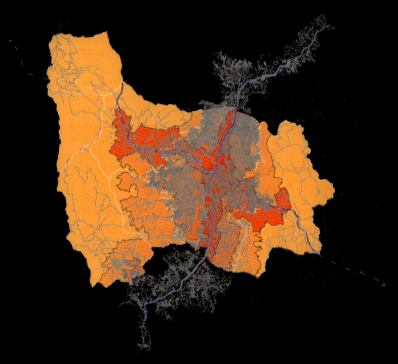

8. Ecological buffer zone encircling the valley, protecting the environmental quality of the Valle de Aburrá, west Medellín

0   4.5   9km

ropolitan Planning Area during Aníbal Gaviria Correa's mayorship, the Plan de Ordenamiento Territorial 2014, POT 2014, is a revision to the POT of 1999, informed by BIO 2030, providing a planning framework addressing the city's projected development over a 12-year period. With a vision for improving the quality of life for Medellín's inhabitants, while adhering to a mandate for an equitable and sustainable city in a era of climate crisis, the POT identifies four main goals: to develop a more sustainable city; provide physical equity across its territory; generate competitive strategies; and to create a city of social inclusion. The plan envisions ways for increasing accessibility, addressing public space and housing deficits; at a local scale the plan promotes social interactions through the landscape, while at a regional scale it also considers the growth of the city through greater cohesion among municipalities, and along the natural amenities of the valley. The POT provides a model for occupation that follows the south-north axis, transversal valleys, and four concentric zones, as classified in the previous POT, yet through an enhanced iteration of the river corridor, not only as central axis, but as a publicly accessible district and ecological basin. This POT affirms the necessity for a high-density residential and mixed-use urban area adjacent to the river corridor, as a compact core, to accommodate housing for the increasing population. The POT also maintains an ascending peri-urban border, for recreation and agriculture, as well as to contain the urban expansion, as an ecological buffer that encircles the valley at 1,800 meters above sea level. This natural shield is defined by the geography and the mountain ranges of the region, protecting the environmental quality of the Valle de Aburrá.[61]

PARQUES DEL RÍO

Áreas de Intervención Estratégica (AIE) include AIE MED-Río, AIE MED-Borde Urbano Rural, and AIE MED-Transversalidades as areas of strategic intervention that identify pilot projects and test the financial and planning feasibility for urban expansion across the distinct geographical typologies of the city-region—the river; urban-rural border; and transverse regions— before being implemented at full scale.[62] Within the AIE MED-Río there are three macro projects, south, central and north, of which the Parqués del Río, the central macro project, has been recently built, as the latest and most ambitious project during the city's near two-decade rebirth.

In 2014, the Municipality of Medellín, in collaboration with EDU and the Colombian Society of Architects launched the Parques del Río project as the Macro Project and as an international competition that sought to re-orient the city's expansion along the Medellín River. In accordance with the recent POT, the competition envisioned connections across the banks, while offering new areas for public space along the river's edge; it addressed how to balance density while providing new areas for public space along the river's edge. The project looked for ways to re-calibrate citizens' perception of the river, both as a public amenity and as an ecological asset.

Parques del Río today, designed by Latitud,[63] offers lively new public spaces in the city center, as an open corridor that invites the public to gather along the river. The linear promenade has a variety of programmatic elements, embankment seating, budding trees and lawn areas, as well as cultural buildings that align the park's procession. This macro project is nine kilometers of a 26-kilometer stretch, which has succeeded in articulating a fanciful public sector for the downtown. The project is not yet fully integrated, however, into the broader, systemic network as part of a more equitable or sustainable city. Parques del Río passes through a central, urban district classified as strata five and six, and it will be important to understand how the connections to the west side are resolved, as well as to the projected northern section of the river project, Río Norte, as part of the "nuevo norte" (the new north) abutting Moravia.

How these connections will be articulated, and if, in fact, the administration will provide funding for the Moravia sector are remaining questions, as here the stratum classification number, one to two, is less glamorous.[64] It is unclear as to whether the project is performing ecologically as much as it could, collecting the stormwater, filtering it, and using it for the park's irrigation; details that if also properly articulated could demonstrate new ways for recycling the water. These practices might link back to environmental considerations benefitting the ecology of the region. Unfortunately, access to the river's edge is impeded, even after all the efforts to re-engage and return this border to the people. The tall concrete embankments, though lushly planted, obscure the view and access down to the water, once again preventing connections with the city's cultural symbol of progress and fertility. This project, no doubt, leaves a lasting impression, as part of the "Medellín Miracle,"[65] with valuable references to the Barcelona model[66] of urban and social renewal, or instead, as an assemblage of NYC's HighLine,[67] beautifully suspended above a cutting-edge mirage of the actual city. This is a delicate matter, since the rebirth of Medellín merits being distinguished by a more inclusive agenda and deeper democratic process on so many more levels.

Right: Parques del Río in Medellín's city center.

SOCIAL HOUSING

One critical aspect to this equation on social urbanism that remains amiss, and one which we must acknowledge as a shared dilemma affecting developing cities worldwide, has to do with the continual expansion of these urban centers and the increasing demand for adequate and dignified housing. The prototypes and "tests" that were introduced and built in Latin America during the 1950s to counter the population surge in countries such as Brazil, Mexico, Venezuela, and Argentina, for instance, are projects we cannot swiftly repeat, as these did not provide a silver bullet. In the mid-20th-century, when reinforced concrete was in vogue, and the architectural writ was about solving large numbers and providing a roof for thousands of people, architects may have missed the mark. As the largest, Conjunto Urbano Nonoalco Tlatelolco, designed in Mexico City in 1964 by Mario Parni, is a prime example of these massive housing projects. This included 130 buildings with 15,000 units to house 100,000 people. With its own schools, hospitals, stores, and amenities Tlatelolco became a city within a city.[68]

In 1966, the UN funded Proyecto Experimental de Vivienda, PREVI, an experimental housing competition geared to solving the housing crisis near Lima, Peru. This competition drew a cast of designers including James Sterling, Charles Correa, and the Metabolists, among others. The deriving solution for PREVI included houses arranged in tightly packed groups, forming courtyards; familiar patterns to the existing customs of the neighborhood, which could be expanded upon informally, upwards, and over time. In the 1980s, public housing primarily transitioned into an economic tool, relocating squatters from prime real estate to the edge of the city, splitting it into multiple, disparate units. This is something evidenced in Rio's favelas, in the barriadas in Caracas, callampas in Chile, and the tugurios in Colombia. Torre David in Caracas, a 45-story banking tower left unfinished in the 1990s, became occupied by 3,000 squatters and turned into a "vertical village."[69] Over the years, the residents of the tower have been able to secure basic services, with water reaching up to the 22nd floor. Though without an elevator, this unintended project does signal a potential model for reintegrating displaced people who are relegated to the edge of the city as the default of these colossal housing solutions.

In 2016, Chilean architect Alejandro Aravena, founder of Elemental, received the Pritzker Prize for his clever concept for a half-built house, a project in Iquique, Chile.[70] This half-house, albeit a project executed on a level terrain, offers a model for an unfinished house, enabling dwellers to invest time and energy while learning how to build, providing them with a greater sense of ownership and dignity as they brand their own units.

In Medellín, there have been recognizable public housing projects, and these have grown in number, capacity, and scale, over time, in an attempt to meet the population demand. La Playa, a public housing project near the Memory Museum, received a design award in 2004 for its imaginative solution; zig-zag facades that break with the traditional monotony that characterizes public housing, and by the inclusion of semi-private and habitable open spaces. In Comuna 13, older housing projects are exemplar for the arrangement of the structures, forming open spaces among them, and for the livable scale that retain the notion that these buildings are for people to live in and thrive. Yet the options on the table for addressing Medellín's current housing crisis are similar to the unsatisfactory and tired solutions to public housing that have been vetted in the past. The spatial limitations of the sloped landscape of the region, notwithstanding, the public housing towers in El Pajarito, Comuna 7 on the northwest side, for example, have forced migrants to live in cold concrete towers, typically five to 13 stories high, wiping out any connections to the ground the residents may have had as agrarian people, or to each other. The structures are nestled midway into the slopes in such a way as to avoid the need to satisfy elevator requirements, but are devoid of any further considerations. Because residents are boxed in, isolated, and removed, they have little ability to interact, let alone greet each other on the streets. These are basic customs that could otherwise promote a deeper sense of community among newly formed neighborhoods that are made up of disparate migrants, in many cases unknown to each other, since they have been displaced from various regions. The towers, moreover, with a meager 32m^2 (345 ft^2) per unit, are faceless buildings, dropped on the ground, with little or no regard for the open and public spaces that could surround them, as part of a more integrated planning strategy responsive to the topography, the hydrology, and the orientation to natural light or to other buildings. Instead, these housing projects are deflected as part of a numbers game framed by the continuous migration and demand for housing and the monopoly of the construction industry, as a new wave of corruption in the urbanization of the city. To compound matters, approximately 30% of Medellín's inhabitants live in slums or informal settlements. Their repeated exclusion, often located in the peripheral comunas, illustrate how these citizens are marginalized and uninvited to taking part of the city.

Even so, the results stemming from the Medellín model on social urbanism are notable. The PRIMED, PUI, and EDU initiatives, the Conserjería de Medellín, the POTs, and the BIO 2030 Plan are invaluable tools for articulating an urban design vision that is socially and regionally framed, extending this unique Latin American city a way forward. A local consortium has resulted from the many collaborations among municipal and academic institutions, from the persistent leadership of liberal politicians who have invited citizens to meet each other in the public spaces of their city, breaking from internal corruption and external exploitation. Social urbanism in Medellín explores social, economic and ecological networks through a dialogue with the community over the reconstruction of a more sustainable city with a regional and national focus, as a metropolis that repositions local energy and restores the spirit of Antioqueños through the shared values held over the landscape, as part of a complete plan for progress.

Poverty rates in the city since 2003 have significantly declined, at 14% in 2018, down from 35% in 2003;[71] homicide rates have dropped dramatically from the tragic figures in 1991 at 365 per 100,000 inhabitants to 20 homicides per 100,000 in 2015.[72] The Gini coefficient for income inequality in Medellín, on the other hand, has increased significantly. In 2018, this number was at 0.475 after having reached a record decline in 2017 at 0.467.[73] This is indicative of the vast divide that Medellín continues to encounter, from south to the north, where the primary PUI projects were initially sited, and which the geomorphology and hydrology of the city amplify by the bisection of the river and the lack of buildable areas, forcing a division between habitable space in the center, in contrast to the precarious east-west slopes at the perimeter of the valley. Political corruption, in some ways a tradition in Medellín, a place where not all mayors are interested in the people as much as in the image of the city, yet where Fajardo, Federico Gutiérrez, Daniel Quintero Calle (elected mayor in 2020), and others continue persisting. Unemployment rates have fluctuated between 9% and 12% over the past few years; where the gross domestic product (GDP) of Medellín alone, ambitiously as in its early days, closely follows the national average of Colombia as a whole at 2.5%, despite a marked reduction since its peak in 2004 at 9.75%.[74] These figures are something to keep an eye on, as these could be related to the fallout of tricky deals as part of tantalizing international free-trade agreements.

The treacherous years of violence and oppression that Medellín has endured stem from multiple strains that are difficult to control or ever fully erase, yet the processes practiced here continue to illuminate a valuable path over the deep connections between the landscape and this special community, as an inextricably bound equation supporting the premises of social urbanism not only as a model, but as a movement guiding the future expansion of the city.

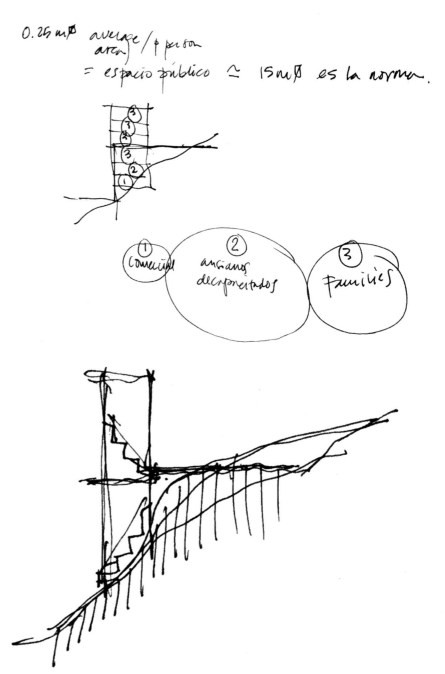

Above: Sketch studies of El Pajarito social housing in context, *María Bellalta*.

Following page: La Playa social housing project in Comuna 9.

NOTES

1   Gabriel Garcia Marquez, "The Solitutde of Latin America," (speech, 1982,) The Nobel Prize, https://www.nobelprize.org/prizes/literature/1982/marquez/lecture/.

2   "Medellín, Colombia Population 1950–2020," Macrotrends, last modified January 2020, https://www.macrotrends.net/cities/20827/medellín/population.

3   Norman A. Bailey, "La Violencia in Colombia," *Journal of Inter-American Studies* 9, no. 4 (1967): 561-75.

4   Ibid.

5   Thomas R. Cook, "The Financial Arm of the FARC: A Threat Finance Perspective," Journal of Strategic Security 4, no.1 (Spring 2011): 22.

6   John Otis, The FARC and Colombia's Illegal Drug Trade (Washington, D.C.: Wilson Center Latin American Program, 2014).

7   Claire Felter and Danielle Renwick, "Colombia's Civil Conflict" Council on Foreign Relations, Council on Foreign Relations, January 11, 2017. https://www.cfr.org/backgrounder/colombias-civil-conflict.

8   Jeremy McDermott, "Revealed: The secrets of Colombia's murderous Castaño brothers." *The Telegraph* (2008), https://www.telegraph.co.uk/news/worldnews/southamerica/colombia/3391789/Revealed-The-secrets-of-Colombias-murderous-Castano-brothers.html.

9   Jeffrey D. Sachs, "New approaches to the Latin American debt crisis" Essays in International Finance, 174 (1989), https://www.princeton.edu/~ies/IES_Essays/E174.pdf.

10   Peter S. Green, "Cocainenomics - The Syndicate; How Cocaine Traffickers from Medellín transformed the Multibillion Dollar Global Drug Trade," *The Wall Street Journal* (2015), https://www.wsj.com/ad/cocainenomics.

11   Amanda Macias, "10 Facts Reveal the Absurd Wealth of Pablo Escobar," *Business Insider*, September 21, 2015, https://www.businessinsider.com/10-facts-that-prove-the-absurdity-of-pablo-escobars-wealth-2015-9.

12   Kate Maclean, 'The Medellín Miracle:' The politics of crisis, elites and coalitions," Developmental Leadership Program, 2014, https://www.dlprog.org/publications/research-papers/the-medellín-miracle-the-politics-of-crisis-elites-and-coalitions.

13   Stanley Stewart, "How Medellín went from murder capital to hipster holiday destination," *The Telegraph*, January 2, 2018. https://www.telegraph.co.uk/travel/destinations/south-america/colombia/articles/medellín-murder-capital-to-hipster-destination/.

14   "Homicide: WHO Global Health Estimates." World Health Organization, accessed October 12, 2016, http://apps.who.int/violence-info/homicide/.

15   Robert McFadden, "New York Leads Big Cities in Robbery Rate, but Drops in Murders." *The New York Times* (1991), https://www.nytimes.com/1991/08/11/nyregion/new-york-leads-big-cities-in-robbery-rate-but-drops-in-murders.html.

16   Kate Maclean, *Social Urbanism and the Politics of Violence* (Basingstoke: Palgrave, 2015), 79, 118.

17   Ibid., 4.

18   "Colombia," Flags of the World, last modified May 20, 2019, https://www.crwflags.com/fotw/flags/co.html#first.

19   Donald T. Fox and Anne Stetson, "The 1991 Constitutional Reform: Prospects for Democracy and the Rule of Law in Colombia," *Case Western Reserve Journal of International Law* 24, no.2, (1992): 144–48.

20   Andrés Dávila Ladrón de Guevara, "Capítulo 2. El Frente Nacional: una transición democrática reformista y conservadora." Chap. 2 in *Democracia pactada: El Frente Nacional y el proceso constituyente de 1991 en Colombia*. Lima: Institut français d'études andines, 2002. doi: 10.4000/books.ifea.3975.

21   Mimi Yagoub, "Alvaro Uribe, when did it all go wrong?" Colombia Reports. January 22, 2014. https://colombiareports.com/uribe-go-wrong/.

22   Maria Alejandra Silva, "Alvaro Uribe; The most dangerous man in Colombian Politics." Council on Hemispheric Affairs. October 20, 2017. http://www.coha.org/alvaro-uribe-the-most-dangerous-man-in-colombian-politics/#_ednref12.

23   The Nobel Prize. "Juan Manuel Santos." The Nobel Prize, accessed November 10, 2019. https://www.nobelprize.org/prizes/peace/2016/santos/facts/.

24   Silva, "Alvaro Uribe," http://www.coha.org/alvaro-uribe-the-most-dangerous-man-in-colombian-politics/#_ednref12.

25   Loic Ramirez, "Peace is Trapped in the Networks of Betrayal." *Le Monde Diplomatique*. September 2018. http://mondediplo.com/2018/09/06colombia.

26   Ibid.

27   Colombia. "Everthing you need to know about the silleteros in Medellín's flower festival." Colombia. July 28, 2018. https://www.colombia.co/en/colombia-culture/folklore/everything-need-know-silleteros-medellíns-flower-festival/.

28   World Population Review. "Medellín Population." World Population Review. Last updated 2019. http://worldpopulationreview.com/world-cities/medellín-population/.

29   Ibid.

30   Ibid.

31   Jorge Perez Jaramillo, *Medellín: Urbanismo y Sociedad* (Colombia: Turner Publications, 2019), 42.

32   Ibid., 23.

33   Eduardo Moncada, "Urban Violence, Political Economy, And Territorial Control; Insights From Medellín," *Latin American Research* Review 51, no. 4 (1993): 230. https://lasa.international.pitt.edu/auth/pub/Larr/CurrentIssue/51-4_225-248_Moncada.pdf.

34   UNESCO, "Records of the General Conference, 27th session, Paris, 25 October to 16 November 1993, v. 1: Resolutions," in UNESCO General Conference (UNESCO, 1993). https://unesdoc.unesco.org/ark:/48223/pf0000095621.nameddest=2.6.

35   United Nations Development Programme Colombia and Secretaría de Desarrollo Comunitario de la Alcaldía de Medellín, PRIMED; Integral Program of Subnormal District Improvement in Medellín (Medellín: UNESCO, 1996), https://unesdoc.unesco.org/ark:/48223/pf0000129776.

36   Pérez, Medellín, 47.

37   Ibid.

38   Jorge Perez Jaramillo, "Medellín; A City for Life," *Biophilic Cities Journal* (2017): 34–39. https://static1.squarespace.com/static/5bbd32d6e66669016a6af7e2/t/5caba2166e9a7f7a1e35562c/1554752024785/Medellín-Columbia-A-City-for-Life-by-Perez-Jaramillo.pdf.

39   Alcaldía de Medellín, BIO 2030 Plan Director Medellín, Valle de Aburrá (Medellín: Alcaldia de Medellín, 2011), 18, http://www.eafit.edu.co/centros/urbam/Documents/BOOKbio2030plandirectormedellín.pdf.

40   J. Pérez Jaramillo, J.M. Patiño, G. Spera, J.C. García, D. Tarchópulos, L. Cardona, Plan De Ordenamiento Territorial De Medellín 2014: Un Modelo Territorial para la Intervención Estratégica (Medellín: Departamento Administrativo de Planeación DAP, Alcaldía de Medellín, 2014), https://upcommons.upc.edu/bitstream/handle/2117/80323/97BCN_PerezJorge.pdf.

41   Francoise Coupe, "Medellín Metropolitan, Colombia." Interview by IN-Between Metropolitan Strategies Programme. International Urban Development Associa tion, 2013. https://inta-aivn.org/en/481-inta/activitities/exchange/roundtables/20122013-inbetween/1686-metropolitan-medellín-en.

42   Observatorio de Politicas Publicas del Consejo de Medellín, Planes de Desarrollo Local (Medellín: Universidad de Medellín and Universidad EAFIT, 2017), http://www.eafit.edu.co/centros/analisis-politico/publicaciones/observatorio/Documents/investigacion-planes-de-desarrollo-local.pdf.

43   "Manifesto Compromiso Ciudadano," El Independiente (2019). https://www.elindependiente.com/wp-content/uploads/2019/11/Compromiso_Ciudadano.pdf.

44   Alcaldia de Medellín, Del Miedo a la Esperanza, (Medellín: Alcaldia de Medellín, 2008), https://acimedellín.org/wp-content/uploads/publicaciones/del-mie do-a-la-esperanza-2014.pdf.

45   Ibid.

46   James Brooke. "Vigilantes Fight Crime in Colombian Cocaine City." New York Times. February 16, 1992. https://www.nytimes.com/1992/02/16/world/vigilan tes-fight-crime-in-colombian-cocaine-city.html.

47   Juan Forero. "Medellín's Effort Against Crime Prove Fleeting." Washington Post. June 13, 2013. https://www.washingtonpost.com/world/medellíns-efforts-against-crime-prove-fleeting/2013/06/12/4852323e-d374-11e2-b3a2-3bf5eb37b9d0_story.html.

48   Liliana Bernal Franco and Claudia Navas Caputo. Urban Violence and Humanitarian Action In Medellín. Rio de Janeiro: Humanitarian Action in Situations Other Than War (HASOW), 2013, 7, accessed June 12, 2018.
http://www.cerac.org.co/assets/pdf/Other%20publications/Hasow_6_Urban%20violence%20and%20humanitarian%20action%20in%20Medellín_(6jun)_CN.pdf

49   Kate Maclean, Social Urbanism and the Politics of Violence (Basingstoke: Palgrave, 2015) 47, 83.

50   Sully Maria Quinchia Roldán, Luis Carlos Agudelo Patino, and Armando Arteaga Rosero. Urbanismo en Medellín, Siglo XIX: Aportes a la Discusión (Medellín: Universidad National de Colombia, 2018).

51   "Urban Design Prize; Medellín Introduction," Harvard University, accessed October 12, 2018, https://urbandesignprize.gsd.harvard.edu/porto medellín/about/.

52   Peter Brand and Julio Davila, "Mobility Innovation at the Urban Margins," City: Analysis of Urban Trends, Culture, Theory, Policy, Action,15: 6 (2011): 1, ac cessed September 14, 2018, DOI: 10.1080/13604813.2011.609007.

53   Julio D. Dávila and Diana Daste, "Poverty, participation and aerial cable-cars: A case study of Medellín." Paper presented at 12th NAERUS Annual Conference "The city at a human scale", Madrid, October 2011, 4. https://www.ucl.ac.uk/bartlett/development/sites/bartlett/files/davila-daste-naerus-2011.pdf

54   Mine Sato. A Fresh Look at Capacity Development from Insiders' Perspectives: A Case Study of an Urban Redevelopment Project in Medellín. Tokyo: JICA Research Institute, 2013, accessed May 14, 2018. https://www.jica.go.jp/jica-ri/publication/workingpaper/jrft3q00000024w6-att/JICA-RI_WP_No.60_2013_2.pdf

55   Danny Andres Osorio Gaviria, Moravia; The Story of a Slum on a Hill of Garbage. Human Settlements, 2014, accessed October 12, 2019. http://www.aca demia.edu/10623171/Moravia_The_story_of_a_slum_on_a_hill_of_garbage.

56   Interview with Moravia resident, August 8, 2019.

57   Kate Maclean, Social Urbanism and the Politics of Violence (Basingstoke: Palgrave, 2015)

58   Perez, "Medellín", 75–93.

59   Joey Jacobson. "How EPM Group Is Reclaiming Medellín's Infrastructure as Public Space," 15 Jun 2015. ArchDaily, accessed 2, Jan. 2019, https://www.arch daily.com/642184/how-epm-group-reclaimed-medellín-s-infrastructure-as-public-space/.

60   Alcaldía de Medellín, BIO 2030.

61   J. Pérez Jaramillo, J.M. Patiño, G. Spera, J.C. García, D. Tarchópulos, L. Cardona, Plan De Ordenamiento.

62   Universidad EAFIT and URBAM. Metodología de Trabajo Colaborativo, Alrededor de la Transformación de Río Norte, Medellín: Universidad EAFIT, 23.

63   Constanza Cabezas. "Latitud, primer lugar del concurso público internacional Parque del Río en Medellín." ArchDaily. November 30, 2018. https://www.plata formaarquitectura.cl/cl/tag/latitud-taller-de-arquitectura-y-ciudad.

64   "Moravian History," G4Moravia (blog), May 2, 2007, http://g4moravia.blogspot.com/2007/05/historia-moravia.html.

65   Kate Maclean, Social Urbanism and the Politics of Violence (Basingstoke: Palgrave, 2015)

66   F. J. Monclús, "El 'modelo Barcelona' ¿Una fórmula original? De la 'reconstrucción' a los proyectos urbanos estratégicos (1997–2004)," Perspectivas Urbanas /Urban Perspectives 18, no.4 (2003): 399–421.

67   James Corner Field Operations. "The High Line." James Corner Field Operations. https://www.fieldoperations.net/project-details/project/the-high-line.html.

68   Mely Morfin. "Architecture Classics: Nonoalco Tlatelolco/Mario Parni Housing Complex." ArchDaily. August 26, 2015, accessed July 13, 2018, https://www.archdaily.mx/mx/772426/clasicos-de-arquitectura-conjunto-habitacional-nonoalco-tlatelolco-mario-pani.

69   Alfredo Brillembourg, ed. Torre David: Informal Vertical Communities, (Zurich: Lars Muller, 2012).

70   Veronica Adler, et al. Vivienda ¿Qué viene?: De pensar la unidad a construir la ciudad. (Banco Interamericano de Desarollo, 2018) 472–73.

71   Colombia Reports. "Medellín." Colombia Reports. July 20, 2019. https://colombiareports.com/medellín/.

72   Jeff Paschke, "Is Medellín Safe? Security in Medellín and Safety Tips – 2019 Update," Medellín Guru (blog), March 17, 2019, https://medellínguru.com/medell in-security-safety-tips/.

73   Colombia Reports. "Medellín."

74   Ibid.

FROM THE FIELD

Cross-Cultural Studio - Medellín

4

FROM THE FIELD
Cross-Cultural Studio - Medellín

Deriving from over five years of international collaborations in Latin America, I have had the opportunity to build agency through expanding worldviews by immersing my students in a diverse cultural, spatial, and ecological arena. By engaging with faculty and students from the Boston Architectural College, School of Landscape Architecture, and the Universidad Pontificia Bolivariana, Escuela de Arquitectura y Diseño, through the participatory processes with local community leaders, and the many excursions we have explored all over Medellín and its astonishing landscape, together we have reshaped a pedagogical approach to spatial design.

Ongoing research and studio work focused on the processes and projects associated with social urbanism investigate how urban design, planning, architecture, as well as site design parameters within an extraordinary geographical and ecological region of the Global South are structured, and how these could excel through re-envisioned social and spatial strategies. At varying scales, natural systems are overlaid against the dense urban fabric to provoke, and see, the viable planning frameworks that can inform the challenges affecting the continued expansion of the city and its developing communities. Through a deeper understanding of the region's terrain, as described earlier, and through its layered history, moreover, a rationale behind the economic inequality and rapid speed at which the city has grown is contextualized. These studies offer insight into the socio-cultural and political underpinnings behind the "form" of the city's development, and to the precarious disconnect that exists with the natural ecology of the area—conditions that must be repositioned through enhanced planning, including social considerations.

Through in-situ observations, these studies re-frame traditional planning practices within a context of a landscape that would otherwise remain unfamiliar, limited by references and perceptions predominantly stemming from the Global North, tinged by colonial and capitalist views. A closer analysis of the local landscape and regional characteristics provide the opportunity for deeper explorations, a priori, when searching for viable solutions for expansive urban growth within a landscape that cannot yield so easily, given its physique, to such anthropogenic demands. Finally, the pedagogical process for guiding emerging spatial design professionals through these cross-contextual/cultural experiences offers renewed perspectives with inclinations toward socially responsible design, leading to the formulation of a global design paradigm, fueled by the more socially and spatially inclusive premises of social urbanism.

Over the years, the studies have included excursions all over Medellín, to analyze the environs, moving through an intensive agenda to experience the city. Visits to Medellín's civic plazas as part of the innovation area downtown, Parque de los Deseos, Jardín Botánico, Parque Explora, Parque de los Pies Descalzos across from the Empresas Públicas de Medellín (EPM)—the Intelligent Building at Alpujarra; as well as Plaza Botero, the Palacio de la Cultura, and the Museum of Antioquia at Avenida Bolivar, as older areas, have provided information on the urban core and grit of this growing metropolis. It has been essential to travel by Metro, Metrocable, and the Transvia, as integral mobility components and as part of the POT's framework, in order to experience the layout and circulation throughout. Moving by hired bus to remote, inaccessible areas where the Metrocable has not arrived, has also been invaluable for experiencing the peripheral areas of the city, as well as to interact with local drivers who share hidden stories and customs. Visits to many comunas and neighborhoods have permitted close interaction with the community and its constituents, where conversations with residents have widened the view of what life in Medellín may be about, more clearly understanding how the urbanization or the progress of the city is affecting the locals, in both positive and negative ways.

Comuna Popular - Comuna 1, has been an important site visit, to understand the density and character of the city's "nuevo norte" (the new north district), and to introduce students to the Metrocable and Biblioteca España, as a first PUI project, with elements of accessibility and urban acupuncture inserted into the Santo Domingo neighborhood. El Perro, an UPB architecture student and talented graffiti artist has led us through San Javier - Comuna 13, the Escaleras Electricas (electric stairs), which have permitted passage up to this tough neighborhood, home to Operación Orión, as mentioned earlier, where the transformation from year to year changes drastically. The scale and context of this and each PUI project visited—Bibioteca Belén, the Guayacanes, and El Pajarito UVAs, to mention only a few—illustrate a range of contexts and architectural and urban solutions, adding to the read and understanding of the city, further informing the projected areas of study each year.

Conceptual projects within the studio have ranged in scale and scope, from in-depth analyses of natural and constructed systems that examine the dramatic topography and hydrology, slope profile and areas of high risk, to the extensive flora and soil structure, for instance. Projects extend to urban design and planning realms, with master plan proposals for housing and public open space, for transit and connectivity between natural and built elements, mixed-use planning, including institutional, cultural and commercial programs, among others. Study sites have been located in the north-west, in El Robledo - Comuna 7, as part of the Pajarito neighborhood, where public housing towers continue to be deployed. Comprehending the social implications to the neighborhood's residents, displaced from disparate regions, and the concrete jungle overtones that radiate from here are poignant truths, aspects spatial designers must witness and consider prior to intervening. Looking at Quebrada Santa Elena in the old city, between Candelaria and Buenos Aires - Comuna 10 and 9, and how to re-connect the dividing stream as part of a communal and cultural public space, has been a significant socio-ecological project that emerges from the city's genesis and attempts to repair the fundamental fracture between the landscape and the cultural values of the native Aburrae settlers. Villa Hermosa - Comuna 8, in the La Ladera, on the eastern slopes, has been another important site and PUI project where an open-air library in place of a former prison building sits at the tip of a conflicted site, with two divisive neighborhoods bordered by streams, where both physical and social challenges have been studied. La Sierra - Comuna 8, is a dense, informal neighborhood where the most recent Metrocable line has arrived (Line H); climbing by foot, one can reach the Jardín Circunvalar (Greenbelt), connecting to Trece de Noviembre, another informal neighborhood of Comuna 8.

These sites have been key in understanding the profile of the city and the ascending circles that form part of the bowl, and of the POT. Additionally, these locations have been areas of proposed housing, institutional and cultural programming, and connectivity. Parques del Río—in the center of the city—with its new programming and polished construction are examined as part of the context for the latest studies at Aranjuez - Comuna 4 and the Moravia neighborhood mentioned earlier. Here, analyses and master plans for institutional, cultural, and public open spaces have been proposed to address the community's need for enhanced programming, local commerce, schools, and vocational training facilities mixed with local art museums and green play spaces for Moravia—elements that are both at stake and in demand when considering the gentrification threats posed by the adjacency to Parques del Río. Lastly, the reconfiguration of the Medellín River, deconstructing its profile, and reintegrating it as part of the ecological and cultural performance of the city, as a complete stream and blue-green system, has also been part of the studies in this central area.

The projects that follow partly reflect the analyses and planning proposals developed by students over the years. Each project represents a glimpse into investigations that consider the natural systems of the region, the fabric of the city, as well as the communities who inhabit these spaces. The work continues to be instrumental as an ongoing pedagogical approach and design methodology, informed by on-the-ground, cross-cultural perceptions over the urbanization of Medellín, and which posit on the development of neighboring areas in Latin America.

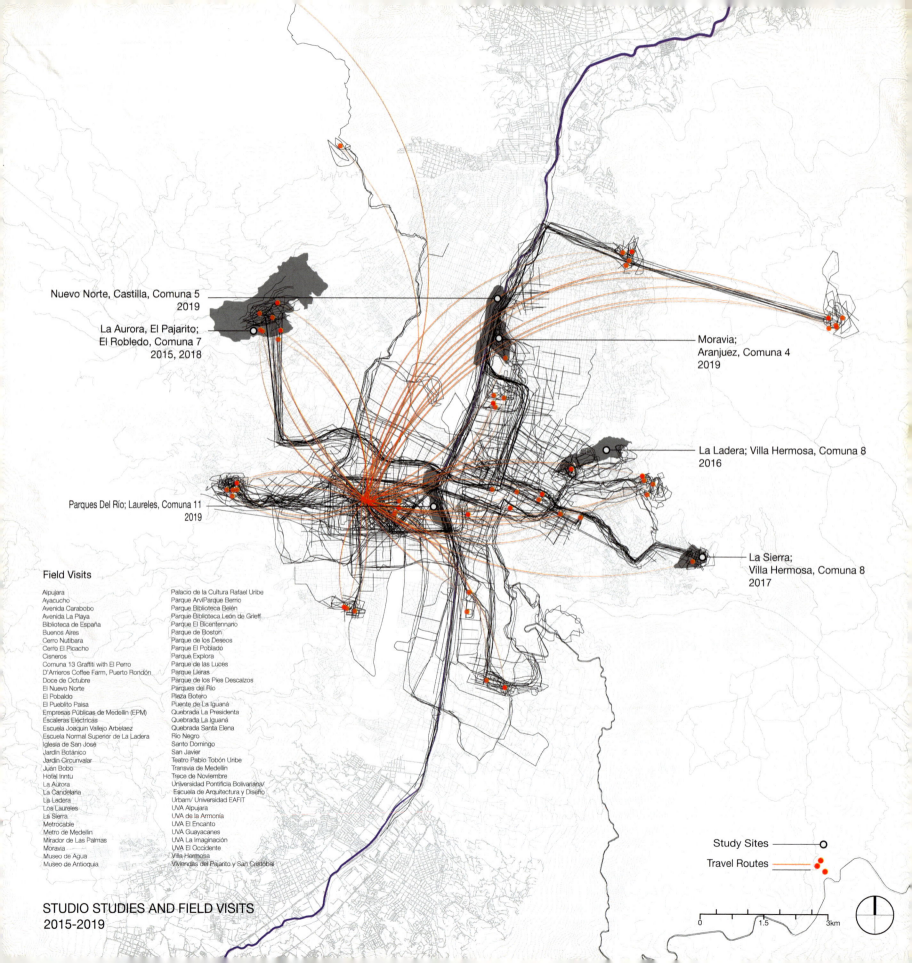

Nuevo Norte, Castilla, Comuna 5
2019

La Aurora, El Pajarito;
El Robledo, Comuna 7
2015, 2018

Moravia;
Aranjuez, Comuna 4
2019

La Ladera; Villa Hermosa, Comuna 8
2016

Parques Del Río; Laureles, Comuna 11
2019

La Sierra;
Villa Hermosa, Comuna 8
2017

Field Visits

Alpujara	Palacio de la Cultura Rafael Uribe
Ayacucho	Parque Arví/Parque Berrio
Avenida Carabobo	Parque Biblioteca Belén
Avenida La Playa	Parque Biblioteca León de Grieff
Biblioteca de España	Parque El Bicentennario
Buenos Aires	Parque de Boston
Cerro Nutibara	Parque de los Deseos
Cerro El Picacho	Parque El Poblado
Cisneros	Parque Explora
Comuna 13 Graffiti with El Perro	Parque de las Luces
D'Arrieros Coffee Farm, Puerto Rondón	Parque Lleras
Doce de Octubre	Parque de los Pies Descalzos
El Nuevo Norte	Parques del Río
El Pobaldo	Plaza Botero
El Pueblito Paisa	Puente de La Iguaná
Empresas Públicas de Medellín (EPM)	Quebrada La Presidenta
Escaleras Eléctricas	Quebrada La Iguaná
Escuela Joaquin Vallejo Arbelaez	Quebrada Santa Elena
Escuela Normal Superior de La Ladera	Rio Negro
Iglesia de San José	San Javier
Jardín Botánico	Santo Domingo
Jardín Circunvalar	Teatro Pablo Tobón Uribe
Juán Bobo	Transvia de Medellín
Hotel Inntu	Trece de Noviembre
La Aurora	Universidad Pontificia Bolivariana/
La Candelaria	Escuela de Arquitectura y Diseño
La Ladera	Urbam/ Universidad EAFIT
Los Laureles	UVA Alpujara
La Sierra	UVA de la Armonía
Metrocable	UVA El Encanto
Metro de Medellín	UVA Guayacanes
Mirador de Las Palmas	UVA La Imaginación
Moravia	UVA El Occidente
Museo de Agua	Villa Hermosa
Museo de Antioquia	Viviendas del Pajarito y San Cristóbal

Study Sites

Travel Routes

STUDIO STUDIES AND FIELD VISITS
2015-2019

0   1.5   3km

LA SIERRA - Comuna 8, eastern, central slopes, elev. +1,800 m. (6,000 ft.)

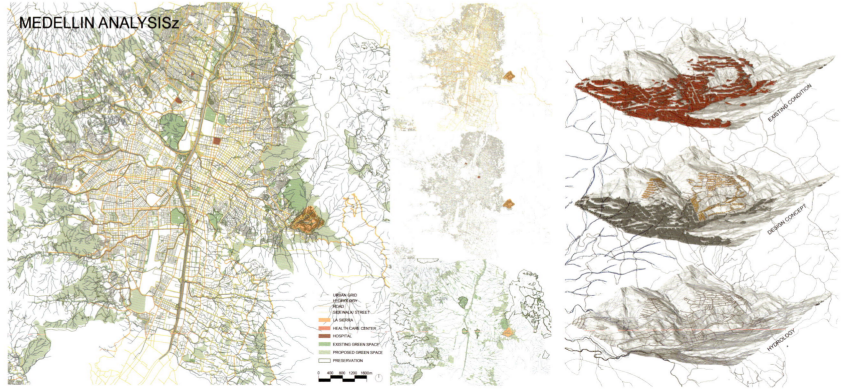

MEDELLIN ANALYSISz

| URBAN GRID |
| HYDROLOGY |
| ROAD |
| SIDEWALK/ STREET |
| LA SIERRA |
| HEALTH CARE CENTER |
| HOSPITAL |
| EXISTING GREEN SPACE |
| PROPOSED GREEN SPACE |
| PRESERVATION |

0 400 800 1200 1600m

ANALYTICAL STUDIES of the MEDELLÍN VALLEY and LA SIERRA
Top to bottom: Erin Fitch, Chien-Yu Lin

The informal settlement of La Sierra; housing and mix-institutional use programming.

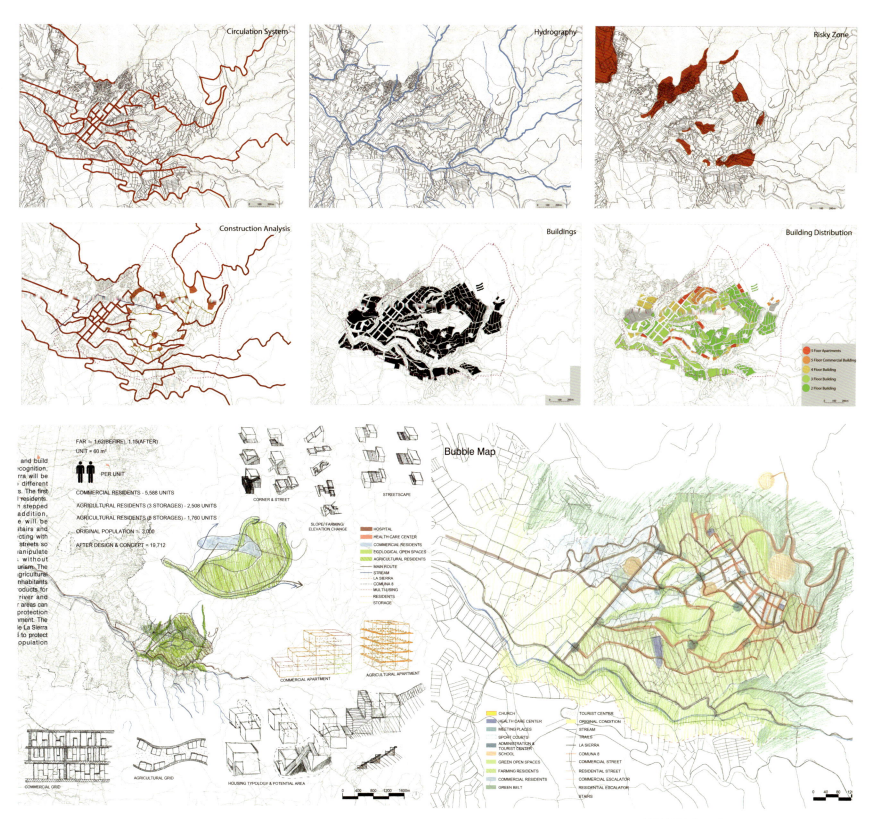

Circulation System

Hydrography

Risky Zone

Construction Analysis

Buildings

Building Distribution

FAR ≈ 1.62(BEFIRE), 1.15(AFTER)
UNIT = 60 m²

🚶🚶 PER UNIT

COMMERCIAL RESIDENTS - 5,588 UNITS

AGRICULTURAL RESIDENTS (3 STORAGES) - 2,508 UNITS

AGRICULTURAL RESIDENTS (5 STORAGES) - 1,760 UNITS

ORIGINAL POPULATION = 3,000

AFTER DESIGN & CONCEPT = 19,712

CORNER & STREET

STREETSCAPE

SLOPE/FARMING/
ELEVATION CHANGE

HOSPITAL
HEALTH CARE CENTER
COMMERCIAL RESIDENTS
ECOLOGICAL OPEN SPACES
AGRICULTURAL RESIDENTS
MAIN ROUTE
STREAM
LA SIERRA
COMUNA 8
MULTI-USING
RESIDENTS
STORAGE

COMMERCIAL APARTMENT

AGRICULTURAL APARTMENT

COMMERCIAL GRID

AGRICULTURAL GRID

HOUSING TYPOLOGY & POTENTIAL AREA

Bubble Map

CHURCH
HEALTH CARE CENTER
MEETING PLACES
SPORT COURTS
ADMINISTRATION &
TOURIST CENTER
SCHOOL
GREEN OPEN SPACES
FARMING RESIDENTS
COMMERCIAL RESIDENTS
GREEN BELT

TOURIST CENTER
ORIGINAL CONDITION
STREAM
TRAILS
LA SIERRA
COMUNA 8
COMMERCIAL STREET
RESIDENTIAL STREET
COMMERCIAL ESCALATOR
RESIDENTIAL ESCALATOR
STAIRS

ANALYTICAL STUDIES for LA SIERRA
Top to bottom: Chen-Chen, Chien-Yu Lin

La Sierra site analyses, including housing typologies, hydrology, mobility, and risk assessment.

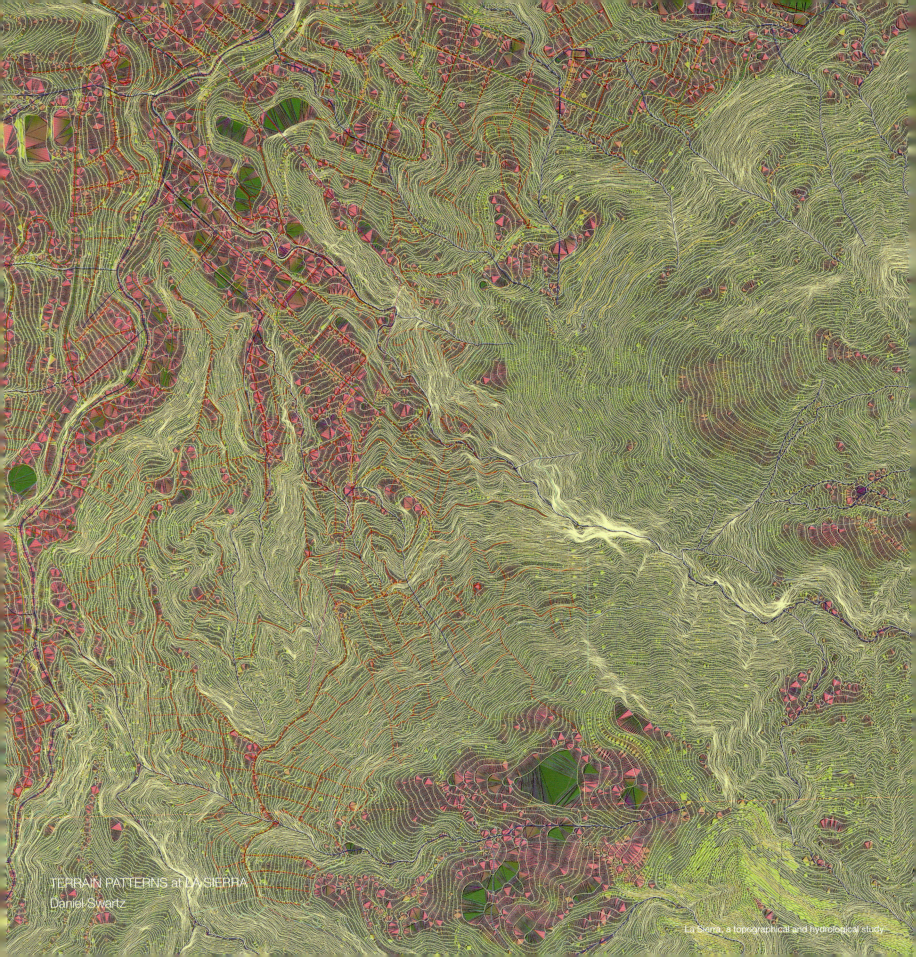

TERRAIN PATTERNS at LA SIERRA
Daniel Swartz

La Sierra, a topographical and hydrological study

Section C
Scale: 1:50

Section D
Scale 1:100

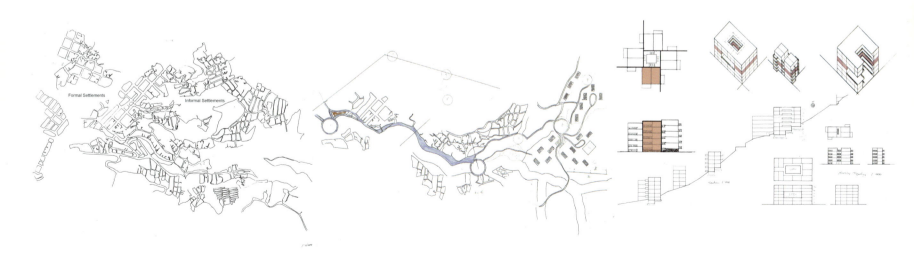

ECOLOGICAL FACTORS of NEW HOUSING PATTERNS in LA SIERRA
Top to bottom: Chien-Yu Lin, Joshua Brown, and Allan Robinson

Master plan and sectional studies: propoosed housing and conservation landscape.

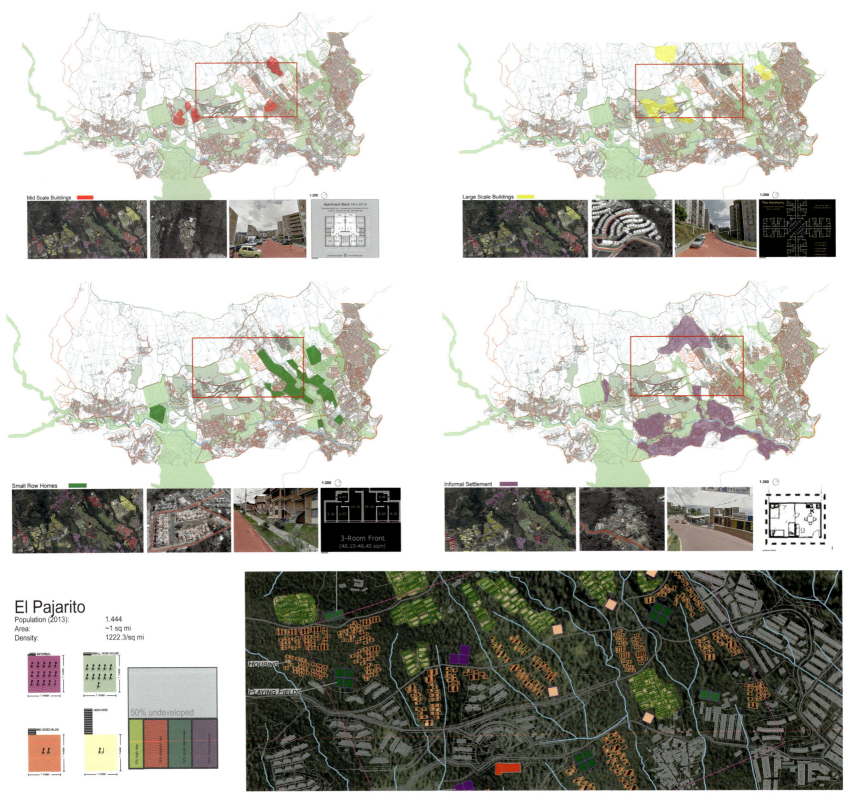

EXISTING and NEW HOUSING TYPOLOGIES in EL PAJARITO

Top to bottom: Judy Timpa, Meredith Juliana

Housing typology analysis in El Pajarito, ranging from large social housing towers to informal settlements.

HOUSING with ECOLOGICIAL and TOPOGRAPHICAL ASSETS in EL PAJARITO
Group project: Stephan Godanis, Meredith Juliana, and William Gardner

Formalization of existing housing typologies as new models for development with inclusion of ecological elements and practices.

HOUSING and FUTURE GROWTH of the CITY

Jonathan Cave

Regional studies for housing and development derived from topographical patterns.

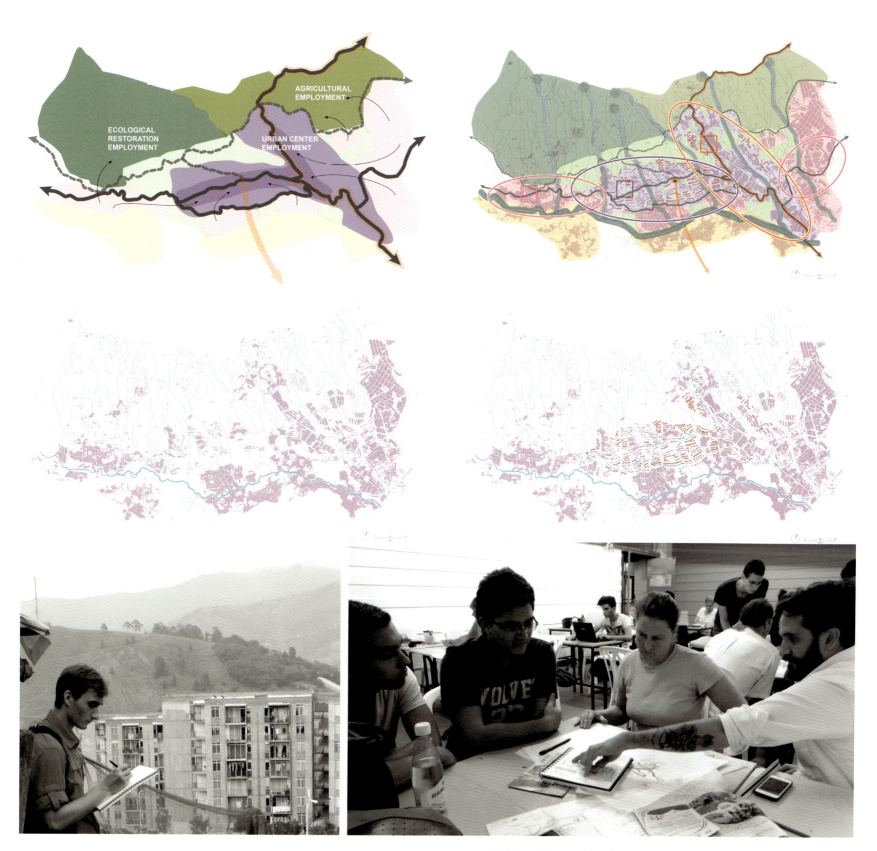

ECOLOGICAL RESTORATION EMPLOYMENT

AGRICULTURAL EMPLOYMENT

URBAN CENTER EMPLOYMENT

HOUSING and AGRICULTURAL MASTER PLAN for LA AURORA

Erica Quigley

Master plan studies for proposed housing, including local economy derived from agricultural programming.
Photos: Housing densities are examined throughout formal and informal neighborhoods.

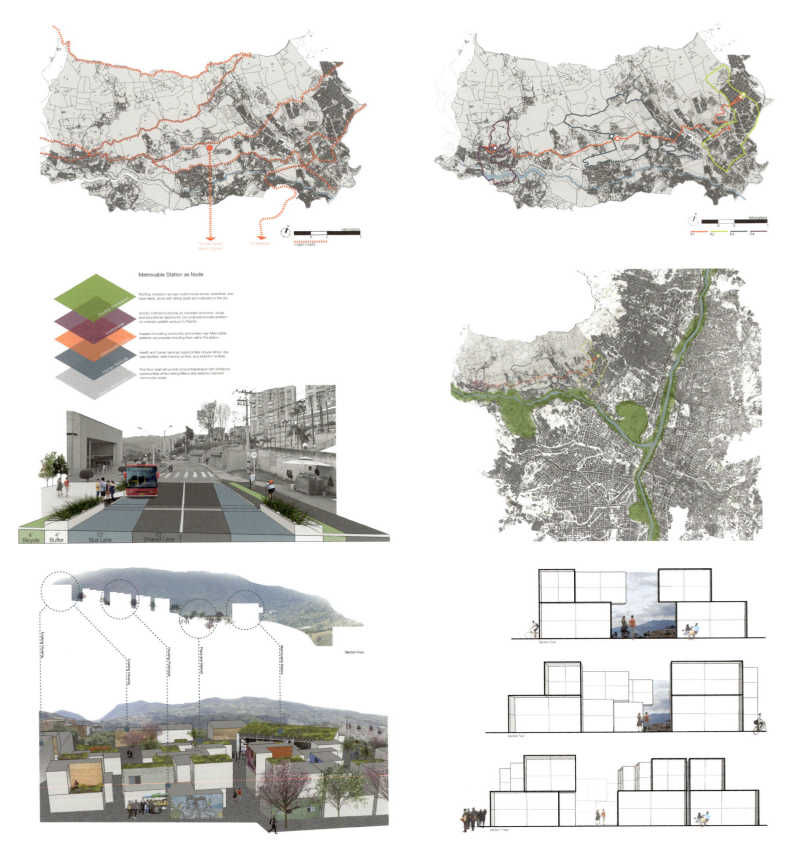

TRANSPORTATION MASTER PLAN for LA AURORA

Thomas Klein

Transportation-led housing and planning project to address lateral connections between existing Metrocable station and proposed pedestrian, cycle, and bus loops.

Illuminating Pathway

Recreational Moments

Enjoyment of Goods

Daily Resources

NEIGHBORHOOD IDENTITY and NECKLACE in EL PAJARITO
Olivia Stasin

Public space intervention lining communal areas throughout El Pajarito via an installation that activates, gathers, and serves to connect citizens.

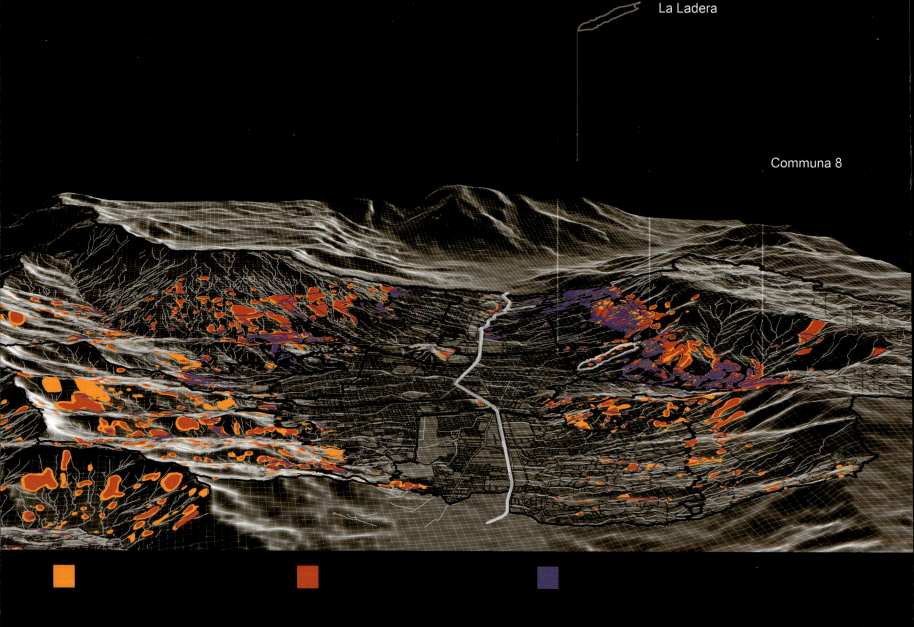

La Ladera

Communa 8

RISK ANALYSIS and ECOLOGICAL CONSERVATION
Jacob Ferreira

Landslide risk analysis in relation to existing site amenities and surrounding formal and informal settlements in La Ladera and Villa Hermosa.

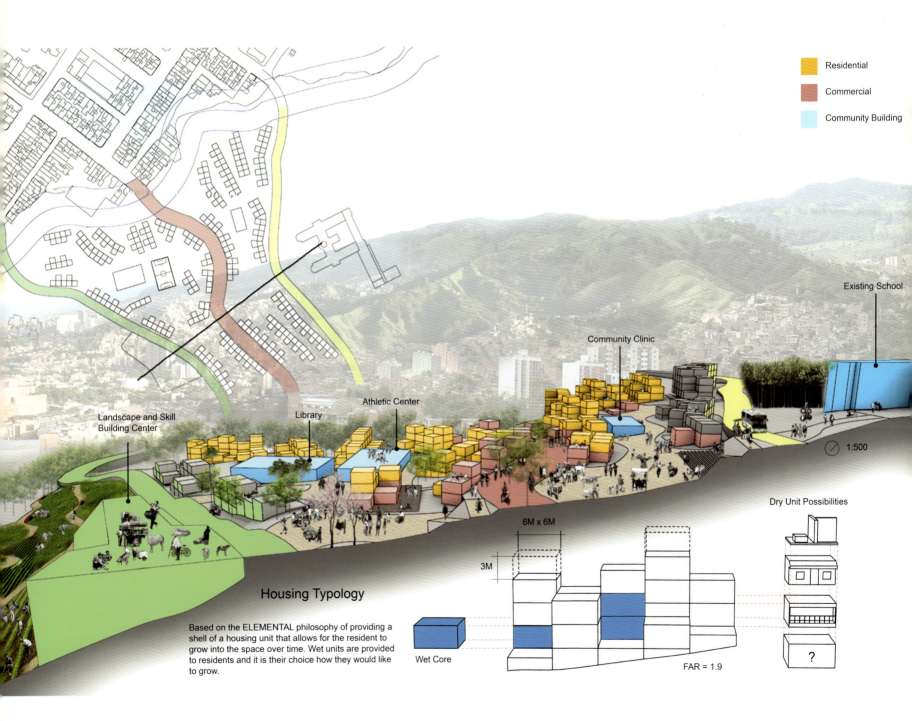

Residential

Commercial

Community Building

Existing School

Community Clinic

Landscape and Skill
Building Center

Library

Athletic Center

1:500

Dry Unit Possibilities

6M x 6M

3M

Housing Typology

Based on the ELEMENTAL philosophy of providing a
shell of a housing unit that allows for the resident to
grow into the space over time. Wet units are provided
to residents and it is their choice how they would like
to grow.

Wet Core

FAR = 1.9

?

HOUSING and PUBLIC AMENITIES THROUGH ECOLOGICAL INTEGRATION

Jacob Ferreira

Housing and institutional programming proposal to mitigate social and topographical divisions along the steep topography of La Ladera and Villa Hermosa.

TOPOGRAPHICAL PLANNING and HOUSING in VILLA HERMOSA

Top to bottom: Benjamin Strong, Brittany Dixon

La Ladera bordering hydrological networks and remediation techniques serve to repair polluted waterways along existing and new housing.

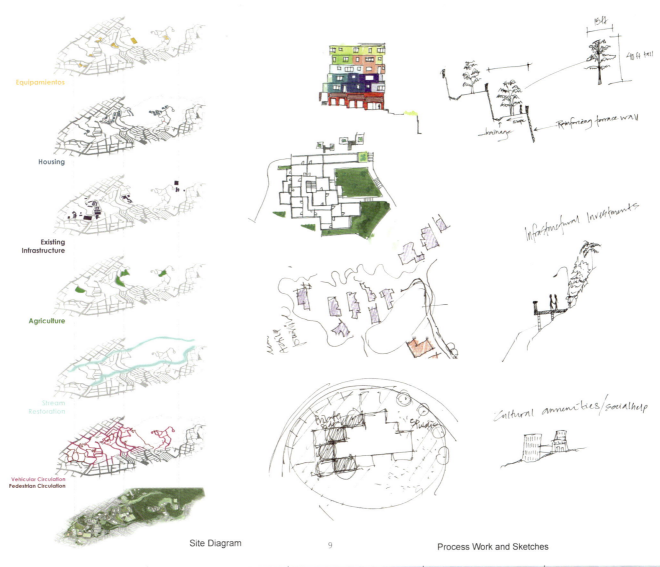

Equipamientos

Housing

Existing
Infrastructure

Agriculture

Stream
Restoration

Vehicular Circulation
Pedestrian Circulation

Site Diagram   9   Process Work and Sketches

15 ft

40 ft tall

drainage   slope   Reinforcing terrace wall

Infrastructural Investments

Cultural amenities/socialhelp

Scale = 1:500

HOUSING BUILDING BLOCKS in LA LADERA
Sarah Kresock

Housing studies integrate open and built units with stackable neighborhood programming along La Ladera slopes.

MASTERPLAN
La Ladera
Medellin, Colombia

SECTION CUT A-A'

SECTION CUT B-B'

SECTION CUT C-C'

TRANSPORTATION NETWORKS for LA LADERA
Fanny Behrends

Proposed circulation connections link divided neighborhoods from the northwest and southwest sides of La Ladera.

1:2000

2600m

ituated in the middle of the Tropical Andes Biodiversity region,
edellin is home for an enormous variety of native species

olombia is the second most biodiverse country in the world

round 10% of the world's known species live in Colombia

1400m

TOPOGRAPHY as PLANNING ASSET at LA LADERA

Mary Burke

New housing proposal integrates existing urban areas with added recreational spaces via access paths into the surrounding forested regions.

217

QUEBRADA SANTA ELENA - Comunas 9,10, eastern, central slopes, elev. +/-1,550 m. (5,085 ft.)

UPPER ZONE 1540M-1850M

MIDDLE ZONE 1453M-1540M

INTERVENTION ZONE 3
LAS ESTANCIAS AND
BARRIO JUAN PABLO

CERRO PAN DE AZUCAR
"SUGARLOAF MOUNTAIN"

INTERVENTION ZONE 2
ESTACION ORIENTE AND
BARRIO VILLATINA

NATURAL CONDITIONS:

- HIGH CONCENTRATION OF TRIBUTARIES REACH-ING THE QUEBRADA SANTA ELENA
- AVERAGE SLOPES OF BETWEEN 40 % - 60%, INCREASING WATER VELOCITY
- POOR SOIL INTEGRITY, LARGELY CLAY UP TO 1 METER THICK
- LANDSLIDE RISKS AS RESULT OF POOR SOIL AND HIGH WATER FLOW AND VOLUME
- QUEBRADA SANTA ELENA IS EXPOSED, WITH NATURAL EDGE CONDITIONS AND DEEP RAVINES
- HEAVY VEGETATIVE COVER ALONG THE CREEK

SOCIAL CONDITIONS:

- MEDIUM TO LOW DESNITY URBANIZATION
- PREVALENCE OF INFORMAL SETTLEMENTS
- PRECARIOUS LIVING CONDITIONS WITH RISK OF NATURAL DISASTER, POOR ACCESS TO PUBLIC SERVICES AND POORER ECONOMY
- TERRITORIAL BARRIOS WITH HIGHER LEVELS OF GANG ACTIVITY
- HIGH NUMBER OF INTERNALLY DISPLACED PEOPLES

MIDDLE ZONE 1540M-1850M

LOWER ZONE 1453M-1540M

NATURAL CONDITIONS:

- HIGH CONCENTRATION OF TRIBUTARIES REACHING THE QUEBRADA SANTA ELENA
- AVERAGE SLOPES OF 0% TO 20%, WITH LOWER WATER VELOCITY
- SOILS RANGING FROM CLAY SILT IN HIGHER ELEVATIONS TO ALLUVIAL SOILS ON A MOSTLY FLAT VALLEY BASIN AT THE RIO MEDELLIN
- QUEBRADA SANTA ELENA ENTERS AN UN-DERGROUND CULVERT BEFORE EMERGING AT THE RIO MEDELLIN
- HIGHLY CONTAMINATED DUE TO POOR WASTE REMOVAL, CONSTRUCTION WASTE, INDUSTRIAL WASTE, AND A CONCENTRATION OF CONTAMINANTS AT THE LOWEST ELEVATIONS

SOCIAL CONDITIONS

- HIGH DENSITY URBANIZATION
- MIXED HOUSING TYPOLOGIES FROM FORMAL TO INFORMAL
- HIGHER QUALITY LIVING CONDITIONS WITH LOW LEVEL RISK, ACCESS TO PUBLIC SERVICES, AND MORE AFFLUENT ECONOMY
- MORE CONSOLIDATED NEIGHBORHOODS
- MIXED ECONOMY WITH HIGHER ACCESS TO EDUCATION

INTERVENTION ZONE 1
PARQUE BICENTENNARIO
AND MUSEO CASA DE LA
MEMORIA

BIRTHPLACE OF MEDELLIN

RIO MEDELLIN

SOCIAL and ECOLOGICAL RESTORATION along the STREAMBED

Daniela Coray

0m 150 300 450

Repairing social and ecological degradation at the Santa Elena streambed corridor

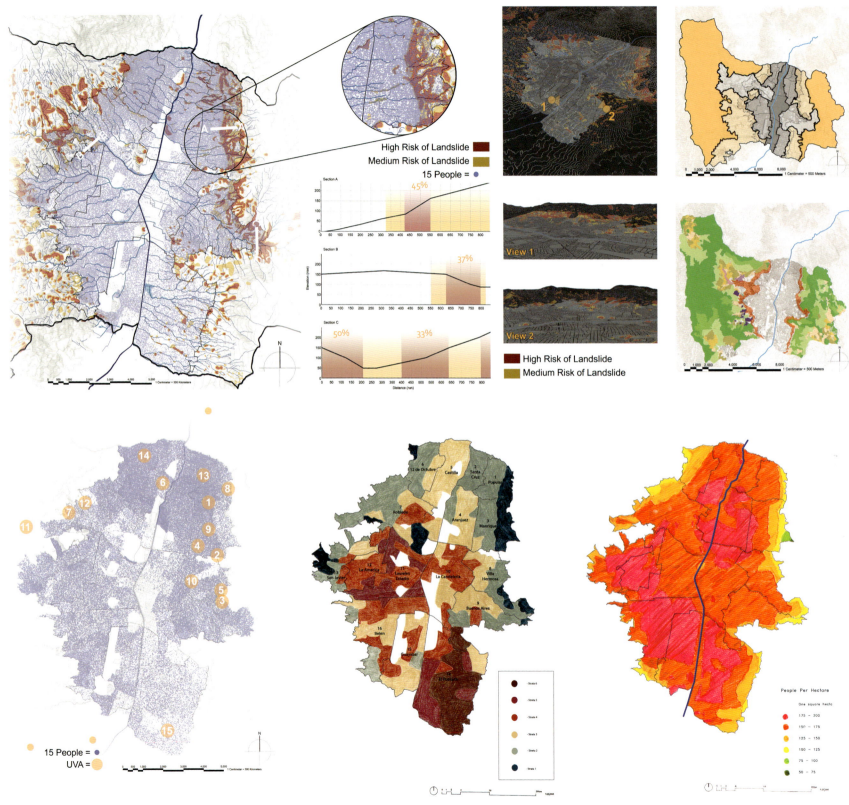

High Risk of Landslide
Medium Risk of Landslide

15 People =

45%

37%

50%   33%

View 1

View 2

High Risk of Landslide
Medium Risk of Landslide

15 People =

UVA =

People Per Hecta

One square hecto

175 - 200
150 - 175
125 - 150
100 - 125
75 - 100
50 - 75

SITE ANALYSES and DATA ASSESSMENT for MEDELLIN

Top and bottom left: Scott Leboeuf. Bottom middle and right: Damon Stewart-Souris

Topography, landslide risk, informal settlements, density and social strata measured against impacts of future urban development.

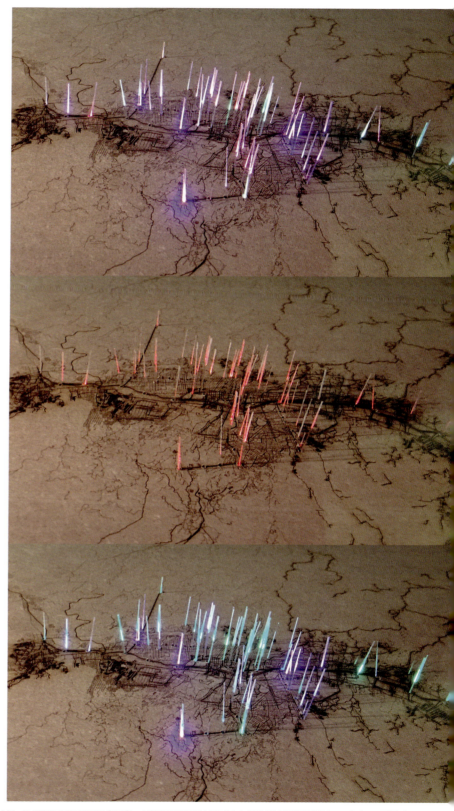

CONCEPTUAL INTERPRETATIONS of TOPOGRAPHY, LIGHT ENERGY and the CITY
Left to right: Lindsey Douglas, Andrew Mitchell

Topographical studies of La Quebrada Iguaná, and urban density explored through lighting studies.

221

CULTURAL and ECOLOGICAL CONNECTIONS ALONG the RIVER

Shiqi Dong

Master plan proposal abutting Moravia with new cultural and ecological loops connecting to the city.

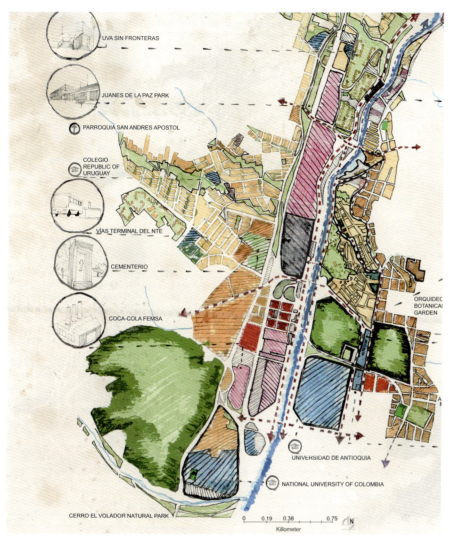

UVA SIN FRONTERAS

JUANES DE LA PAZ PARK

PARROQUIA SAN ANDRES APOSTOL

COLEGIO REPUBLIC OF URUGUAY

VÍAS TERMINAL DEL NTE

CEMENTERIO

COCA-COLA FEMSA

ORQUIDEO BOTANICAL GARDEN

UNIVERSIDAD DE ANTIOQUIA

NATIONAL UNIVERSITY OF COLOMBIA

CERRO EL VOLADOR NATURAL PARK

0   0.19   0.38   0.75
Killometer   N

FARMERS MARKET

PLAYGROUND

WETLAND PARK ZONE

CULTURAL CENTER

PROPOSED PEDESTRIAN BRIDGE

VÍAS TERMINAL DEL NTE

GREEN CORRRIDOR

TRAIN STATION

NEW PEDESTRIAN CROSSING BRIDGE WITH RAMP

MORAVIA

RIO MEDLLIN

CERRO EL VOLADOR NATURAL PARK

N

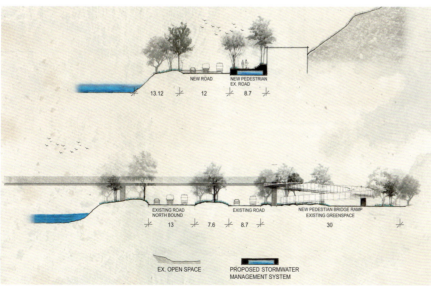

NEW ROAD   NEW PEDESTRIAN EX. ROAD

13.12   12   8.7

EXISTING ROAD NORTH BOUND   EXISTING ROAD   NEW PEDESTIAN BRIDGE RAMP EXISTING GREENSPACE

13   7.6   8.7   30

EX. OPEN SPACE   PROPOSED STORMWATER MANAGEMENT SYSTEM

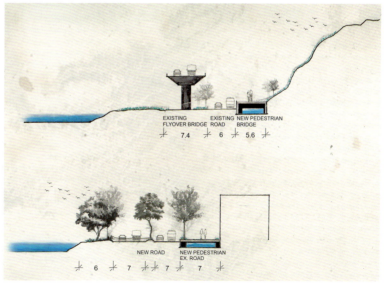

EXISTING FLYOVER BRIDGE   EXISTING ROAD   NEW PEDESTRIAN BRIDGE

7.4   6   5.6

NEW ROAD   NEW PEDESTRIAN EX. ROAD

6   7   7   7

GREEN CORRIDOR in MEDELLÍN'S NEW NORTH
Washie Khan

A natural water collection and spatial project that performs ecologically while integrating the neighborhoods in the "new north" of the city.

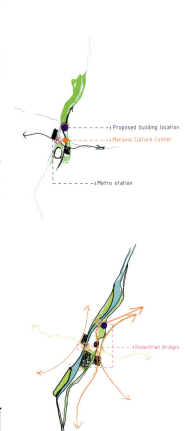

Building #4
Performance Space
Music Rooms
Gallery

Building #3
Workshops/Community Kitchen
Study Rooms
Library

Building #2
Recycling Workshops
Study Rooms
Theater

Building #1
Moravia Exhibition
Library
Study Rooms

Proposed building location
Moravia Culture Center
Metro station

Pedestrian Bridges

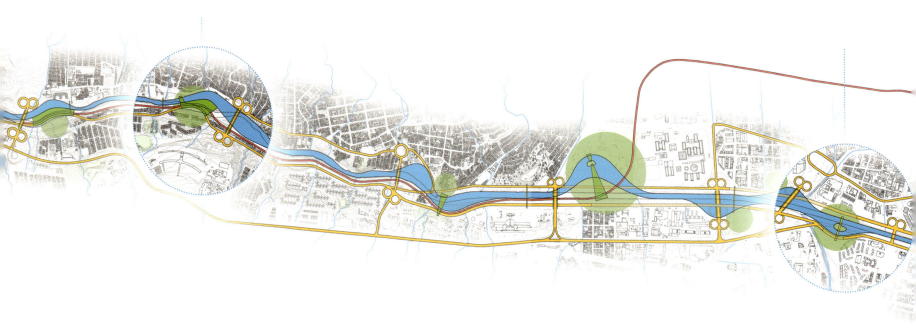

CULTURAL ENCOUNTERS ALONG the RESTORED MEDELLÍN RIVER

Top to bottom: Sara Alshankiti, Laura Feddersen

Proposed community center and artists's workspace/museum are sited along the river to integrate Moravia.
Dechannelization and restoration of the river increase the ecological performance of the natural systems in the city.

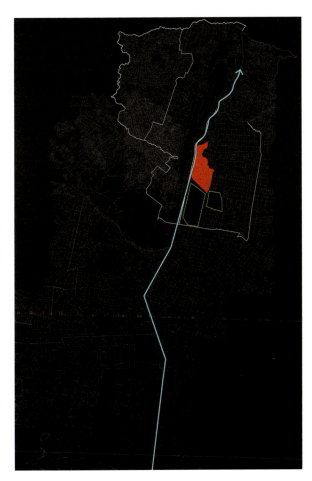

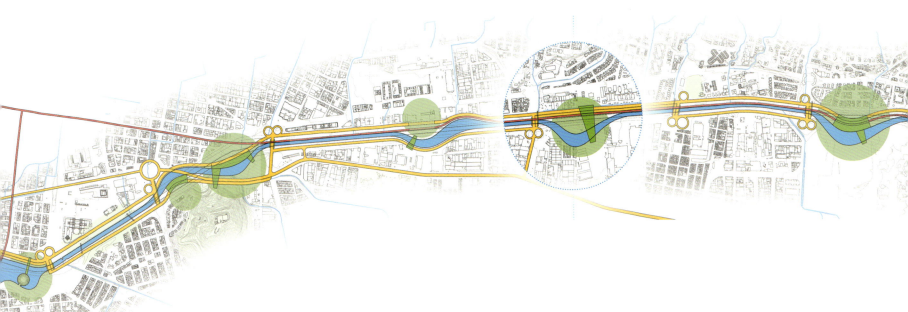

PROPOSED CULTURAL BUILDINGS for MORAVIA
Sara Alshankiti, Anna Vaivoda, and Laura Feddersen

New cultural and recreational buildings engage the Medellín river as a social connector.

INVITED VOICES

Across the Disciplines

5

INVITED VOICES
Across the Disciplines

The thesis of this book has offered an overview of Latin America's geographical characteristics alongside a historical recount of its land development for over more than five centuries. Augmented through a more focused view of the socio-economic and political underpinnings of Colombia, and finally, of Medellín's urbanization over the last century, the rationale behind a progressive strategy for urban growth has been revealed. Social urbanism in Medellín has demonstrated the reconstruction of the city and of its society through building trust, and by inviting the community in as rightful and integral members of their urban spaces. As a methodology for the continued expansion of this and other similar global urban centers, however, this planning strategy must be broadened by deliberately folding in the regional geography of each particular arena, as the building blocks of cultural and social norms, and therefore of a fully integrated urban development approach.

In this chapter, the points of view of expert colleagues across varying fields provide introspection on re-occurring themes affecting the challenges of urbanization in Latin America. Influenced by their geographical and cultural contexts, each author identifies the social values of their tremendous work through meaningful interpretations of social urbanism, forming part of a shared vision and "collective culture" for re-framing spatial design today and for the future.

FROM SOCIAL URBANISM TO CULTURAL URBANISM
Construction of cities is evolving, and with that, many people continue to be left on the fringes. These spatial patterns are driven by economic—rather than social and ecological—incentives, which point to the missing cues of planning practices. Nature and the deriving local customs are often not considered in design, prompting the existing models on social urbanism in Medellín to fold in the ecological systems of the area, not as residual aspects of the built city, but as the drivers of a culture formed by the richness of the tropics, and as part of our response to the urgent climate crisis.

GOLD AND MEDELLÍN
Gold mining has shaped the landscape of Colombia and the community's relationship with the land, particularly in Medellín, leading to continued myths and discussions over the true meaning of the "city of gold." The history and impact of slave mining and Colombia's innocuous independence, its rise and decline due to industrialization, coffee exports, and stigmas over the violent years, has been followed by a new surge, which places the country at the center of gold mining again due to large-scale resource extraction as a new wave of economic development, where small-scale miners and the ecology of the region are at stake.

MEDELLÍN AND THE ABURRÁ RIVER
IN SEARCH OF A CITY FOR LIFE
Unraveling the urban processes of resilience and inclusion, and the role of urban planning, architecture, and infrastructure as social tools for promoting accessibility, offers a closer view into the methodology of social urbanism in the recovery of the city. What characterizes the precarious urbanization of Medellín, its historical violence, informality, and illegality, and the lessons from the reconstruction of democracy are discussed. New territorial plans that organize the city as it prepares for expansion through more sustainable and equitable frameworks focus on accessibility and availability of public open space for everyone.

CROSSING THE LINES OF WATER IN MEDELLÍN
Medellín's inhabitants' relationship with the edges of the water, as a profuse element representing the geomorphology of the region, is traced as the dividing line through historical references and symbols in the landscape. Recognizing the city's inequality, manifested in the industrialization of the river and the rift created by the natural basin, we have extended an invitation to the community to engage with the water—seeing it as a point of connection to relieve social tensions rather than as a border.

SOCIAL URBANISM
A STRATEGY OF SELF TRANSFORMATION IN MEDELLÍN
Social urbanism in Medellín has been possible through an open and continuous public management process by government administrations and community participants as part of an inclusive and democratic exercise. These practices have created a more resilient city with physical and social spheres that overlap.

MEDELLÍN'S SOCIAL INNOVATION
As the UN Habitat's World Urban Forum host city in 2014, many of the architectural projects have placed Medellín on the global design spectrum and superseded its deadly reputation as murder capital of the world. A

review of projects such as the Metro, Biblioteca España, the Greenbelt, and Parqués Del Río offer insight into how these elements are, in fact, only partly responsible for the urban transformation though. Deeper conversations with politicians affirm that the process of healing has required the participation of many, with a long way to go still, and that spatial equity and the distribution of resources is an ongoing agenda for the city.

SOCIAL URBANISM?
Breaking away from typical city systems, social urbanism explores tactics for encouraging social interaction as an enhancement to everyday urban experiences. A trip through "a day in the life" in Mexico City offers a glimpse into the bustling character of the city, advocating, as a result, for the addition of "urban oases" as new platforms providing essential services such as quick food and phone recharging, with room for pause, where social engagement can flourish.

ENVIRONMENTAL CONFLICTS AND DEGRADATION IN THE LANDSCAPE OF MEDELLÍN
The irrefutable degradation of the landscape and the inequality of natural resources, clean water, air quality, waste water disposal, access and distribution of land-use, and biodiversity loss are pushed to the fore, and are no longer incidental matters of urban development that we can ignore. Medellín's renaissance is evident, but the lack of awareness of the environmental impacts of urbanization must be addressed alongside this as well. While the city continues to modernize, nature implores, and we must realize the urgency to reconsider our actions.

SOCIAL URBANISM
WITHOUT SOCIAL URBANISM, AN URBAN REALITY RIGGED TO IMPLODE
Colonial oppression is studied in Brazil, particularly Rio de Janeiro, which today is a divided city symptomatic of the inequality in Latin America. The author takes a look at how citizen action in Rio's favelas have mobilized to create structured communities providing socio-economic functions for the livelihood of the community, and how these communities are categorized beyond the informality—by which they are condoned. Land trust systems—a progressive concept on social urbanism—are considered as they go well beyond misconceived notions of failing urbanization mechanisms by recognizing city structure in emerging communities today.

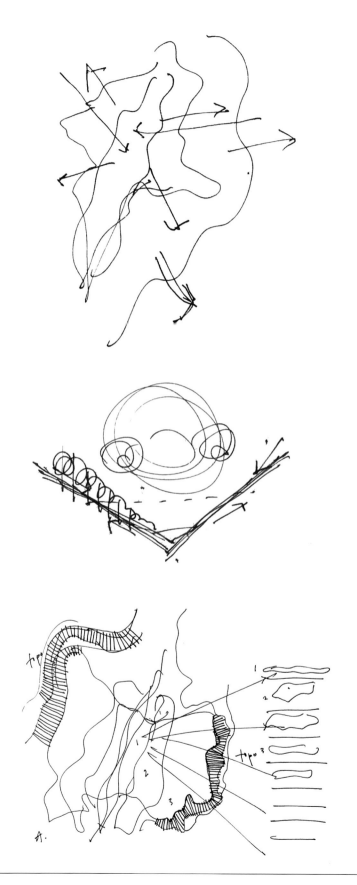

FROM SOCIAL URBANISM TO CULTURAL URBANISM

Gloria Aponte Garcia

Life does not stop, and of course neither does culture—the engine of all human collective results—which includes, among other shared manifestations, the way that every society runs to carry out its understanding of nature, use of resources, cultivation of natural products, manufacturing processes, production of material artifacts, the disposal of waste, building and urbanization, among others. The term "culture" has a widened meaning now, and does not belong just to elites as it used to. Now we are in the "culture of the liquid modernity world," as Zigmunt Bauman states.[1] All can be mixed and everything changes at an unimagined speed. Quoting Bordieu, Bauman reminds us that culture should not be a preservation of the status quo, but an agent of change, more precisely, a navigation instrument to guide the social evolution toward a universal human condition.

Some cultural manifestations evolve faster than others, and those that leave solid evidences of their course in time, provide wider opportunities to be examined and also to be improved upon, hopefully, as credible agreements among all social actors. One of the most outstanding of these is urbanism, the built habitat for most of the world's population. Urbanism as a single word reflects a generalized way of seeing the construction and evolution of cities. Traditionally, urbanized has meant organized and neat places for residence, but which are not always affordable, while non-urbanized has been the term of reference for peripheral areas where poor people settle in a disorderly fashion, usually outside of the declared urban polygons defined by planning norms or authorities.

Nevertheless, there is another sort of urbanism, perhaps not so clear, related to the countryside activities or services: that of "agrarian-urbanism," which is increasing in the nearby countryside of many Latin American cities—and especially in Colombia. Wild or agrarian land is made up of private property that is predisposed from engineering or rigid geometries, bringing urban style and commodities to the countryside in a sort of "new colonization" trend. The practice of condominium gathering, usually made up of second homes that demand all sorts of services in the urban system and styles of provisions, bring little apart from litter to the specific place; neither to the human relationships within the neighborhoods, nor any kind of harmonic coexistence.

What is the urge causing society to produce the stuff that ultimately makes up the urban labyrinth? Unquestionably, it is the economy that drives the building industry, and consequently decides the route for the activities of urbanization, and the shape and general character that, later, the settlement will accomplish; a sort of palimpsest engendering a particular urban style, not necessarily previewed or planned in an integral manner. This compelling occupation becomes, often, outdated over time. The construction industry in Ibagué, Colombia is a good example of this. Ibagué is an intermediate city, located in the very geographical heart of the country, with a population of around 530,000 inhabitants (less than in 2015). Although an urban settlement representative of a developing country that continues to grow, last year's census showed that growth had slowed to less than 10% of what was expected. Concurrently, new housing towers keep going up because of the optimism of the construction business though. Real estate promoters hope for the reverse of the decrease in population, and even if they are not optimistic, they have too much invested to stop their activity abruptly. Rent and sale announcements abound, and more new housing continues to flood the market. The city is alive, dynamic, in progress, but it is not growing as fast as commercial dynamics or on pace with "the speculative voracity of the land value or the buildings."

Social urbanism, a movement derived from the adaptation of Barcelona´s acupuncturist technique, in good time, emerged tending to recognize and attend less favored people within the urbanization maelstrom. This new expression could be interpreted in two ways. Firstly, that of what is being accomplished by collective added work, planned or unplanned, legal and illegal; that is to say, the actual physical result of the summary of the continuous building dynamic that predominantly characterizes cities in the still-called 'developing countries'. And second, the 'culturally' conceived urbanism that is to be accomplished; in other words, what public authorities or public professional staff strive to guide and, finally, establish decisions in the name of the local authority bodies.

In Colombia, particularly in Medellín where the movement was properly established as the local interpretation of the New Urbanism, social urbanism has been understood as a new movement driven by an desire to achieve certain equity by providing urban services to peripheral areas. The movement started in 2004 as an expression of public policies with emphasis on proposed processes to move forward with the city's rebirth a demonstration of resilience after a very hard and prolonged period of violence. Many worthy social projects were carried out at the periphery as pointed interventions—as forms of urban acupuncture—toward equity in space. The feeling that something was missing remained, a consequence of the autonomy of these plans and objects throughout the urban area, and still with the menace of indefinite expansion looming. This drove local authorities to think about a new project that would connect the various projects in a cohesive whole

This is the origin of the three-stripe project up on the hills, which more or less parallels the river. The goal of this was to stop urbanization up there. It was called Jardín Circunvalar de Medellín (JCM), similar to a "chastity belt, an impenetrable limit to protect the city" as described by Montaner and Muxi. It is not a garden as it lacks the requisite amount of plants; it is not a bypass, as it does not enclose; and it does not belong to Medellin, because it covers, at least in plan, the nearby municipalities that form part of a greater metropolitan area beyond Medellín. The JCM was designed to invite recreation through pedestrian and cycling trails in two of the three lines, and to provide transportation facilitation in the third one with the implementation of a monorail. It was an excellent initiative in an effort to address the peripheral communities, along with enhancing the image of the city to attract investors and tourists. Unfortunately, the project's downfall was that it ignored the nature of its place. Those social urbanism infrastructure tactics were drawn on plain paper, and consequently imposed on the wrinkles of the slopes of the mountains that go down to the Aburrá River valley, ignoring the numerous streams that run toward the river from east to west, and interrupting the natural processes and dy-

namics. During the construction phase improvised solutions appeared to face this incompatibility. There is a lot to be learned from this attempt. In a place where nature is capricious and unfolds in many features that create a wide variety of spaces and sub-spaces, with the added particularity that those features are seen, appreciated, enjoyed, or identifiable as places of suffering, the slope on which the JMC is located is not viewed as a mirror of the city on the slopes and below in the valley, but must be a reflection of the personal and shared experiences of nature and the people that inhabit it.

Social urbanism is defined by Montoya in the 2008–2011 Municipal Development Plan as one of the areas of urban transformation management in Medellín, and is strategically proposed as a model of territorial intervention that simultaneously includes physical transformation, social intervention, institutional management, and community participation. There is nothing mentioned about the environment, nature, or even the local ecology and conditions. When a foreign model from a temperate zone brought onto a tropical, wrinkled valley without any corresponding logical consideration, the desired results will not translate.

It is clear that social urbanism (as previously described) does not employ environmental and sustainable planning and design. Rather, it highlights the disregard of people. How can one think about local people and how to solve their problems without recognizing the natural environment that supports them? What is obvious tends to go unnoticed. How many times a day do people think about breathing? But should one try not to breath for even a few minutes, see what happens. As gravity ties us to the earth, good design should be tied to the Earth. But some designs seem to float on air, neglecting the natural features of a place, of nature, and the watercourses related to the place. These must be noticed, recognized, assessed, valued, appropriated, preserved, and enhanced.

Why not make nature the basis of design?

The respect for nature within the collective culture—the one that dictates so many of our daily activities—is no longer considered for development, even during the present context in which sustainable development is trending. The importance and value of nature have to be brought back into the our daily lives and all data, and must be respected—as it deserves—as the principal determinant for evolution, particularly in urban contexts as indigenous people did and still do. This is imperative for our future, which often seems chaotic in this age of environmental uncertainty climatic crisis.

It is not enough for social urbanism to consolidate the urban conglomerates that Mother Earth deserves or withstands. A persistent mistake is to urbanize, disregarding the land and nature that support life, and often masquerading with meaningful or fashionable names. In that sense, and in a perhaps an optimistic proposal, research was carried out on what could and should be the role of streams in the structure of urbanization on the slopes of Medellín with, "Edge landscape: the structuring role of the streams on the slopes of Medellín." The aim was to provide a guide for landscape intervention along the streams on the slope, specifically at the juncture that represents the urban-rural edge. From a landscape optic, seen as both integral and balanced, the specific purpose was to guide the consolidation of streams as a local landscape structure based on the following:

> The landscape is a sensory or perceptual image of a certain medium. The effects of the scene and the urban environment, not because they are insufficiently studied, are less impressive in the spirit and the mood of the citizens, nor do they cease to be basic motivators of their behaviors.

The results of this study went unnoticed and were disregarded. Some of the minimum requirements expressed were as follows:

• Will and commitment to solve environmental and socio-cultural management problems with clear repercussions on the landscape;
• Investment and support for research, and the hiring of qualified professionals dedicated to finding attainable solutions;
• Allocation of resources to the landscape cause;
• Guarantee of continuity during the processes, and assurance that longterm projects transcend periods of public administration and politics.

At present, urbanism cannot be considered apart from nature and its consequences on the landscape, especially in contemporary times as humanity faces increasing environmental issues. As Waldheim reminds us, there is an urgent need to reconcile the design of the city with its ecological and social functions, and a need to reconcile the soul of each inhabitant of the city with the collective spirit of the community.[1]

I dare to say that it is the time for a "cultural urbanism," but as a culture from and for everybody that includes the proposals contemplated by the social urbanism movement, but also on the essential basis of recognizing and valuing nature as the foundation along with the overall ecosystem, not just seeing these as elements of the built city or areas to be designed over, around, or upon. Understanding natural cycles and processes, following them, and confronting climate change are of key importance in the urban design process. This is a standard to follow everywhere, and especially in cities that are located in rich and diverse biospheres.

NOTES
1   Zygmunt Bauman, "La cultura en el mundo de la modernidad líquida," *Dianoia 59*, no. 73 (2013).
2   Zygmunt Bauman, *Ética posmoderna* (México: Polity Press Ltd, 2005).
3   Javier Maderuelo, "El paisaje urbano," *Estudios Geográficos* LXXI, no. 269 (2010): 575–600.
4   Charles Waldheim, *Landscape as Urbanism: A General Theory* (New Jersey: Princeton University Press, 2016).
5   Josep Maria Montaner and Zaida Muxi, "Los modelos Barcelona, de la acupuntura a la prótesis," *Journal of Hispanic Cultural Studies* 6 (2002): 265.
6   Nataly Restrepo Montoya, "Urbanismo social en Medellín: una aproximación a la utilización estratégica de los derechos," *Estudios Politicos,* no. 45 (2014).
7   Ibid.
8   Universidad Pontificia Bolivariana, "Paisaje de Borde el papel estructurante de las quebradas en las laderas de Medellín," (2013), Unpublished.
9   Ibid.
10 Ibid.
11 Charles Waldheim, *Landscape as Urbanism: A General Theory* (New Jersey: Princeton University Press, 2016).

GOLD and MEDELLÍN
A Regional View

Elizabeth Ferry, Ph.D.

In 1897, Elisée Reclus wrote in his encyclopedic work of "universal geography" *The Earth and its Inhabitants: South America, that Medellín:*

> standing at an altitude of 4,860 feet, within the temperate zone, with a climate in which the enterprising inhabitants retain all their characteristic energy…Medellín is an active centre of the gold-mining industry, and much vigor is displayed in working the gold and silver mines in the district and farther east along the unfinished line of railway running north to the Magdalena. By this route are forwarded the gold and silver ingots destined for England.[1]

This paragraph aptly characterizes the ways observers have linked Medellín's climate and geographic situation with the (supposed) character of its people and with its place as a center of gold production and export. In this brief essay, I describe some ways that gold has shaped the city of Medellín and its surrounding region.

Colombia has some of the largest and richest gold reserves in the world, and gold has been central to its history. Pre-Columbian cultures, such as the Tayrona, Muisca, Quimbaya, and Tierradentro, developed advanced technologies and aesthetic practices with gold, which were fundamental to their ritual and political life. Europeans' search for gold in the Americas crystallized in the legend of a city of gold, known as El Dorado (in Spanish, "The Golden One"). This famous myth arose from a misunderstanding; the Spaniards sought a golden city, but really the term referred to a Muisca ritual held on Lake Guatavita, north of what is now Bogotá. In this ritual, as recounted in 1636 by the colonial chronicler Juan Rodríguez Freyle, the heir to the chief was covered in gold powder and transported by boat into the middle of the lake where he threw in offerings of gold, emeralds, and feathers. Rodríguez Freyle concluded his description by saying, "From this ceremony was taken the celebrated name of 'Dorado,' which has cost so many lives." In search of El Dorado, the conquistadores plundered countless native towns and graves.

Throughout the 16th century, indigenous populations collapsed because of disease, forced labor under brutal conditions, and warfare with the Spanish. To replace their labor, the Spanish imported thousands of Africans as slaves, especially to mine gold in the Pacific and Antioquia regions. Many escaped and formed marooned communities that supported themselves through mining, fishing, hunting, and agriculture. Others, although, remaining enslaved until emancipation in 1852, also engaged in these economic practices.

To finance Colombia's War of Independence, Simon Bolivar leased major gold mines, such as those in Marmato and Segovia in the Antioquia region, to British concerns. In the republican period, steam technology, and later, railroads, helped to establish underground mining as a major source of Colombian wealth. For most of the 19th century Colombia was the world's largest producer of gold.

The Antioquia region and the city of Medellín developed over the course of the nineteenth and first half of the twentieth centuries as the most successful commercial area of Colombia, with Medellín as the entrepôt for gold and, beginning in the last quarter of the 19th century, coffee. The region was also much more consistently white and/or mestizo than the large neighboring region of Cauca. In the course of the twentieth century, through which Colombia, along with Brazil, dominated the world coffee market, Antioqueños from Medellín and surrounding areas began to spread south and west. They sought lands to grow coffee and to control the flow of gold from Cauca to Medellín where is was smelted and refined for export. In 1905, the department of Caldas was created, including regions rich in gold and in land with propitious altitude and soil for coffee production. Colonization has traditionally been portrayed as a benign or benevolent civilizing mission, or as the peaceful settlement of empty lands by "enterprising inhabitants" like those described in the quotation with which I opened the essay. In fact, the lands that were settled had been inhabited for centuries, often by afro-descendant or indigenous Colombians. Even when the presence of these people was acknowledged by the state or by elites in Antioquia and Cauca, it was often framed in terms of a desirable "bettering" or "whitening" effect on the local population. Over much of the 20th century coffee boomed, while gold mining regions and the Colombian production of gold in general, languished, as a major industry—many thousands of Colombians continued to work gold at a smaller scale and to build livelihoods and communities through their work.

Up until the late 20th century, with uncertain and often low gold prices, the antiquity of mining infrastructure and the violence of civil conflict made foreign gold companies reluctant to do business in Colombia. However, beginning in the early 2000s a combination of high prices for metals, more efficient technologies, and greatly improved security conditions have made Colombia newly attractive for transnational corporations. The Colombian government prioritizes large-scale resource extraction as a central feature of its economic development agenda. Between 2005 and 2011, the Colombian government issued over 9,000 mining titles for exploration and production, with nearly 1,000 for precious metal mining.

These new concessions and projects were bound to come into conflict with the (at least) 350,000 Colombians make their livelihood directly through small-scale gold mining activities, and so they did. For the most part, these licenses were issued without informing or consulting with miners already working in these areas, nor with agricultural, indigenous, and Afro-Colombian communities who are often opposed to large-scale projects in their territories. This has led to many confrontations and to the displacement of people on a large scale, leading to suffering and unrest. At the same time, the rise in gold prices led Colombia's insurgent armies, the Revolutionary Armed Forces of Colombia (FARC) and the National Liberation Army (ELN), along with paramilitary militias and numerous criminal gangs to get involved in gold mining, causing tremendous violence in certain areas of the country, including in the Antioquia region. In what follows, I sketch a picture of a few places in Antioquia, Caldas and Cauca to give a sense of how gold runs underneath the region and through the lives of people.

Rich gold deposits—both placer (on the surface and in rivers) and lode (underground)—run through the Cordillera Central (a branch of the Colombian Andes) that passes through of Antioquia, Caldas, and Cauca. Numerous historical mining centers cluster around these deposits, and the Nechí, Cauca, Magdalena, San Juan and other rivers have been places for extensive gold panning for hundreds of years.

Segovia

The Segovia mining district, which includes around 375 mines and hundreds of small-scale miners and *barrequeros* or *mazamorreros* (gold panners), exemplifies how gold and civil conflict have intertwined in Colombia. In the 1980s paramilitary groups and the FARC and ELN moved into the Frontino mine—the largest employer and producer in the zone, organized as a worker-owned cooperative—, after the U.S. company left the mine to its workers in the face of low gold prices and increasing violence. In the years 1982-1997 Segovia suffered 14 massacres at the hands of paramilitaries and state forces, and 200 more political murders carried out by all parties to the conflict. Paramilitaries allied with state forces ultimately prevailed and guerrilla forces largely withdrew to the rural areas around Segovia. In 2004, Colombian president Álvaro Uribe offered Frontino to the Canadian-owned Gran Colombia Gold Corporation in 2010 for close to $200 million (and the payment of outstanding debts). Gran Colombia Gold cut back on workers' benefits and laid off much of the permanent work force. Seeking to keep ownership of the mine in the hands of workers, leaders of the miners' trade union took the case to Colombian judicial system, but so far the company maintains control. At the same time, in the face of a number of successful legal and popular opposition movements against transnational gold companies and the instability of the peace process, Colombia has lost much of its "shine" for external investors.

Segovia's processing plants (*entables*) and gold panners have used mercury to process gold for many years and the region around the mines has one of the world's highest concentrations of the element, which binds to human and animal fat and causes toxicity, organ damage, and death. Recent legislation to ban mercury use and to provide training and capital to some mining operations has begun to reduce these concentrations, but there is still a long way to go.

Marmato

The town of Marmato is located in the department of Caldas, and has an officially recognized population of about 9,000, though residents estimate it is about 30-50% larger than this, as its gold mines attract displaced people from other parts of Colombia and recently from Venezuela. According to the census of 2005, 56% of the inhabitants consider themselves "afro-descendent" and 16.7% indigenous. Gold mining in the region predated the arrival of the Spaniards, but the presence of gold attracted colonization, including the importation of Africans as slaves in the 17th and 18th-centuries. Marmato had a growing community of free blacks in the 18th-century, and it has tended to attract people from outside for much of its history. The mines were conceded to the British for a large part of the 19th and early 20th-centuries, originally in return for help in the wars of independence from Spain.

In 1954, a federal law formally divided the mountain on which Marmato is built into two parts, designated as the lower and upper zones. The lower section continued to be mined by a parastate company, Mineros Nacionales,S.A., and the upper part grew into a bustling center of ramified tunnels, with small mines at each entrance and small-scale processing mills below many of these mines. Currently some 300 small mines and over 100 mills operate in the upper zone, while a transnational corporation, Gran Colombia Gold, runs the mine that used to be owned by Mineros Nacionales. This corporation has been trying to dislodge the miners from the upper zone for some years, and while it has succeeded in purchasing many mining titles, it also provoked a powerful and organized social movement, and has arguably helped to unify Marmateños against a common threat. Local buyers purchase the gold extracted and processed in these mines and take the product to the smelters in Medellín. From there it is sold to international refiners.

Corregimiento de la Toma, Cauca

The tributaries of gold that flow to the city of Medellín also originate farther to the south in the Department of Cauca. In contrast to the high number of descendants of Europeans in Antioquia, Cauca is home to many afro-descendant and indigenous Colombians, and the region is traditionally, and currently significantly poorer than its neighbors to the north. Many of the communities in the coastal region of the department practice alluvial gold mining in the rivers, along with fishing, hunting, and subsistence agriculture, as well as coffee cultivation. During the colonial period, this area fell under the political and economic sway of the city of Popayán.

The families that live in the five towns in the Corregimiento de La Toma—Yolombó, Gelima, El Hato, Dos Aguas, and La Toma—like many Afro-Colombian communities in this region, govern by means of an autonomous community council. Their ancestors have inhabited this region on the Pacific coast of Colombia since the early 17th-century when they were brought as slaves to work the Gelima gold mine, and surrounding farms. The gold from Gelima and other smaller mines enriched Popoyán, and the whole Real Audiencia de Quito, which included parts of southern Colombia, current-day Ecuador, and northern Peru. The Jesuits mainly owned the mines until their expulsion from the Americas in 1767. With the expansion of antioqueño settler-colonists into the coffee areas in the

19th and 20th-centuries and the construction of the railroad, the Cauca region came under the influence of the city of Cali and, especially for the gold economy, Medellín, where ancestral miners now send their gold. La Toma and towns like it have faced two major threats to their lands and livelihoods in recent years, first from large-scale transnational mining companies, in this case AngloGold Ashanti, and second, and perhaps more immediately and devastatingly, from criminal groups who strip the banks of the Ovejas and other auriferous rivers using backhoes. These miners do not commercialize their gold through the established channels in Medellín or Cali (at least not officially) but seek informal channels that have been severely curtailed since the tightening of regulations in 2015. A 2018 OECD report, "Due Diligence in Colombia's Gold Supply Chain: Where does Colombian gold go?" surmises that gold mined outside of the legal supply chain infrastructure (which is often, though not always, mined by criminal groups or their suppliers) leaves by plane from Medellín and Dogotá to Curaçao, Aruba, and Barbados, or over land to Ecuador or Brazil.

Topographically, biologically, geologically, and historically, Colombia is a tremendously diverse country. Its diversity has been channeled by the three Andean cordilleras, by the distribution of mineral deposits and of lands apt for coffee and other export crops, by histories of conflict and inequality, and by mobilization and rootedness. All these shape how gold comes out of the rocks and rivers and moves to, through and from Medellín.

NOTES

1   Elisee Reclus, *The Earth and its inhabitants: South America* (New York: D. Apple ton,1894), 199-200.

MEDELLÍN
and the ABURRÁ RIVER

In Search of a City for Life

Jorge Pérez Jaramillo

Medellín is recognized worldwide as an interesting case study, with references to urban processes, where resilience and social inclusion are fundamental. The city is valued for the role it plays in urban planning, architecture, and infrastructure, as part of the social tools for promoting accessibility and the right to the city. When more deeply analyzed, Medellín is a city that has overcome an extreme urban crisis, not only due to the infamous violence that has derived from crime and drug-trafficking, but also as the results of the precarious structural factors of urbanization, informality, the illegality of its growth, the absence of local democracy until only a few years ago, and by the economic system, which together have represented an unfeasible society. The city points to the realities over the quality of life for everyone, in a varied and generally positive direction, suggesting that even miraculous changes can happen, even if the reality is far from being so. This is a case of extraordinary resilience and democratic rebuilding, with many valuable practices and enormous progress in overcoming inequities, with access to drinking water, energy, education, health, recreation, transportation, and many public services; with lower rates of unemployment, less poverty, all within a framework of institutional democracy and strength, citizen participation, and assured outcomes, which tend to be oversimplified. There have been many valuable challenges and complexities, with immense gaps and difficulties still to confront, even so, making us believe that the positive steps until now, should and could continue to evolve.

Medellín has an important track record for small-scale urbanism projects, for urban acupuncture favoring social inclusion that has offered a framework for bridging gaps. Yet, when analyzed at a strategic and structural level, the city has accumulated a series of failures in its attempts to formulate planning models to address critical aspects of socio and spatial segregation. The growth toward the periphery and the ensuing demands for mobility and expanded infrastructure, coupled with the insurmountable challenges that come with properly managing the metropolitan city, have led to the ability of the construction industry to bypass the issues, as well as to a certain a level of institutional inertia, framing a difficult system reaching the objectives for sustainable development with goals for addressing climate change.

Since its planning, the Medellín metropolitan agenda has proposed many challenges for reconciling urban development with balanced solutions in sync with the city's natural origins, including its mountains and its rich flora, fauna, and hydrological qualities, as an opportunity for reconnecting to the river and its basin, to tend and preserve the water, and, above all, to overcome the atmospheric degradation and sustainable mobility challenges. These need to happen through a clear framework demanding the entire community to engage and overcome a growing complacency in order to be able to revise the current situation.

In this brief text, I share reflections derived from my recent book *Medellín: Urbanism and Society*, where I propose a broader and more complex analysis of the process of the city.

1. In the mid-1970s, Medellín was a very precarious city, within a framework of apparent beauty, making it a mirage rather than a reality. The vision of an urban society that would prioritize the environment and public life of people, over the construction of infrastructure for machines became constant. I gradually learned to understand the structural problems of our growing urbanization in terms of its precariousness and informality, where a high concentration of land ownership and real-estate speculation promoted a socio-spatial segregation and a progressive path of economic impoverishment for the majority of the community. There were other evident problems such as the absence of municipal democracy and the deterioration of the regional economy, the disappearance of the railroad, the growing illegality and informality—economic and social issues that became extreme over the years.

Our generation's interests over urban issues led us to quickly understand specific problems and to become conscious of the role of planning, engineering, urban design, and architecture, toward the concept of the city. Because Medellín was conceived and framed exclusively for road and motor vehicle functions, and for the real-estate business, a more integrated view that looked at urban design and social issues was not in the agenda.

To speak of the environment, public space, and citizenship, and to mention architecture and public life, the interior of the city, or the ability to promote equitable urban development in which everyone can coexist, fueled dreams and an understanding across architecture, urban design, and planning scales through many decades. The extreme social, regional, and economic hardships, and the violence that resulted during the last decades of the 1980s, were conducive for the foundations of our city over the following years to be tested, where the power structures and prevailing ideologies entered into a crisis. During the violence and denial of public life that characterized Medellín during this period, as inhabitants we lost our city and we were left isolated and locked up, under the empire of crime, amid the immense poverty and precarious urban state.

This crisis coincided with various processes, such as the emergence of local democracy in 1988, the public dialogue derived from the Conserjería Presidencial, Medellín's Presidential Council, between 1990 and 1995, and the new framework offered by the New Constitution in 1991. A phase of critical review permitted many ideas to surface, making room for the gradual ambition to transform the area and the society. Renewed leadership implemented various urban projects, such as centers for urban living and the improvement of neighborhoods, and later the Parque de los Pies Descalzos (Park of Bare Feet), Museum of Antioquia, Plaza de las Luces (Plaza of Lights) at Cisneros, and Parque de los Deseos (Park of Wishes) toward the end of the 20th-century, demonstrating how to create alternatives for providing a city for everyone. The Metro, with a conflicting history, included an infrastructure that accommodated public spaces, complementing its transit service with a civic agenda of "metro culture," with a significant impact over the city, from where a gradual and alternative vision for how to build a different city became possible. During this period, we dreamt over the reintegration of our community and a coexistence within a context of greater inclusivity and equality. We initiated planning efforts through the Strategic Plan and the first Territorial Ordering Plan (POT) in 1998, with the hope of containing the segregation at the periphery, and of promoting urban reintegration through an interior densification of the river and the city's central area. We thought it was

possible to prioritize the Metro and the connecting transit system over private vehicles. We also believed we could develop an agenda for urban development that capitalized on available areas for urban opportunities, characterized by lower densities and little economic productivity for the city or the land owners. These were instead envisioned for public services and cultural amenities, with greater economic utility between what these could provide in contrast to the land value, all within a plan of providing a right to the city for everyone, through greater accessibility, public life, and better services for the citizens.

Over time, the traditional discourse over the city evolved, from perspectives fundamentally driven by real estate, motor vehicles, and mobility to considerations over the quality of life, and to ideas favoring the promotion of public spaces, social services, multi-modal mobility, and housing for everyone. Various experiences around planning and public dialogue taught us how to take action through acupuncture, with small architecture and urban design projects, little by little helping to qualify the life for everyone in the barrios, while also providing lessons that undoubtedly contributed to living in a better city. Nonetheless, local forces managed to prevail with an agenda for urban expansion that continued toward the periphery, with Medellín then continuing to grow in an unstoppable fashion toward the mountains and into neighboring municipalities.

In 2014, with the enactment of the Territorial Ordering Plan of Medellín (POT), as part of a community consensus process through the Consejeria de Medellín that reached an 80% approval rate, we finally agreed to intervene with a framework that outlined strategic interventions for prioritizing the agenda in a context of climate change, with objectives for sustainable development, with greater emphasis on controlling the urban expansion and segregation of inhabitants toward the high mountains to protect them from the risks of inappropriate settlements, as well as to preserve what is left of the rich ecology of the area. The POT defined a renewed path for the city's development, promoting greater accessibility, right to the city, sustainability, and more interaction in order to supersede the divisions over social integration; to articulate, moreover, the metropolitan valley within the region, together with new infrastructure at a proportionate scale, all within a context of improving connections with the natural environment.

2. The POT Territorial Planning Plan that has been in effect since 2014 was structured based on a detailed diagnosis of the urban evolution over the last decades, the consequences incurred, a complete analysis of the attributes of the territory, and the definition of current issues. New questions and proposals for alternative solutions to the plan addressed greater awareness over the natural wealth of the landscape and the search for how to reconcile urbanization with nature-based solutions as part of the agenda on climate change and sustainability changes. An agenda was formulated and we agreed, among many elements, on the need to prioritize ways for harmonizing Medellín within the region, preparing the city's urbanization through the integration of new regional and national infrastructures, and by reincorporating the railroad. Likewise, the plan developed multimodal structures to integrate the city—including not only traditional modes of transportation, but an extensive network for pedestrians and cyclists—with ambitious goals for 400 kilometers of new bikeways, turning the river into an articulating node for the entire metropolitan valley.

On the other hand, the dangerous aspects of public space endowment in the city were recognized, more extreme even when green areas and parks are considered, suggesting less than $1m^2$ and $4m^2$ per inhabitant depending on various sectors of the city. The analysis indicated that this condition could only be resolved by incorporating new park areas along the Aburrá River corridor or beyond the city limits at the edge of the mountains. The POT, therefore, projected public space areas in as many areas as possible, making this a priority, and including the Jardín Circunvalar, as part of the Metropolitan Green Belt project and the master plan for Parqués del Río. These became concepts for the city's urban renewal, with complex management challenges as well as structural and social paradigms.

In response to the successful river sanitation program advanced by EPM and financed by citizens for several decades, we are also looking for mechanisms for promoting ecological connectivity between the eastern and western mountains, integrated through the streambeds, the hills, and the green corridors, regenerating the river in order to attract wildlife and the quality of environmental conditions promoting equality, social integration, and sustainable solutions.

Through the POT, the potential for developing innovative urban management tools have existed within our legislature, yet seldom tapped within the planning strategies of our city. These help to promote the financial backing of the municipality and favor the ability to fund additional programming and public amenities, including the various phases of Parqués del Río. The macro projects, including 36 partial plans for urban renewal, have been formulated and coordinated with the Parques del Río Society, a new public management company that aspires to implement the overall transformation of the area.

The strategic plans with greatest impact have to do with Parques del Río. Until now, our infrastructure had been conceived as a limited entity, unlike presently, where the simultaneous aspects of a project are envisioned including the multi-modal mobility elements, public space, urban renewal, ecological connectivity, ecological restoration, the greening of the river, and, above all else, the integration of the project at the city-wide scale. The POT proposes powerful changes to the traditional concept of the city. To make decisions based on goals that will affect everyone's future is difficult. For this reason, assuming complex management goals for a given community is rare. Implementing projects that rely on commitments spanning several administrative government terms is unpopular. Likewise, innovation with financial and management models creates resistance. Political and social changes will be necessary to take on these challenges. What has caused Medellín to advance in such a substantial way despite all of its difficulties? This would take too long to explain, however, one clear aspect has been the collective capacity among socio-political players to agree to carry forward certain agendas over long periods of time. This commitment and shared leadership stems from many governments that have worked to make these demanding and impactful projects viable.

Parques del Río is the most ambitious environmental project proposed to date in Medellín. No other program has the same scale or reach as the elements and benefits that it provides and which affect so much of the life of the metropolitan residents. We have not identified a path with the structural changes for the urbanization and management of our region that include an environmental preservation agenda and which could reconcile nature and the natural foundation of the city. We had not strategically planned for how to strengthen the multimodal mobility corridor of the river, though this time we have understood, in every capacity and dimension, that we are not only part of a machine age, but that we are also social human beings.

The POT framework, strategically integrated into Parques del Río, proposes greater, more equitable programming and financing for the city as it utilizes the mechanisms captured through the management of available land areas in the Colombian legislature. The POT promotes urban renewal through partial plans, including an inclusive system of public housing and public space; it proposes the investment of the pyramid of mobility, connecting the entire city through networks that prioritize pedestrian and cyclist's mobility with public transit; it seeks to control the borders of the city with regulating processes that improve neighborhoods and include PUI's, integrated urban projects. These diverse experiences and lessons reflect the goals of an agenda that promotes the city as a social engagement, and the region as a complex, integral object of management.

Over several decades of experimentation and territorial action, Medellín has the opportunity to undertake structural changes as part of its agenda. In times of complacency, as today, during a phase of popularism and demagogy, there is confusion over the processes the city has carried out for decades. We have the opportunity to project ambitious challenges that will truly change the inertia in place of a new agenda, in order to carry out the changes that the city's transformation is requesting; renewed leadership, change in scale with adequate instructional management. Our environment and our economy offer us opportunities that directly affect our lives in the city, through a project of similar impact over the problems than it will resolve: inequality, poverty, pollution, sustainable mobility; politics over public housing and environmental conditions, the deficit of civic and green spaces, water sanitation and the watershed, among many aspects.

Throughout the decades, one clear aspect that has been key for Medellín has been to work with the proper political leadership in order to successfully manage significant projects over the course of several terms of government. However, during recent years, the master plan for Parques del Río was suspended, as was the Jardín Circunvalar, along with other projects, the UVA's, Articulated Life Unit projects, as part of political complicity among State environmental agencies led by Medellín. In general, the POT has been poorly implemented, with the largest goals of mobility, such as the Tranvia and the ciclo-routes, having not been built. These are difficult times for Medellín. The new phase of government that begun in January, 2020, marking a period of uncertainty as well as of opportunity for reaction. Hopefully, Medellín can move forward and break free of this seemingly new crisis, out of which we can re-appropriate our agendas to create frameworks geared toward equality of life in the city.

NOTES

1   Alcaldia de Medellín, Medellín, la transformación de una ciudad. Medellín: Alcadía de Medellín, 2011.

2   J.R. Mejia Botero, et al, "Mejoramiento Integral del Hábitat para la Región Metro politana del Valle de Aburrá". Medellín: AMVA y UPB. (2007).

CROSSING THE LINES of WATER in MEDELLÍN

Lina Escobar Ocampo

This text is the result of continued reflection on a topic of personal and professional interest, which also has sensitive connotations, as it addresses the city where I grew up—its watercourses, mountains, and the landscape, which have significantly influenced who we are in Medellín. The landscape has emerged in our current context and as a central part of our contemporary thinking, and has lead to a practical and sensitive perspective and rethinking of the human environment, and particularly of the urban landscape. This research illustrates how the past relationship of the inhabitants with the water's edge in Medellín in comparison with today. These relationships are determinants of many dynamics, including the "urban image" that we perceive of Medellín.

Nature is defined by lines and contours, soft and subtle, but also strong and marked. These borders and contours are usually more about transitions, ecotones, meeting places of two or more ecosystems that result in a new convergent ecosystem with spatial expressions and environmental conditions of its own. The landscape is composed of a combination of these lines and edges in nature that structure it, shape it, give it character and identity, and define its dynamics through matter and energy flow.

Water is perhaps one of nature's most powerful lines, which manifests itself on many occasions, such as waves and curves in the landscape, leaving characteristics and undeniable traces sculpted into the earth. Water is a multi-functional element in the landscape, and offers habitat and energy transport systems to minerals and organic matter. At the same time, water represents a symbolic connection with nature and is associated with well-being, freedom, and, often, with a high spiritual and ritual significance. The history of humanity has been associated with water since the beginning. Water landscapes are mainly cultural landscapes, since water has provided the possibility for human existence, and it has also been a fundamental part of the identity of the communities.

In Medellín, these water lines are abundant and diverse, such as contours and structuring edges of the landscape, where water is always present, shaping the relief of the valley and the texture of its slopes. This wrinkled landscape, very characteristic of the city, has been a fundamental factor in the way urbanization has developed and how the urban relates to the surrounding natural environment, transforming the structure and function of the landscape over time. These water and urban lines make up a highly intricate system. Medellín is located in an inter-Andean and sub-tropical valley where the water carves the relief and the spring-like climate favors the presence of lush vegetation. Water is one of the most relevant bio-physical aspects of the local landscape character.

The city was founded at a crossroads, but also at a water crossing, between the Aná stream-bed and the Aburrá River. Water has always been part of the history of the valley and its inhabitants, but this relationship has changed over time. It has had different meanings, sometimes more functional and sometimes more symbolic, but always as a determinant in the urban structure and the relationship of the city with the landscape. Water has been a provider, a vital resource for the development of the city. Sadly, water has been highly impacted and transformed by accelerated urban growth and undesirable territorial planning that has ignored the local landscape values, as the baseline for land use planning and in favor of the natural patrimony.

In fact, these natural contours, those lines that make up the landscape, such as water edges, have become territorial lines, limits, borders, and sometimes even barriers. Water lines have been used as part of the territorial control of some areas of the city, many of them in isolation or with difficult access—a condition that facilitates crime. These water borders have been, on many occasions, ambiguous divisions of the territory, separating instead of congregating people. They are margins, which contain and differentiate one side from the "other," although both are part of the same landscape. The unavoidable consequences of this condition have been pollution and environmental degradation, mainly of the water basins in the valley. Streams have been used as sewers, and many times covered with asphalt to make new roads, and other infrastructure and services typical of mid-20th-century urban-planning practices widely used today. The water currents structuring the landscape of Medellín have been mistreated since the beginning of the urbanization of the valley. Some streams have been completely covered or their channels rectified with concrete, preventing the infiltration capacity of the soil, among other water regulation functions. Even worse, the river in Medellín is losing its character as a biological corridor, as well as its social functions as a place of enjoyment and identity for the inhabitants of the city.

Unfortunately, we cannot forget that the watercourses in Medellín have also been associated with a history of violence in the city, and this violent stigma has been transposed to the water engraved in the image inhabitants have of the city and the water edges. Ravines have been places where not only trash has been thrown, but also the dead, animals and people, victims of clashes and conflicts, with corpses that often end up floating in the river. These violent images have removed people from water streams, fomenting an idea of fear over conflicting territories as borders of criminal control. The reconciliation with the watercourses has not been easy, but it has been fundamental in the process of the recent urban transformation of Medellín.

There are still memories and legacies from previous moments, from very difficult times for the city and its inhabitants in relation to water. Nonetheless, the city has opted for spatial interventions that include the natural water course, creating spaces for accessing the river banks, with invitations to cross the streams of water, previously separated, to connect with communities that were otherwise considered as isolated and divided communities. There is still a long way to go, in terms of the recovery of the city's water lines, and we have many challenges in terms of risk management and the decontamination of basins ahead. Encouraging citizens to encounter nature is part of the health of contemporary cities. The landscape reflects the history of the relationship of the inhabitants with their environment, serving as an interface between natural and cultural processes. The landscape of Medellín reflects the relationship between the communities and their environment; open spaces and the natural areas that remain in the city with water; linear parks aligning various streams of the city, and Parques del Río, are projects that help to recover water corridors, giving them renewed significance through their functional and symbolic value.

A project such as La Herrera Bridge between the La Francia and Andalucía neighborhoods located in Comuna 2, Santa Cruz, connects two communities that were previously in conflict. This project represents the power of joining instead of dividing and separating communities. The edges, in the end, connect, becoming transitions rather than borders and boundaries that used to divide and separate, generating socio-spatial segregations. For many people it may be obvious that a bridge has

the power to connect, but for a community like Medellín, with a wrinkled, steep, and sloping relief, a city besieged with violence for a long time, distrustful and afraid, this type of intervention gives value to meeting spaces—once again crossing the water lines and sewing the social fabric back together, truly transforming the city.

The inter-institutional seam has been very important for the formulation and execution of this type of project in the city, yet the participation of communities and social leaders, who are increasingly responsible and committed to the planning of the city, has been an elemental key to building these spaces. Understanding the dynamics of water borders requires a multidisciplinary approach, together with complementary perspectives, to define and characterize these complex systems. This integral approach can be useful in order to identify the opportunities offered by the landscape in these contexts, both for the reconstruction of the social fabric and for the re-establishment of the citizens' relationship with nature.

Reflecting on these water spaces, through the hyper-dynamic lines and fringes, becomes urgent to the extent that the landscape must be considered as a resource; a natural, economic, and social element that drives human development at the local, regional, and national levels through the recognition and management of its values, and as the basis forming geographical and cultural identity.

We should give priority to the water edges, the creeks, and the streams as the foundations of urban planning in Medellín. We must promote these as public spaces for all to enjoy, and restore the water's environmental importance, ultimately connecting to the landscape character of the city. It is of utmost importance to understand the water streams as transitional fringes rather than lines or limits. Finally, it is necessary to comprehend the true nature of streams as symbols of our identity and history and as venues for the future. Planning strategies for the city, for ordering the territory, must understand the character of the landscape and its water currents, as ever so present and important in Medellín, and to the relationship that the inhabitants have with the creeks and streams of the city. These will be the determining factors, and therefore social urbanism also needs to recognize the environment, to reconnect people with nature, as the basis of all of our urban landscapes, and as the strengthens of our social identity.

SOCIAL URBANISM

A Strategy of Self Transformation in Medellín

Samuel Ricardo Vélez González, Ph.D.

Medellín went from being the most dangerous and violent city on the planet in the 1990's,[a] an unfeasible city with no future, to becoming a global reference for its social and urban transformation, deserving of several international recognitions, including "the most innovative city in the world" in 2013 by the Wall Street Journal. In March 2016 the city was awarded the Lee Kuan Yew World City Prize for its urban and innovative commitment. Trip Advisor awarded the city with the prize for best tourist destination in South America. The urban intervention in the poorest neighborhoods was recognized in 2018 with the Autodesk Excellence Award. In June 2019 Medellín won the Ashden International Award for "Cooling by Nature," for the city's green corridors; in July of the same year, it was recognized by Le Monde in a new edition of its awards for urban innovation for offering real project solutions to the problems of its citizens, and for the manner in which the city is facing climate change as it stays ahead of the Fourth Industrial Revolution and is a leader in processes and programs related to technology. Later, the city received the innovation award given by Nearshore Americas as City of the Year 2019. How has this transformation been possible?

Since the middle of the 20th-century Medellín, as "the industrial capital of Colombia," was not only the location for many industrial plants and factories, but also a settlement area for thousands of migrants who arrived in search of better economic opportunities, due to the internal displacement caused by political violence in the Colombian countryside. The increase in construction activities within the Aburrá Valley—a geographically limited space for urban growth—was based on the demolition of the old colonial and republican city, causing a loss of heritage, and the drastic change in the natural characteristics of the landscape, its mobility, cultural heritage, and values. Despite having relied on a pilot plan formulated between 1948–1950 by Wiener and Sert, and after the establishment of a city planning department, the rapid growth of urban areas on the city's hillsides could not be controlled.

The troubled political situation of the country derived from the growth of drug trafficking, its permeability into society, and the political fear in the country; with incremental deterioration of conditions since the 1980s, including public safety, economic growth, and the general quality of life throughout the Colombian territory, but particularly in Medellín, where one of the richest, most powerful and violent drug cartels originated. Medellín was the stage of a bloody internal war in the region. The city lived in fear, terrified, waking to bombings and murders, whereby its communities and neighborhoods became divided by natural, invisible borders in areas controlled by various drug-trafficking gangs that confronted each other, the government, the police, and armed military forces. Civil society was the victim of an internal conflict, where the official authorities' presence barely mattered. This posed a difficult situation to confront in how to adapt to the loss of hope and protection while searching for survival and clinging to social values that remained that could permit some return to a collective path forward.

The national panorama began to change in 2002 with the election of President Álvaro Uribe Vélez and his proposal for "Democratic Security" to regain control of the country and its governance. In Medellín, Sergio Fajardo Valderrama was elected mayor of the city in 2004, with a municipal administration program based on transparency, social participation, and oversight; the recovery of citizen culture in search of a peaceful coexistence; ways to improve education and social equality as a gateway for a more just and modern society and a safer city with public space as an asset for equity and coexistence.

The moment of change for Medellín initiated in 2004, propelled by the election of independent political alternatives, over traditional parties, that contributed new visions and ideas for gaining institutional credibility and the citizens' confidence. The Development Plans (Planes de Desarrollo) formulated for the capital of Antioquia in the periods 2004 to 2007, and 2008 to 2011, established actions for land use based on urban regulations through more socially inclusive approaches in order to "reduce deep social debts and the chronic violence of past decades," overcoming unsustainable economic growth and weakness of certain democratic governances. A new model of intervention in the city was formulated—social urbanism.

---

a   On March 10, 1991, the *Washington Post* included Douglas Farah's report "Record Murder Wave Overwhelms Medellín: Medellín, Colombia" noted: "A record tide of violence here —including 1,200 murders in the first two months of this year —has been sparked by feuding drug gangs, vigilante justice groups, cocaine cartel wars, and personal vendettas, civilian and military authorities say. 'It is very difficult to definitively interpret what is happening in Medellín,' said President Cesar Gaviria at a press conference. 'In part, there are changes in the power structure of the criminal organizations that operate there, but I do not think that is the sole cause of what is going on in Medellín…It transcends drug trafficking, and it will take a relatively long time to secure public order there.'" https://www.washingtonpost.com/archive/politics/1991/03/10/record-murder-wave-overwhelms-medellin/5e7f1080-1ea0-46e8-bfef-1ab4df9d53d0/

There were many advances in connectivity and mobility through the construction of the Medellín Metro, which opened in 1995; the construction of the Metrocable, a rapid cable-car transit system suitable for urban mobilization in sloped areas, with its first line inaugurated in the northeastern part of the city in 2004, followed by the western Metrocable, the Metroplús, the Tram-way, the EnCicla bike-hub, and the Integrated Transportation System of the Aburrá Valley (SIT), under continued development today, and in accordance with the Territorial Ordering Plan (POT). The Development Plan "Medellín, commitment to all citizens" of 2004–2007, has in its scope: the construction of public spaces for leisure, education, and citizen participation, as foundations for the poorest and most vulnerable sectors, to be included as part of citizen advancement agendas, thus generating conditions for safer, participatory, and sensible development, generating an "equal city for all, where citizens could build relationships stimulated by a city rich in culture, services, and public space."[1]

The academic community investigated the urban areas to understand and diagnose the living conditions of the inhabitants of the sectors with the highest rates of violence and insecurity in order to gain knowledge of the morphological, natural, geographical conditions, the state of public services and amenities, as well as the living conditions. This information served the mayor's office in the formation of the Integrated Urban Projects (PUI) in order to implement the different variables proposed by the Development Plan, including: education, mobility, habitability, safety, coexistence, public space, economic development, recreation, and social inclusion as the structuring pillars of social urbanism in areas with high rates of violence, as well as social and urban vulnerability.

The PUI's were accompanied by the Integral Neighborhood Improvement Projects (PMIB)[b,2] as initial steps for implementation and catalysts in the process of the city's transformation. Through the diagnosis of the area, small infrastructure projects were designed to mitigate the natural risks of urban settlements on the hillsides and around the streams running down from the mountains of the Aburrá Valley into the Medellín River; specifically, the PUI of the northeast communities and the Juan Bobo stream bed, building on land outside the areas of environmental risk, yet within the same sector, and resettling vulnerable residents in the immediate area.

The synergy between the professionals, technical experts, and the community gave way to a viable process, and to the implementation of projects within these communities. The most significant result was the fact that through the PUI and the PMIB projects, the sense of belonging among residents of violent sectors was established. Physical links, bridges, roads, public spaces, and sports fields were built to break the invisible borders established by criminal gangs, and the authorities were able to regain control to guarantee the safety of the inhabitants. A sense of identity and hope for a better future were regained, aspects that were necessary for reintegration into the community.

Achieving high social, economic, safety, and welfare outcomes, as well as mobility and citizen satisfaction, was possible during the first phase of social urbanism through an integrated community approach. Both types of projects, PUIs and PMIBs, moreover, as implemented in areas of conflict, favorably impacted several indexes, including public safety, settlements in risk zones, quality of life, mobility, and accessibility to public amenities, education, and health. Urban benefits were evident, from political and economic perspectives, and particularly relative to the development of community inclusion and the perception of quality of life.

Social urbanism begins by recognizing the community as an active member in the process of urban design and architectural interventions, where trust and bonds are created among actors, and where organizations within a civil society are strengthened. Community leadership, with the support of the private sector, defines the projects and guarantees their continued implementation. This last point being of utmost importance for the city, given that the past two municipal administrations have continued to develop the strategies in their Development Plans.

Social urbanism in Medellín has made it evident, and believable, that only through an honest, transparent, and continuous public management process, through consecutive municipal administrations, and with the participation of the community—as part of full citizenship exercise—within a democratic and inclusive model, it is possible to face the challenges of reversing social, environmental, and urban degradation. Only through such a process is it possible to build a resilient city, with the synergy of an integrated design approach, where both physical and social components exist.

---

b   The Neighborhood Integral Improvement Projects (Spanish acronym: PMIB) is an analytical methodology for urban areas as products of the informal growth of the city of Medellín formulated through the Laboratory of Architecture and Urbanism, Research Group LAUR of the School of Architecture, Universidad Pontificia Bolivariana in Medellín (today registered with Colciencias as a Group in Architecture, Urbanism, and Landscape: GAUP) in order to diagnose and formulate specific project interventions that allow for improved conditions of habitability, including community consolidation and destination of land for community amenities, with social, environmental, and economic sustainability criteria. This methodology was transferred to the Urban Development Company—EDU of Medellín—for its implementation in different sectors of the city.

MEDELLÍN'S SOCIAL INNOVATION

Jared Green

In 2014, Medellín, the second largest city in Colombia, hosted the UN Habitat's World Urban Forum, which attracted more than 15,000 leaders from around the world. This was a major accomplishment for a city that had the highest number of homicides in the world just a decade earlier. At the forum, then Medellín Mayor Aníbal Gaviria Correa explained the city was not even in the top 50 ranking of dangerous cities. How did Medellín turn it around to win the title of the world's most innovative city? The answer is complex, but the mayor said its amazing progress is really due to "social, not technological, innovation."

Medellín is the largest city in the Antioquia province. Nestled in a valley some 5,000 feet up, the city had a population of around 250,000 in the 1940s. Through "informal expansion," the population exploded to 2.5 million today.

Without a clear urban growth plan, slums took root in undesirable locations along the slopes, while the prime real estate down in the valley was claimed by the wealthy. People from the countryside moved to the slopes to flee the Colombian civil war, which killed some 220,000 people and displaced five million since the conflict began in the 1960s.

Pushed up the slopes, these newly urbanized people experienced major displacement, resentment, and, later, incredible violence, fueled in part by drug lord Pablo Escobar and the many drug gangs. Landslides could also take away their home in an instant.

Mayor Correa called 1990 to 2000 the "decade of violence." Across the country, 48,000 people were murdered, with Medellín accounting for more than 20% of those deaths. Correa said it was no coincidence that during this decade Medellín had areas of extreme poverty, and the city was characterized by high inequality. In a clear warning to other developing world cities now seeing their slums expand, he said violence and inequality are deeply connected. To climb out of that dark place, Mayor Sergio Fajardo, who was in office from 2004 to 2008, began to create a "structure for public participation" designed to bring all long-neglected residents into a planning process, even in the midst of Colombia's ongoing civil war.

Three successive mayoral administrations continued the same good policies, creating momentum for the city's long-term vision, which was to become a "city of life," with a high-quality public transportation system, parks, and libraries accessible to all.

Empresas de Services Publico (EPM), a public-private utility that provides power, water, sewage, sanitation, and other services to the city, also played an important part in making the dream a reality. EPM provides hundreds of millions to the city each year, supporting the development of iconic projects like the Metro subway, but also the extended "Metro plus," which includes a cable car system that provides connectivity to low-income areas on the north side of the city. On the Metro system, which is now the largest public transportation system in Colombia, Mayor Correa said "there is a real pride of the Metro, a culture of respect when you are in this space."

The city also tapped leading Latin American landscape architects and architects to build fantastic "library parks," which offer both green space and a place to access educational and recreational opportunities. The area where the Biblioteca de España (Spanish Library Park) was built in the hills of Santo Domingo used to be such a dangerous place the police would not even venture there.

Two important new pieces of green infrastructure under development include an extensive new riverfront park system, which will provide people with access to the Medellín River that cuts through the center of the city, and a connected greenway system, which will provide a "green belt" around the city, helping to reduce landslides and flooding for the poor communities along the steep slopes and perhaps pause sprawl. In 2014, the Medellín city government launched an international design competition to envision a new Parques del Rio (Medellín River Park). The competition asked firms to create a master plan for the entire length of the river as it cuts through the city and then to focus in on the central zone— the nine-kilometer stretch through the core of the city.

Medellín-based firm Latitude won the competition with their concept for a "botanical park that recovers connections to water systems through a revitalized biotic metropolitan corridor." The park developers are taking the concrete channel out, burying an adjacent highway, and creating a new, lush green spine, with tendrils spreading throughout the valley.

Mayor Correa said green spaces are needed for both ethical and aesthetic reasons. If parks are found in all neighborhoods—rich or poor—they improve the ethical make-up of the city. Public green spaces provide "the civic realm where people can become citizens. It's where everyone can be equal." Parks also provide urban beauty, which Mayor Correa said is also "necessary for urban coexistence."

Another important symbol of how the city is addressing persistent inequality: new day care centers. Mayor Correa said 80,000 children have accessed these new facilities, where they get free meals and a place to play, so their parents have opportunities to go out and work. The city's goal is to provide 100,000 children services through 20 centers.

At the other end of the educational spectrum, the city is planning two new universities that will serve low-income populations in the city. Mayor Correa wants those young people working in new innovation districts.

Medellín still has a long way to go. The city is still unequal, even though there have been steps toward equity, more so than other cities in Colombia. (Unfortunately, this is not saying that much, given that Colombia is one of the more unequal countries in South America, which is the most unequal continent on earth).

After Mayor Correa spoke, UN-Habitat experts from around the world commented on whether Medellín can really serve as a model for other cities:

The Swedish ambassador to Colombia Marie Andersson de Frutos said Medellín is a replicable model because its city government worked as a team with the private sector and non-profits. Medellín shows "there is no quick fix. Prescriptions can't come from a doctor, they have to come from the whole hospital."

Jose Carrera of the Development Bank of Latin America said Medellín correctly identified that violence was tied to inequality. The city removed one destructive aspect of inequality by providing clean drinking water for the whole city, rich or poor. However, he added, Medellín, like many others in Latin America, still needs to do a better job of creating new jobs for unemployed youth who face double the unemployment rates of adults just at a time when they should be most productive.

David Sims, a partner with urban design firm Gehl Architects, applauded Medellín for "incorporating terms like love, trust, equality, and pride" in its city charter. He said these concepts are difficult to measure but vital goals. Sims said Medellín has learned that true innovation comes from "different people meeting each other and having a conversation." He also thought the city was focusing on the small things that matter—how people get to work, how they live. "There is a great balance here between the tangible (the physical infrastructure) and the intangibles (the culture)."

A version of this article first appeared in The Dirt, the blog of the American Society of Landscape Architects (ASLA).

SOCIAL URBANISM?

Francisco Luna Ugarte

What is social urbanism? It is an interesting concept to discuss in modern 21st-century Mexico City, one of the largest and most crowded cities in the world (with a population of almost 25 million, divided in 16 municipalities, and having a density of over 8,000 inhabitants per m$^{2)}$, with different boroughs composed of varying social classes. It is a city of contrasts, where the richest people in the world can live two blocks away from poor, who can barely afford to eat.

To understand the city and in order to discuss social urbanism we have to choose what colored glasses we are willing to wear. We can talk about culture, education, and social relationships, addressing them from economical or historical points of view; we could spend a lifetime talking about mobility and equality issues, yet never fully grasp the problems, solutions, or the proposals that we could affect change. This is true globally, but especially when considering Mexico City, where there is such a diverse array of opinions, points of view, and opportunities.

In order to understand the city, you have to live it—to move from one side to the other. Given this, I invite you to take a trip, from one side to the other, from east to west, as the sun moves, to review some form of an autonomous social urbanism that is occurring throughout the city.

First, we start at the crack of dawn sometime around 5:00 a.m. The alarm goes off in a household in Ciudad Neza, where the planes start flying at 5:00 a.m. and won't stop until 3:00 a.m. the following day. We have to wake up and get ready for the day. It is a Tuesday morning. The woman of the home usually wakes up first to take a quick shower and prepare breakfast, shouting in order to wake the kids and get the family ready for school, which is just five or six blocks away. Some of them will go to another district near their parents' work. The city begins to light up. Kids roam the streets, accompanied by their parents on their way to work or their grandparents. Cars and public transport, or *"peseras,"* as the buses are called, are already running up and down the streets. There are 28,000 buses with 106 different routes. It is now 6:00 a.m. and school starts at 7:00 a.m. Nearby, there is a convenience store, a *"papeleria,"* where children stop to buy junk food to take to school, or paper and a pencil if their teacher has requested so. We pass by *"puestitos,"* little informal shops that sell food, homemade bread and natural juices, where family members can finish their breakfast and buy lunch after dropping the kids at school. Family members have improvised parent-teacher-association meetings outside the school, holding coffee and bread, discussing what is happening and what will happen in the school festival. Parents converse with teachers about their kid's performance while the school principal makes last minute announcements before the doors are closed. An improvised town-hall is set outside the school just before everybody sets off to work.

Suddenly, hands start rising to hail cabs, or heads face down to look at smart phones to call an Uber. There are public transit stops where pick-ups and passenger drop-offs occur at 250-meter-intervals, in a city where city blocks are typically ten meters long. One can spot people eating, reading the paper, or just listening to music, where everybody is heading west, either to Santa Fe, the business district, or to the historic downtown, El Centro, where the shops are located and where all are well dressed and groomed. Most are late to work, as the public transportation stops at different subway stations, which span 230 kilometers collectively and run all over the city, with 12 different routes and 195 stops that carry 5.5 million people each day. Outside the subway stations, one sees all kinds of vendors, and, depending on the season, one can buy food, umbrellas, gifts, bags, wrapping paper, or anything one can think of. People greet each other commenting on the news, politics, sports, or entertainment. The street acts as a make-shift shopping mall, built of wood and tents, and are nearby every subway station or bus stop.

The city is awake. By now, everybody is either at school or on their way to work, and we see business people at cafés, shops opening and selling, and people moving up and down the streets. At 1:30 to 2:00 p.m., as lunch nears, the smell of delicious foods begin to fill the city streets. Cars with open trunks outside office buildings sell tacos, little corners and pocket parks are transformed into *comedores* (dining-halls), where people gather to chat, do business, and rest while people watching, whereas the restaurants and cafeterias are busy, full of people waiting in line for a *"comida corrida,"* a home-cooking style with a fixed menu sold in restaurants *(fondas).* After the rush, it is back to work, but before returning, the kids are picked up from school and sent to their homes where they can eat, do their homework, and go outside to play with friends until the sun sets. Kids play in the streets or in nearby parks, or spend the afternoon indoors.

Meanwhile, it is business as usual until 7:00 p.m. when everyone heads back home. Different stores are now open and there are different restaurant menus, smells, and noises, and we can see lights and color in the streets, as well as tired faces after long hours of work. Televisions with soccer games are on, and sometimes the news; couples are dining out or going to the movies in the big shopping malls inside the city (there are more than 209 shopping malls with 6.2 million square meters of commerce in Mexico City). The public transportation bustles until 10:00 p.m. when *merenderos* begin selling quesadillas and tacos, and the night bars are open with laughter, and a few brawls here and there. By 11:00 p.m. everyone is getting ready for bed, but before, people catch up on the latest news, chat, and go to sleep to the sirens and the nightly murmurs of a bustling city.

The next day, the process is repeated all over again. While Mexico City may seem chaotic or devoid of order to a western onlooker—as do many cities in Latin America—these cities present the perfect places for examining how social urbanism can truly function. In Mexico City, as in other similar places, everything is ordered according to the social and economic status and interests of the city and its inhabitants, where food and the casual social interactions shape the landscape and layout of the city.

We initially saw our family gathering around a breakfast table, only to enter the street where breakfasts and lunches are served in formal and informal settings all around, throughout the day, and culminating with the *fondas*. All of this happens in pop-up restaurants along the streets or plazas, with vendors creating public spaces and people gathering around food. Most social interactions take place outside: be it outside the school, the office buildings, or in open shopping malls. Open-air gathering is facilitated in part by average temperatures in Mexico City—and similarly so in many Latin American countries—being 20° Celsius. One can witness various activities taking place in different surroundings, but one thing is common to all: each is improvised, be it on the way to or from work. In this respect, a type of social urbanism is happening along the streets and the main spaces where mobility occurs. These spaces are reconfigured to the shape the city, appearing and disappearing throughout the day as needed.

Here at Buró Verde, we are proposing to build pit stops as a type of urban oasis within the city. Instead of making social interactions simply incidental, we hope to build infrastructure elements that will enhance social interactions at higher and more sustainable levels, adapting to the ever-transient shifts of the city and its multiple users. These urban oases offer the potential for infrastructure ports along the main pedestrian corridors, between bus stations or metro stations, places of work and schools, and which frame a series of archipelagos to form a network of basic services for the inhabitants of the city. The intent is to provide accessible and essential daily sources of power, Wi-Fi, and seating, as well as garbage disposal, neighborhood alarms, and protected areas in case of rain or too much sun exposure. The goal is to make the city horizontal, an even playing field, extending the necessities of everyday life to all people.

We are taking advantage of the weather and the existing infrastructure of a city, trying to detect the main pathways to and from the various access points to the buses and subways to initiate another network of services along the streets that will reinforce social interaction and encourage businesses and people in the neighborhoods to care for their surroundings.

The greatest problems in large cities are not always the most complex, like transport or garbage disposal, which are related to the scale of the city. The toughest issues are often much smaller; at the neighborhood scale where people do not realize they are part of a large network of services, seeing themselves instead as mere individuals with little impact on their city. One of the ideas of the urban oasis is to give control to individuals, making them aware of how an urban network operates, and how this system can affect people in minimal to extreme ways no matter how incidental their contributions or actions may seem. These functions will take place through information panels in the oases, as part of an urban haven or hub, providing different services and improving the quality of life for the community.

The urban oasis will work as a beacon and node for social infrastructure in order to reinforce the autonomous modes of social urbanism that are occurring in Mexico City and that take advantage of weather conditions, public and private mobility, and cultural behavior. The oasis will provide basic urban services, safety, and general urban network information.

We have the ability to create memorable spatial experiences, while simultaneously retrieving the city from the "system," using it for the community, where social and everyday collaborative encounters can occur, making people proud of their surroundings and aware of their urban context. These opportunities will promote a more humane experience of living in the city, and thereby more livable. We believe that it is from these everyday social experiences that we can rebuild the urban tissue of the city in order to make it more functional for all citizens.

ENVIRONMENTAL CONFLICTS and DEGRADATION in the LANDSCAPE of MEDELLÍN

An Overdue and Necessary Reality Check

Juan Camilo Jaramillo

Like most cities in the world, Medellín has an array of conflicts, including environmental issues intrinsic to the global economic model in place. With close to four million people living in a relatively small and deep inter-Andean valley, the city struggles to maintain its environmental integrity, while complying with the existing regulations that should guarantee a future for generations to come that provide the minimum necessary eco-systemic services for today's inhabitants. Not an easy task when the ecological footprint of Medellín is as high as 50 to 100 times the size of its urban area. These challenges usually occur due to competition for resources, and the result is, invariably, the progressive degradation of the natural ecosystem, and that of the extended region necessary for proving the food, water, and other fundamental services for the growing population. Only too often, local politicians are either "greenwashing" their administrations, or are offering a euphoric and triumphalist "sustainable-city" discourse. However, reality contradicts these officers daily, who make up claims of an innovative and model city that are difficult to support, particularly when considered from an environmental perspective. It is, therefore, necessary to have a long-overdue reality check of the current environmental status of the city. The conflicts that generate the continuous environmental deterioration of the Aburrá Valley in which Medellín sits, together with nine other cities that define a large metropolitan area, is a clear ecological overshot that triggers several issues, yet for this essay, I will focus primarily on air quality, water access and waste-water disposal, land use, and biodiversity loss.

Air Quality

The quality of the air is perhaps the most important issue for the citizens, since it has become a real problem for their health and it is evident every day of the year. Sitting in a 1,000-meter-deep valley at 1,500 meters above sea level, in the northern Central Cordillera of the Colombian Andes, Medellín has—due to the heat-island effect—dramatically altered the circulation dynamics of the valley that are already less than favorable for the dispersal of particulate matter, which is abundant in the city. Prevailing winds from the northeast to the southwest over the mountains, among other factors, prevent the rising particulate matter generated from sources on the ground, such as cars, buses, trucks, motorcycles, many polluting industries, construction sites, brick factories, and the burning of trash and litter from passing through the valley, instead lingering in the air and accumulating throughout the day in "pulses" of regular and contaminated air quality that suffocates the population. Other external factors, including forest fires in different parts of the country, or even the continent, greatly affect the city as well, especially during seasonal periods, usually twice a year during the transition between dry and wet seasons, as part of a bimodal climate regime. A combination of geography and a huge car fleet, high pollution, humidity, and other relevant factors make Medellín the city with the worst air quality in the country, and perhaps the continent. Particulate matter of 2.5μ exceeds the OMS norms (Organización Mundial de la Salud; World Health Organization) by a factor of four or even five times in many seasons of the year during most of the day. Because of this, health issues abound, especially among the elderly and children who are the most affected by a pervasive atmospheric pollution stemming from the city.

There is no doubt, that the monitoring of the air quality in Medellín is the best in the country, and perhaps the region. The city has an efficient and comprehensive network of data collection and monitoring stations around the urban areas of the valley. However, observation alone does not guarantee the improvement over the quality of the air. The chronic problems are not being addressed properly: automobile and motorcycle sales; strict enforcement of air quality and other environmental regulations for citizens and industries; and corruption around the issues of construction permits, particularly related to the obligatory yearly emissions' testing for cars that are five or more years old. These problems, when combined with local weather patterns that are also altered, are preventing the indicators from becoming significantly better. The increase in new car sales and motorbikes is evident, and no matter what the city does, if that situation continues as it is, the quality of the air will invariably decrease further to even more menacing levels than experienced today. In Medellín people are dying as a result of air pollution related diseases and syndromes at unprecedented rates, with no clear solution in place for the short or long-term future.

Water Access and Disposal

The northern Andes in Colombia, where the city was established more than 300 years ago, is a humid mountainous place. Because of this, water is plentiful and flows all year round from hundreds of streams and creeks that converge on the central Aburrá River, running at the bottom of the valley northbound—toward the Cauca River, and eventually to the Caribbean Sea. Access to clean, potable, domestic water is, generally, provided for most citizens, with the exception of a few settlers at the high parts of the hillsides who have no access to treated water. There are plenty of reservoirs around the valley to supply Medellín with good quality water, but the proper disposal of it after it has been used is still a big dilemma. Although there are two modern treatment plants that are intended to mitigate this water quality problem, returning the used water in a better state than simply raw sewage, the reality is that many thousands of houses, particularly the informal settlements on the slopes, do not have a collection system. The sewage from these homes is directly disposed into the creeks that carry it straight to the river, and which never reach treatment plants. What runs down the Aburrá River is a combination of sewage, trash, pesticides, industrial waste, and dead animals that people still throw in it, along with all kinds of solid and liquid residues. It is not rare to see a mattress or a couch among the things being disposed of in the water streams. This, of course, is a monumental problem when the rainy season arrives, because the clutter causes the creeks to swell and overflow, inundating neighborhood streets, and sometimes killing people. As the growth of the city continues over the next decades, water scarcity will be a major issue around the valley, a condition that no amount of innovation or technology will be able to solve, and the social conflicts around this problem will only worsen as other examples around the world have demonstrated over and over.

Land Use

The main problem with land use in the city is the fact that there is no more space for growth, except on the higher parts of the slippery hillsides—already saturated with rapid urban development—or the few open spaces left for development at the bottom of the valley, at the cost of the highly stressed and degraded local ecosystem. According to the OMS, there should be at least one tree per person in every city. Some capitals, such as Madrid in Spain, or Curitiba in Brazil, have up to fourteen trees per person. However, in Medellín, that figure is dramatically lower, at 0.39 trees per person. There is a huge deficit of green space, which, when combined with the poor air quality, can be very detrimental to both the physical and emotional health of its inhabitants.

The next big issue with land use is inequality. This is a chronic problem in Colombia, and Medellín is no stranger to this issue. The best land in the city is in the hands of the few who can afford it, while the majority of the people struggle to build small vertical houses next to each other on the steep hillsides. This leaves no space for trees or other vegetation, or for habitats and wildlife. This fact is highly evident from satellite pictures, where the prevailing color of the valley resembles that of the color of the bricks and the local earth of which they are made. There are very few green corridors and natural areas for animals to live. The city looks somewhat "impermeable"—like a slab of cement—from a couple of kilometers, as viewed from high up.

Biodiversity Loss

Biodiversity loss is by far the least studied environmental problem in Medellín. In my view, this is worst of all. Unfortunately, there have not been nearly enough systematic or chronological studies on the assemblage of animal and plant communities in the valley to be able to understand the true magnitude of the loss of biodiversity in the last 100 years. If judged by the same parameters as those related to the current global biotic crisis—as one of mass extinction—a great percentage of our fauna and flora have been affected, particularly vertebrates, such as mammals, reptiles, fishes or amphibians, but also insects and plants. Insect loss in the valley and the city, in particular, is very worrisome, even in the least populated rural areas. In the urban landscape, it is very evident that the total population of flying insects is greatly diminished, perhaps by more than 60% to 70% judging from the almost total absence of flying insects around the street lights at night, something that was a norm with many insects only 20 or 30 years ago. Habitat loss and light pollution are the likely causes for insect loss, along with the use of pesticides and agro-chemicals in residential gardens. Moreover, the relentless increase of average local temperatures—between 1.0 to 3.0 C°, as global temperature increases, plus heat island effects—and the fast-shrinking habitats due to urban expansion is contributing to the evident insect population demise. However, insects are not the only group affected. Wildlife in general, except for the most resilient species of birds, has disappeared from the urban grid due to chronic habitat loss. Virtually all reptiles such as snakes, turtles, mammals—big and small—and countless plant species have vanished completely since the industrialization and the ongoing and exponential population growth of Medellín. The increase in temperatures has promoted the mobility, or forced migration, of species, whereas some have been showing up coming from lower warmer lands, while many others have disappeared from the valley altogether because it is too hot for them. To a distracted observer, this could be interpreted as species recovery, but that is likely a case of false hope. The truth is that the overall biodiversity and abundance of species and wild populations in the valley, as in the rest of the planet, has been declining, and will continue to do so, as the global climate crisis presses on.

Environmental Reality

The euphoric discourse of politicians and city planners over the innovation, progress, and sustainability of the city may hold a partial truth in terms of human comfort, although we are, by no means, the "model" city that has been portrayed in the news for the last 10 years. But one thing is absolutely true: nature cannot be included in that discourse. In Medellín, and in the whole world, for that matter, while humanity thrives, nature withers. In 1908, only about 15% of the population of Antioquia lived in Medellín, and those only accounted for about 100,000 people. Today, more than 60% of the current six million people of Antioquia live in the valley. Medellín has been the fastest-growing city in Latin America for many years now, and clearly, there is a persistent disconnect among the politicians in charge, who rarely take the environment as a "reality" into consideration. This is evident even in the most publicized "green" citywide projects, that keep the reoccurring reference to chlorophyll as a tool for city branding, despite being mostly empty and futile. In the end, the relentless degradation of the local ecosystem due to the exponential expansion of the city is a fact that cannot be denied, nor stopped, within the current economic and planning model in place. For the last 20 years Medellín has become a city with lower levels of violence, better access to public services, less poverty, more education, and renewed optimism. Tourism, for example—an abstract index on city approval—has been steadily growing, and the future seems bright. However, nature has its limits on what it can provide, and those margins do not appear to coincide with the actual growth rate of the urban areas, and the manner in which the local administration is handling matters. Yes, there has been tremendous progress in terms of many social and economic aspects of the city, but nature has not gained anything at all; on the contrary, it has been pillaged and plundered; it has been stomped on by the same innovative progress of which the city is so proud.

SOCIAL URBANISM

Without Social Urbanism, an Urban Reality Rigged to Implode

Theresa Williamson Ph.D.

Perhaps nowhere is there a better textbook case for the need—or potential—for social urbanism than Rio de Janeiro. A city that was the largest slave port in world history, which left a legacy of structural inequality so deep that few Cariocas have the awareness to recognize it as the primary culprit of the city's woes, even today. Ask a local if they know this history; for more than 95% the answer is no. Rio was, in fact, a principal port to the primary slave-holding society in human history. Brazil imported 10 times as many enslaved Africans as the U.S. and slavery here lasted 60% longer. Yet rarely is this taught or discussed, even in 2020.

It is no wonder that the city of Rio, now 455 years old, has experienced 71% of its history as an intensive port of entry to enslaved peoples, is the way that it is. Unlike Germany, which teaches the Holocaust to all its schoolchildren to ensure history does not repeat itself; or Chile, which conducted its Truth Commission immediately following the dictatorship resulting in a Museum of Human Rights visited by all Chilean youth; Brazil, and Rio in particular, live in collective amnesia that works only to perpetuate and deepen its structural divides with each passing year.

Rio, called both Cidade Maravilhosa ("the marvelous city") and Cidade Partida ("the divided city" or "the broken city") is known globally for these two extremes: its natural beauty and apparent light, festive party atmosphere (i.e., marvelous); and its stark inequality, represented primarily by the city's favelas, or informal settlements, as compared to its wealthy areas, often located in proximity to one another (i.e., divided). With these histories and realities increasingly coming to a head in recent years, it is time to add a third descriptor to the dramatic list: panela de pressão (pressure-cooker). Rio's social turmoil has been brought to a boil in recent years and few venture to imagine alternative ways to release the pressure other than by way of an all-out explosion. Rather than turning down the heat and taking the time to slowly remove the lid and take a close look at what's in the pot, Carioca society does what it has always done: it shakes the pot harder. The privileged few protect and strengthen their system of entitlements and reinforce their security systems. Meanwhile, the majority reacts in innumerable ways (from surviving through the pursuit of faith or multiple jobs, to violence and sinister activities), though what almost all those who are marginalized have in common is a foundation of despair. This is where social urbanism comes in. Without tools and determination to shed light on the city's history, dissect it collectively, provide an opportunity for the broad society to drop its collective conditioning—wherever they may be cast in the play—and opt out of this cycle in favor of something equitable and sustainable, Rio will continue proceeding robotically down a very dark tunnel with no end in sight.

I expect you've heard some of the headlines or statistics. In 2019, Rio de Janeiro police killed more people than they had in any past year on record, primarily in the city's favelas. In the lead up to the 2016 Rio de Janeiro Olympic Games, 80,000 people were evicted from their homes in the city's favelas. Rio's wealthiest neighborhood of Lagoa is only 1.5% black while the city's favelas are majority black

Rather than pursue productive policies based on social justice to recognize and integrate Afro-Brazilians and rural migrants on an equal opportunity basis, Rio de Janeiro's public administrations have marginalized and enacted laws and programs that have kept afro-descendants and many working class residents in a precarious state over the last 132 years since abolition. Racial inequality persists, not necessarily through an explicit race-based policy, but rather by repression and neglect of what are termed "illegal" and "insalubrious" settlements and behavior. In effect, the city has been built and conditioned to maintain the functional logic of a slave-holding society where slavery has been abolished, with the privileged benefiting from cheap labor while not servicing that same population. Tenuous realization of land rights, criminalization, etc., serve as levers that can be pulled to keep these communities "in their place." Through various levels of denial of rights and precarization of favela life, favela communities, and their residents are kept from realizing their potential.

Unfortunately, over the long haul the result is a growing quagmire of apparently unsolvable complexity, confusion, and chaos. Current trends indicate more of the same. In fact, fear and a sense of insolvability run so deep that in the last few years they have generated an even greater rise in neglectful policy, vigilante justice (militia and otherwise), zero transparency, policies encouraging police killings with near-guaranteed impunity, disinvestment in the infrastructure necessary to prevent deaths and promote life, and continuous eviction pressures.

Such policies are always met with healthy and necessary resistance, however, reflecting the commitment of the human spirit to realizing a better future. If properly channeled, this can result in fruitful and transformative participation, but in Rio, it is being repressed, resulting in anger. In turn, the revolutionizing potential of anger (i.e., protest) is being squandered, since officials are also repressing protest and participation in various forms. The result is violence and crime, perpetuated by citizens and authorities alike. The main difference being that when the authorities engage in violence (i.e., militias), citizens have no official security force to turn to. This is yet another way implosion may happen in Rio: corking resistance to the point where it explodes under pressure.

After raining on the marvelous parade, I'd like to turn to unraveling the divided city and seeking light in unexpected places: the favelas themselves. Proclaimed as the source of the city's woes by its elite, it may just be that favelas are, instead, the future source of its reawakening.

The existence of favelas in their early form—as squatters, slums, or shanties—is based on a failure of policy to guarantee affordable quality housing and connected livable neighborhoods. However, once favelas consolidate urbanistically, socially, economically, and otherwise, the source of policy failure is just the opposite; it is the failure to recognize, solidify, and build on a community's achievements while addressing its challenges. Residents are those most fit to identify whether their community is consolidated to this point, what elements should be solidified, and what challenges need to be addressed.

The majority of Rio's favela residents today live in communities that are over two-generations old, and sometimes up to five or more. Over 90% of households are built of brick, concrete, and reinforced steel, with indoor plumbing, electricity, and water. Residents build their homes based on need and develop wealth over time, benefit from strong solidarity networks, and produce the city's vibrant culture and much of its commerce. They are poorly serviced by the city government, however, experiencing interrupted or insufficient services, poor sanitation infrastructure, and insufficient upgrading, but they are consolidated communities nonetheless. In fact, favelas are simply how cities were always built until recent centuries: informally, by hand, using local materials as available. They are self-built cities—in a way, a sort naturally occurring social urbanism.

Being labeled slums, etc., after their consolidation, does these communities a huge disservice: it paints the solution as repression, eviction and public housing, when actually the solution lies in further investing in the communities on their own terms. There are today eleven community museums and more to come in Rio's favelas, working hard to make clear that their communities not only have history, but that they are an integral part of the city and are here to stay.

In Rio de Janeiro, a movement has been taking shape in recent years, and is set to grow intensely in the coming years: thousands of favela community organizers are developing their own solutions to the wide array of community challenges. In particular, they are working to solve energy issues, sanitation concerns, waste and a host of other environmental challenges through decentralized community-led programs. Together forming the Sustainable Favela Network, some of these organizers could pave the way for a sustainable urban future that builds on the qualities of consolidated informal settlements like favelas, from the inside, through local knowledge and local control. Network-supported self-organizing around decentralized solutions for sustainable development is a point of hopeful light in today's Rio de Janeiro.

Rio has also taken inspiration from San Juan, Puerto Rico, where residents of eight informal settlements along the Cãno Martín Peña canal opted not to receive individual land titles from the government, and instead formed a Favela Community Land Trust. The neighborhood is quickly developing socio-economically but does not risk losing its history, community or assets to gentrification, even though it is located next to San Juan's financial district, because they collectively own and manage their land, and have written into residents' home sales procedures the guarantee of permanent affordability. What the Caño declared is what Rio de Janeiro's Vila Autódromo favela declared when a group of residents resisted Olympic evictions and pay-offs: "Not everyone has a price." In fact, when sharing with Rio de Janeiro organizers during a peer exchange in 2018, a Caño leader turned to her Rio peers, declaring, "You have a sense of belonging! You, yes, can form a Favela CLT!" Favela CLTs are a legitimate titling option for residents of informal settlements for whom legal title is desired as a path to remain where they live and affirm their belonging to a community, for those residents who do not view their land as a dollar sign but rather as a place called home.

Solutions are out there. These are just a few. Resistance, heritage conservation, sustainable infrastructure, recognizing and building on all community assets—not just financial ones—are in fact a source of hope in Rio's current hardships. As we aim to move forward, we must seek alternative options that can be explored in greater depth. If we bother to stop and take the time, slow down, and reevaluate we can pursue so much more. We can create a renewed model that others will want to follow. The future of sustainable urbanism may just lie in Rio's favelas.

21st-CENTURY CHALLENGES

Our Collective Culture

6

21st-CENTURY CHALLENGES
Our Collective Culture

Since 2014, I have quietly observed the changes displayed throughout Medellín, and with each visit understand more about the layout and character of the valley, the multitude of projects that continue to be built—a new age of urbanization that takes the community into consideration and invites the people to take part in the cultural spaces of the city. The speed of progress is evidenced by an ever-expanding footprint. Engaging with locals across the various comunas, learning from their daily experiences testifies to the successes of these rebuilding projects and inclusive processes that have been extended to Medellín's community, affirming and humanizing an approach to urbanization through social urbanism.

Medellin still has many dilemmas to confront as the city continues to grow and with the increasing number of inhabitants living in sub-standard, precarious conditions. The POT and its intension to control sprawl into the rural and ecological zones of the valley has not fully succeed. The unstoppable migration and density, which has resulted in dual complications of safety to dwellers and preservation of the ecological region, are compounding the factors stressing the urbanization of the area. The issues with construction and corruption appear to go hand in hand, as mentioned earlier, perpetuated by a relentless equation between supply and demand. Vehicular congestion heavily marks the character of the central area of the city, where dense housing simply cannot meet the numbers for projected residents in this zone. As such, air quality is also compromised, and given the valley's deep profile, the pollution has little chance of passing through. Some projects come and go, start and stall, such as the Jardín Circunvalar and subsequent phases of Parques del Río, indicating the loss of energy in the process of Medellín's development.

One aspect that certainly continues to be remiss is the inequality across the city. Medellín struggles with its inherent topographical qualities, details that cannot be overlooked, nor that humankind should strive to alter. These conditions have resulted in a naturally divided city, characteristics mentioned through narratives of the river and the invisible borders created by the watercourses throughout the region, yet exacerbated by class struggles and supremacy over the land, condoned even today. The separation occurs across a number of lines and systems; most noticeably from real estate in the low-lying center of the city to the outskirts at the top of the slopes where the informality is most pronounced. East and west are also kept apart, by the river, and the still largely impassible links

across, deepening the cut rather than stitching the two sides together. Likewise, the city elicits divisions from the south to the north, between affluent neighborhoods in El Poblado where the strata classification are in the five-to six-range, with comparably high percentages of open space ($7m^2$ per person). By contrast, in the north of the city, Santo Domingo, at strata one and two, represents one of the densest areas, with only one m^2 per person; the city's average is $3.6m^2$ per person.[1]

When one considers the global population increasing from the existing 7.6 billion inhabitants, to the 9.77 billion projected by 2050,[2] together with the lack of available space for housing this number of people worldwide, the answers for solving these parameters begin to narrow, well beyond our imagination. Today's anthropogenic period is intensifying, with 56% of the current population living in cities, and with this number expected to grow to 68% over the next 30 years.[3] The space deficit is real, as are the complexities for remedying these askew matrices. A billion people already live in informal settlements across the globe, of which 130.9 million, or 20.4%, are located in Latin America.[4] In Colombia, 80% of the population lives in cities, with 20% to 30% located in precarious settlements;[5] in Medellín, the degree of informality has also reached a 30% ratio.[6] The UN Habitat defines slums,[7] or Colombia's tugurbios in this instance, as areas of informality where one or more of the following basic living conditions are evident: inadequate access to safe water; inadequate access to sanitation and other infrastructure; poor structural quality of housing; overcrowding; or insecure residential status (susceptible to land eviction). The numbers of inhabitants living in these sub-standard conditions will continue to rise, with the spatial challenges compounding exponentially.

Having touched upon the state of the city, the behavior of the community in Medellín and its related years of utter violence and catastrophic homicide rates, we have moved on to looking at the shape of the city and its form, which further informs the future frameworks for approaching spatial design in the 21st-century. In the context of the colonial city, the deliberate orthogonal grid, banal as it is, is repeated throughout Latin America as part of the traditional organization of cities and their formal legibility. In Medellín this order is also present, even if seemingly disguised along the meandering slopes, with strong vertical and horizontal axes running south-north and center-east to west along the peripheries and divisions discussed earlier. There is also a boundary around the city, as it once

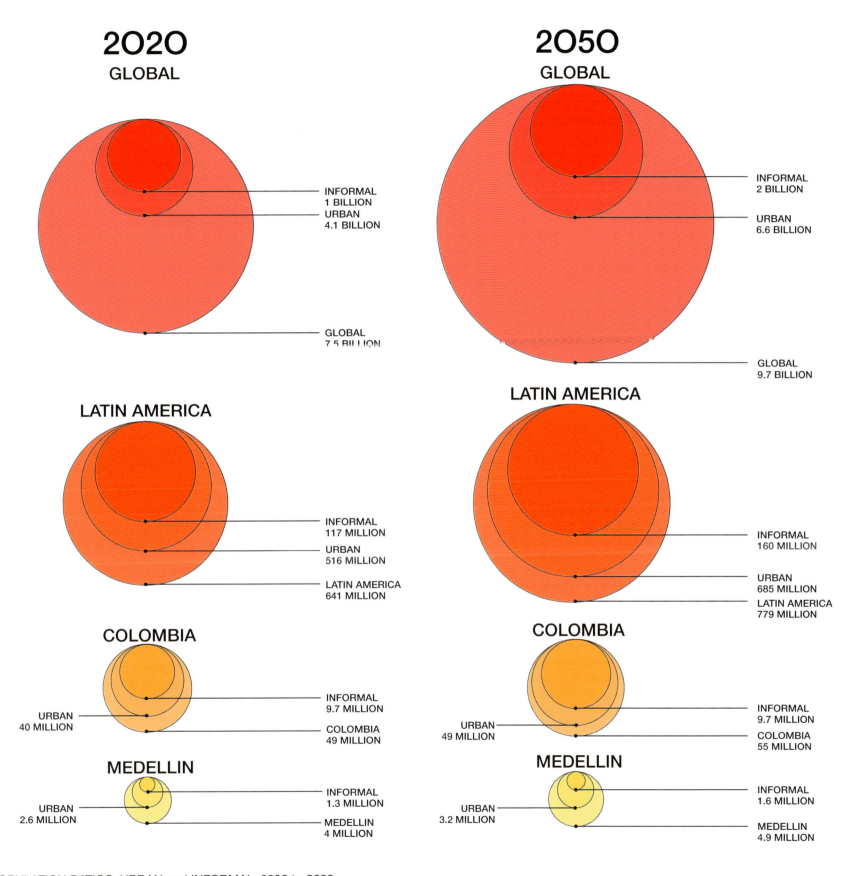

2020

GLOBAL

INFORMAL
1 BILLION

URBAN
4.1 BILLION

GLOBAL
7.5 BILLION

LATIN AMERICA

INFORMAL
117 MILLION

URBAN
516 MILLION

LATIN AMERICA
641 MILLION

COLOMBIA

URBAN
40 MILLION

INFORMAL
9.7 MILLION

COLOMBIA
49 MILLION

MEDELLIN

URBAN
2.6 MILLION

INFORMAL
1.3 MILLION

MEDELLIN
4 MILLION

2050

GLOBAL

INFORMAL
2 BILLION

URBAN
6.6 BILLION

GLOBAL
9.7 BILLION

LATIN AMERICA

INFORMAL
160 MILLION

URBAN
685 MILLION

LATIN AMERICA
779 MILLION

COLOMBIA

URBAN
49 MILLION

INFORMAL
9.7 MILLION

COLOMBIA
55 MILLION

MEDELLIN

URBAN
3.2 MILLION

INFORMAL
1.6 MILLION

MEDELLIN
4.9 MILLION

POPULATION RATIOS, URBAN and INFORMAL, 2020 to 2050

DATA POINT	Buenos Aires	Havana	Lima	Medellín	Mexico City	Quito	Rio de Janiero	Santiago	Sao Paulo
Area, sq km	2,681 km²	728 km²	2,818 km²	381 km²	1,484 km²	372 km²	1,437 km²	640 km²	1,520 km²
Population, million people	15.2 mil	2.1 mil	10.7 mil	4.0 mil	21.8 mil	2.6 mil	13.5 mil	6.8 mil	22.0 mil
Density, people/sq km	5,670 p/km²	2,885 p/km²	3,798 p/km²	10,499 p/km²	14,690 p/km²	6,989 p/km²	9,097 p/km²	10,625 p/km²	14,474 p/km²
Informal Settlements, % of population	25%	21%	35%	30%	15%	15% (1992)	19%	9%	31%
Gini Index	0.457	No data	0.470	0.474	0.530	0.307	0.642	0.462	0.560
Gini Index of residing country	0.412	0.380	0.433	0.497	0.483	0.459	0.490	0.505	0.490

LATIN AMERICA
CITY COMPARISONS

Right: Concept on social and spatial equity.

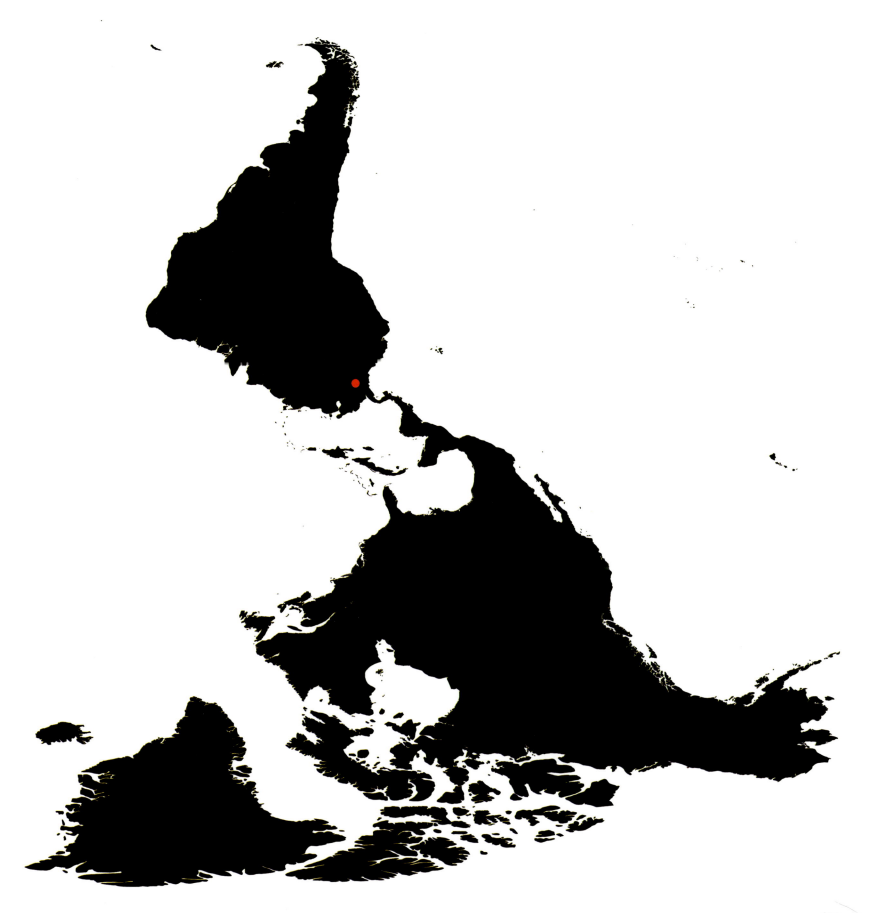

existed at the public square, now partly outlined by the POT and even by the Jardín Circunvalar or Greenbelt project, where inhabitants fall in or out of line with levels of accessibility reaching some, though not everyone. The original framework laid over Medellín dating back to 1675 was socially and physically imposing then, and today the growth of the city is demanding a new type of space with a more organic form shaped by the regional landscape, embracing a marked new number of inhabitants that must have access to the same assets, forming part of the city-region. This phenomenon illustrates a different typology of the city, as a shared condition of urbanization today and as part of the developing world[a] where the population is increasing and the allotted spaces have reached their viable capacity.

The conurbation of Medellín with bordering municipalities introduces another dimension of future cities, in terms of the equal management and fair distribution of assets and responsibilities, together with the need to conserve ecological reserves and protect the environmental quality. Nonetheless, the predicament between space and equity must be addressed further at a macro scale of urbanization where regional connections may be required. At a micro scale, the recognition of peripheral communities as vital elements of the urban city must also be included in the future frameworks for development. Deleting these spaces from the organization of the city would be tantamount to the dereliction of our roles as spatial agents of our time. In Medellín, public housing projects still rely on collecting the masses in building blocks to resolve and control the city's border. On the other hand, efforts to advance the inclusion of informal settlements is, in part, demonstrated by the PUI projects, the Metrocable extensions, and the emphasis on public space. Many of these projects are aimed at maintaining residents in place, over relocating the neighborhoods; supporting the residents, facilitating their existence through as many shared amenities as possible, and through a reliance on their own entrepreneurial character as part of their innate cultural norms. This is a valuable aspect of the work in Medellín, which despite not being able to reach its full realization today given the magnitude of the spatial and social issues, offers significant considerations for other developing cities.

Even after all the work that has been produced through the processes and projects marked by the social urbanism years of Medellín, we have to be mindful not to repeat or promote the past. There is an idealization over infrastructure and iconic architecture becoming the most essential aspects of the work conducted here, with continued reference and emulation of standards in place in the Global North. The public project initiatives, if not carefully implemented, could also fall into this realm, with a continued, greater advantage for the global market as ongoing neo-liberal, capitalist maneuvers stacked against the real goals and merits of social urbanism. Ironically, there is a tendency to mimic the Global North, often by transporting formulaic models of urbanism that in the end prevent the autonomy of progress. As has been a topic throughout, the erasure of a society has been the underlying problem with Latin America's ability to prosper. This imposition cannot be replicated. The correlations that can be drawn from Medellín should not be simplified, and require a deep understanding of the regional geography and the unique customs of each community. Here lies the potential to widen the breadth of social urbanism, expanding the cultural diversity that this work imparts, where the inclusion of, and spatial equity for, communities rank high, making it possible for "non-formal" cities to emerge. Through an exploration of a de-constructed metropolis, a progressive spatial and theoretical vision for Latin America and the developing world offers a renewed spatial paradigm.

Importantly, our focus from the building and the public square as the objects of our work has begun to shift to a comprehensive mission and holistic view of our surroundings, where we abandon our role as designers as demigods, and evolve into designers as agents of collective planning, assisting the development in-situ over implanting external systems. In place of delineating uncontrollable boundaries, not only due to urban expansion, but also to abide by natural systems, we are recognizing the climate crisis era in which we are situated. Through this unified experience we can embrace our collective culture as spatial thinkers, practitioners, designers, and as mentors, in order to explore these conditions across borders, evidenced through the politics, the economics, and the ecologies that no longer separate us.

Social urbanism, stemming from Medellín, offers significant lessons, through the magnificent projects and the greater inclusion of the community, and through the ongoing will to work together, forging the future of the city. Lest we forget the layered history of this productive region, the gold and agricultural riches that have been swiped away, its industrialization as a result, and the physical implications of the landscape and the social structure of its agrarian owners. The violence that Colombia, and Medellín in particular, have endured, mark both the landscape and the

---

a   See diagram on urban informality, page 254

community who wear the scars and carry the weight of a region despoiled by colonization, market-driven economies, internal and international power. Within this context, the social urbanism model can be transformed into a social urbanism movement, expanded and applied elsewhere when the connections between the landscape and the people are valued bonding the two within their unique arena and through their inseparable dynamics, as revealed across global landscapes.

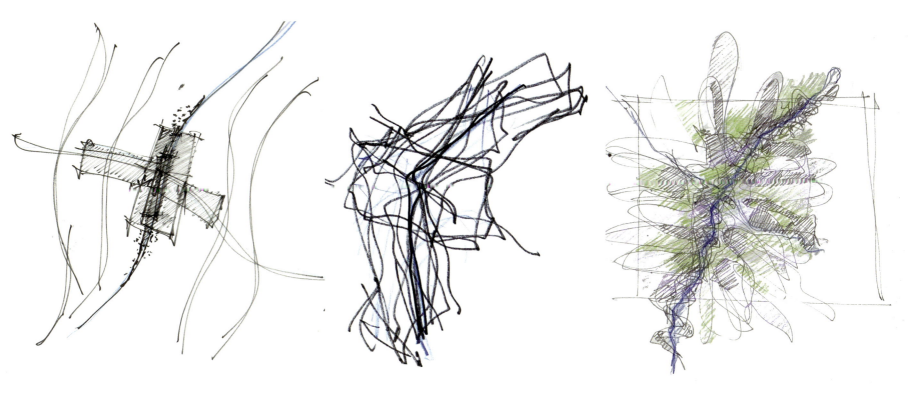

NOTES

1   Diego Zembrano Benavides, "Reclaman mas espacios para goce; Medellín solo cuenta 3,7 metros cuadrados de espacio publico por persona, el ideal seria," *el Colombiano*. February 12, 2017, https://issuu.com/edu-medellín/docs/espacio_p__blico, accessed May 12, 2019.

2   The World Bank, "Population, total," The World Bank, 2019 The World Bank Group, accessed February 3, 2020, https://data.worldbank.org/indicator/SP.POP.TOTL?view=chart; Our World in Data, "Urban and Rural Population Projected to 2050," Our World in Data, Creative Commons, accessed February 3, 2020, https://ourworldindata.org/grapher/urban-and-rural-population-2050.

3   The World Bank, "Urban Population," The World Bank, 2019 The World Bank Group, accessed February 3, 2020, https://data.worldbank.org/indicator/SP.URB.TOTL?view=chart; Our World in Data.

4   The World Bank, "Population Living in Slums," The World Bank, 2019 The World Bank Group, accessed February 3, 2020, https://data.worldbank.org/indicator/EN.POP.SLUM.UR.ZS?locations=CO-ZJ&view=chart.

5   The World Bank; A. Echeverri and F. Orsini, "Informalidad y Urbanism Social en Medellín," *Medellín Environment Urbanism Society*, (2012): 132.

6   Ibid.

7   UN-Habitat, The Challenge of Slums: Global Report on Human Settlements 2003, London: Earthscan Publications Ltd, 2003, https://www.un.org/ruleoflaw/files/Challenge%20of%20Slums.pdf.

CONTRIBUTORS

MARÍA BELLALTA CROMIE

María Bellalta is Dean and Faculty, School of Landscape Architecture, Boston Architectural College (BAC), where she teaches design theory and interdisciplinary studios on social urbanism, with a focus on the emergence of Medellín, Colombia and developing cities of the Global South. María engages in academic collaborations in Latin America with Universidad Pontificia Bolivariana (UPB) in Medellín, and Centro Metropolitano de Arquitectura Sustentable (C+) in México City. María received her MLA from Harvard University, Graduate School of Design, with prior studies in Environmental Psychology at the University of Notre Dame. She has held positions as Design Director with Martha Schwartz Partners, designer with Sasaki Associates, Inc., and project manager at Copley Wolff Design Group. She chairs the Committee on Education, American Society of Landscape Architects. María is originally from Santiago, Chile.

ALEJANDRO ECHEVERRI RESTREPO

Alejandro Echeverri believes in the ethical responsibility of designers to contribute toward a better society. He is cofounder and Director of URBAM, the Center for Urban and Environmental Studies, at EAFIT University in Medellín, Colombia. His experience combines architectural, urban, environmental projects, and planning. He is a Loeb Fellow from Harvard University, GSD, and was given the Obayashi Prize 2016. Since 2010, from URBAM, he has focused on the urban, environmental, and social issues of emerging developing countries, particularly those with weak political and institutional structures. He is also active in design through his studio, Alejandro Echeverri + Valencia Arquitectos, focusing on projects with low environmental impact for tropic regions.

ELIZABETH FERRY, Ph.D.

Elizabeth Ferry is a professor of Anthropology at Brandeis University. Her research areas include mining, finance, resources, materiality, cooperatives, and value, and she has conducted fieldwork in Mexico, Colombia and the United States. She is the author of *Not Ours Alone: Patrimony, Value and Collectivity in Contemporary Mexico* (Columbia, 2005) and *Minerals, Collecting and Value across the U.S.-Mexican Border* (Indiana, 2013), co-author, with Stephen Ferry, of *La Batea* (Icono/Red Hook, 2017), co-editor, with Mandana Limbert, of *Timely Assets: the Politics of Resources and Temporalities* (SAR Press, 2008), and many articles.

GLORIA APONTE GARCIA

Gloria Aponte has run her landscape design firm Ecotono for 20 years while serving as delegate of the Colombian Society of Landscape Architects (SAP) to IFLA, and chair of the Education and Academic Affairs Committee in IFLA Americas Region. She has her MA in Landscape Design, University of Sheffield, U.K. Gloria designed the Master in Landscape Architecture program for Universidad Pontificia Bolivariana (UPB) in Medellín, which she directed for eight years. She promotes landscape education in Latin America, advises leading firms in Colombia, and directs academic research on landscape. She has also been a competition jury, a national and international speaker at numerous events on landscape concepts, design, and management, and has published articles and book chapters.

LINA ESCOBAR OCAMPO

Lina Escobar is program director for the Master of Landscape Architecture program at the Universidad Pontificia Bolivariana, Medellín. Following her degree in architecture and urbanism from UPB in 2001, Lina has been involved in landscape and conservation projects throughout Colombia, including the development of a new nature reserve for Medellín, and the implementation of the city's green belt around to promote ecological and social wellbeing. Her research interests include city border landscapes, urban infrastructure upgrading, and landscape and territorial planning. She sits on the academic counsel and the Curriculum Committee at UPB.

SAMUEL RICARDO VÉLEZ GONZÁLEZ, Ph.D.

Samuel Vélez is an architect, specializing in business management in architecture, and has a Ph.D. in Philosophy. He was dean of the School of Architecture and Design of the Universidad Pontificia Bolivariana between 2004 and 2010, and director of the Architecture Program in 2009, and from January 2015 to date. He is currently president of the Colombian Association of Architecture Faculties (ACFA) from 2004 to 2006, and 2018 to 2020, and vice president of the Association in 2009–2010. He has served as evaluator for the Ministry of National Education of Colombia for the verification of quality conditions in the Architecture Programs from 2006 to date.

JARED GREEN

Jared Green is editor of *The Dirt*, the blog of the American Society of Landscape Architects (ASLA). He is also the editor of *Designed for the Future: 80 Practical Ideas for a Sustainable World* (Princeton Architectural Press). His writing and interviews have appeared in *Metropolis, ArchDaily*, and *China Dialogue.*

JORGE PÉREZ JARAMILLO

Jorge Pérez is an architect and planner in Medellín, Colombia, where he has practiced since 1987, as well as a senior consultant to the World Bank. Pérez is former director of planning for the Municipality of Medellín, 2012–2015, and was coordinator of the Medellín Lee Kuan Yew World City Prize in 2015–2016. In 2019, he was resident at the Bellagio Center of the Rockefeller Foundation, Bellagio, Italy, and a Member of the High Level Advisory Group UCLG-UBUNTU for United Cities and Local Governments. Pérez was a visiting fellow at King's College, Cambridge, United Kingdom in 2017. He was dean of the Architecture Faculties of the Santo Tomás University in 2018–2019, and the Universidad Pontificia Bolivariana, School of Architecture and Design, from 1993–2001, in Medellín. Jorge Pérez recently authored the book *Medellín, Urbanism and Society*, published by Turner Libros, México-Madrid (2019).

FRANCISCO LUNA UGARTE

Francisco Luna is the founding partner and principal of Buró Verde Arquitectura in Mexico City. His work includes cultural landscapes, sports facilities, parks, streetscape/urban design, and institutional planning; BRT Guadalajara for the Jalisco state government, Independencia Street Boulevard, and all the main avenues in Guadalajara; National Renewal Sports park in Azcapotzalco; and the master plan in different boroughs in Mexico City, Polanco, Lomas and Pensil. He currently teaches both at La Salle University where he graduated with a master's degree in higher education, and Tecnologico de Monterrey in Mexico City. Luna has also conducted studies in psychology and urban art that have led him to examine the city, social environment, and their interactions.

JUAN CAMILO JARAMILLO

Juan Camilo Jaramillo is a marine biologist with extensive experience as former curator for the Bird and Reptile collection at the Miami Seaquarium; and former research assistant at the Rosesntiel School of Marine and Atmospheric Sciences at the University of Miami, Florida, where he obtained his Master of Marine Affairs and Policy degree. Jaramillo is former director for the Harbor Branch Oceanographic Institution, Microalgae Laboratory. He returned to his native Colombia as a consultant for multinational institutions, and lectures on the effects of climate change on ecosystems and society, and on complex issues of our global environmental crisis. He currently lectures at the Instituto Tecnológico Metropolitano de Medellín on topics of environmental conflict. Jaramillo has been instrumental in academic collaborations between the Boston Architectural College, School of Landscape Architecture, and the Universidad Pontificia, Escuela de Arquitectura y Diseño as an environmental expert and leader in the Medellín region.

THERESA WILLIAMSON, Ph.D.

Theresa is a city planner and director of Catalytic Communities, an NGO that supports Rio de Janeiro's favelas through asset-based community development. CatComm produces the RioOnWatch.org news platform, a recently launched Rio's Sustainable Favela Network and a Favela Community Land Trust program. Theresa advocates for favela heritage status and resident rights. She received the 2018 American Society of Rio prize for her contributions to the city and the 2012 NAHRO Award for contributions to the international housing debate. Theresa lives in Rio de Janeiro.

APPENDIX

PROFILE

COUNTRY	AREA sq km	POPULATION millions	DENSITY people/sq km	GDP U.S. dollars	MAJOR EXPORTS by order of volume
Argentina	2,780,400	44,271,041	15.95	51,847,500,000	Soybean meal, wine, corn, wheat, cars, soybean oil, beef, industrial chemicals, refined crude petroleum, gold, raw aluminnum
Bolivia	1,098,580	11,051,600	10.06	40,287,647,757	Petroluem gas, zine ore, gold, silver, soybean meal, alchohol, coconuts, brazil nuts, cashews, tin
Brazil	8,515,770	209,288,278	24.58	1,868,630,000,000	Iron ore, crude petroleum, copper ore, soybeans, coffee, corn, raw sugar, cars, poultry, beef
Chile	756,096	18,054,726	23.88	298,231,000,000	Copper ore, iron ore, zinc ore, grapes, apples, pears, fish, wine, animal meal, fertilizers, woodpulp
Colombia	1,141,749	49,065,615	42.97	330,228,000,000	Crude petroleum, coal, coke, coffee, cut flowers, bananas, pesticides, gold, precious stones
Ecuador	256,370	16,624,858	64.85	108,398,000,000	Crude and refined petroleum, bananas, cut flowers, frozen vegetables, fish, cocoa beans
Guyana	214,970	777,859	3.82	3,610,435,299	Gold, railway containers, rice, raw sugar, aluminum ore, fish, rough wood
Paraguay	406,752	6,811,297	16.75	40,842,341,774	Soybeans, corn, rice, wheat, beef, raw sugar, soybean oil, insulated wire, textiles
Peru	1,285,220	32,165,485	25.03	222,238,000,000	Copper ore, refined petroleum, zinc ore, lead ore, gold, tropical fruits, coffee, grapes, animal meal
Suriname	163,820	563,402	3.44	3,427,269,682	Gold, refined petroleum, frozen fish, banana, rice, rough wood
Uruguay	176,220	68,038	19.62	56,160,000,000	Beef, milk, cheese, woodpulp, soybeans, rice, industrial chemicals, plastics and rubbers
Venezuela	912,050	31,977,065	35.06	482,359,000,000	Crude and refined petroleum, acrylic alchohols, iron reductions
Belize	22,970	374,681	16.31	1,925,000,000	Raw sugar, fruit juice, tobacco, molasses, bananas, legumes, fish, crude and refined petroleum
Costa Rica	51,100	4,905,769	96.00	60,126,014,829	Bananas, tropical fruits, coffee, medical instruments, machines, fruit juice, rubber tires
El Salvador	21,040	6,377,853	303.10	26,056,950,000	Textiles, raw sugar, plastics, paper containers, insulated wire, flat-rolled steel
Guatemala	108,890	16,913,503	155.30	75,620,000,000	Bananas, coffee, melons, nutmeg, textiles, raw sugar, industrial chemicals, lead ore, nickel ore
Honduras	112,490	9,265,067	82.36	23,803,230,473	Textiles, coffee, bananas, melons, insulated wire, tobacco, raw sugar, palm oil, coconut oil, fish
Mexico	1964,380	129,163,276	65.75	1,223,810,000,000	Computers, insulated wire, telephones, cars, metals, refined petroleum, petroleum gas, plastics
Nicaragua	130,370	6,217,581	47.69	13,117,859,222	Textiles, beef, fish, cheese, coffee, ground nuts, legumes, bananas, insulated wire, tobacco, gold
Panama	75,420	4,098,587	54.34	61,840,000,000	Refined petroleum, coal tar oil, petroleum gas, bananas, passenger ships, fish, machines
Cuba	109,880	11,484,636	104.50	87,130,000,000	Raw sugar, tobacco, hard liquor, nickel mattes, semi-finished iron, fish, honey, refined petroleum
Dominican Republic	48,670	10,766,998	221.20	81,298,585,403	Gold, tobacco, cocoa beans, hard liquor, raw sugar, textiles, machines, bananas, tropical fruits
Haiti	27,750	10,961,229	395.70	9,658,084,644	Textiles, essential oils, tropical fruits

PRODUCTION

COUNTRY	GOLD PRODUCTION metric tons	SILVER PRODUCTION metric tons	COFFEE PRODUCTION tons	HYDROELECTRIC ENERGY kW/hour, billions	AGRICULTURE Value added, billion $	NATURAL GAS terawatt-hours	CRUDE OIL terawatt-hours
Argentina	56	751	0	31.56	38.97	398	422
Bolivia	12	1,131	28,582	2.35	2.66	238	40
Brazil	81	17	2,804,070	428.33	100.35	239	1,739
Chile	44	1,194	0	19.22	8.97	10	9
Colombia	61	14	728,400	48.88	22.04	92	599
Ecuador	7	17	4,225	11.13	7.94	7	329
Guyana	20	N/A	431	N/A	.54	N/A	N/A
Paraguay	0	N/A	386	57.62	4.02	N/A	2
Peru	145	4,108	222,047	21.57	13.11	162	106
Suriname	27	N/A	4	N/A	.42	4	9
Uruguay	1	N/A	0	6.48	3.65	N/A	1
Venezuela	5	3	48,356	83.67	83.67	271	1586
Belize	N/A	N/A	86	N/A	.18	N/A	<1
Costa Rica	0	0	90,916	7.13	2.57	N/A	<1
El Salvador	N/A	0	41,965	2.01	2.58	N/A	<1
Guatemala	N/A	0	231,536	3.25	5.45	N/A	8
Honduras	0	0	282,230	2.81	2.81	N/A	<1
Mexico	125	5,574	214,667	31.86	40.6	516	1658
Nicaragua	0	17	89,700	.44	1.91	N/A	<1
Panama	0	0	6,688	4.1	1.31	N/A	<1
Cuba	N/A	N/A	9,159	.09	3.25	11	29
Dominican Republic	N/A	96	13,470	1.53	3.34	N/A	<1
Haiti	N/A	N/A	35,232	.12	.12	N/A	N/A

SOCIAL

COUNTRY	SECONDARY SCHOOL % of population	LIFE EXPECTANCY	CHILD MORTALITY RATE %, deaths before 5 years old	LITERACY %, population	WORKING AGE RATIO % employed	POVERTY LINE %, population living below poverty line
Argentina	89.51	77.50	1.11	99.1	56.45	25.70%
Bolivia	77.62	69.80	3.69	92.5	62.19	38.60%
Brazil	82.33	74.30	1.51	92.0	43.47	4.20%
Chile	87.09	79.10	0.83	96.9	45.78	14.40%
Colombia	78.85	76.20	1.53	94.7	45.19	28.00%

COUNTRY	SECONDARY SCHOOL % of population	LIFE EXPECTANCY	CHILD MORTALITY RATE %, deaths before 5 years old	LITERACY %, population	WORKING AGE RATIO % employed	POVERTY LINE %, population living below poverty line
Ecuador	88.25	77.10	2.09	94.4	55.14	21.50
Guyana	83.20	68.90	3.24	88.5	52.21	35.00
Paraguay	64.91	77.60	1.99	94.7	55.71	22.20
Peru	80.54	74.20	1.53	94.2	52.76	22.70
Suriname	58.58	72.80	2.00	95.6	50.08	70.00
Uruguay	82.77	77.60	0.92	98.6	55.56	9.70
Venezuela	69.82	76.20	1.63	97.1	52.00	19.70
Belize	70.47	74.70	1.49	76.9	54.50	41.00
Costa Rica	82.74	78.90	0.88	97.8	45.17	21.70
El Salvador	60.45	75.10	1.50	88.1	55.40	32.70
Guatemala	47.11	71.80	2.85	81.5	65.96	59.30
Honduras	45.44	71.30	1.87	89.0	56.98	29.60
Mexico	77.15	76.30	1.46	94.9	50.43	46.20
Nicaragua	48.92	73.70	1.97	82.8	52.62	29.60
Panama	69.70	78.90	1.64	95.0	54.57	23.00
Cuba	89.67	78.90	0.55	99.8	44.45	26.00
Dominican Republic	66.55	71.30	3.40	93.8	56.93	30.50
Haiti	20.00	64.60	6.70	60.7	60.70	58.50

ENVIRONMENTAL

COUNTRY	FRESH WATER ACCESS % of population with access to safe drinking water	GEOGRAPHICAL FEATURES	HIGHEST PEAK name / height in m	FOREST AREA COVER % of total land area	AGRICULTURE % of total land area
Argentina	99.1	Rich plains, flat to rolling plateau, rugged mountains	Cerro Aconcagua 6,962	9.80	54.34
Bolivia	90	Rugged mountains, highland plateau, hills, lowland plains	Nevado Sajama 6,542	50.29	34.79
Brazil	98.1	Flat to rolling lowlands, plains, hills, mountains, coastal belt	Pico da Neblina 2,994	58.93	33.93
Chile	99.0	Low coastal mountains, fertile valley, rugged mountains	Nevado Ojos del Salado 6,880	24.26	21.17
Colombia	91.4	Flat coastal lowlands, highlands, high mountains, lowland plains	Pico Cristobal Colon 5,730	52.70	40.26
Ecuador	86.9	Coastal plain, highlands, flat to rolling jungle	Chimborazo 6,267	50.21	22.21
Guyana	98.3	Rolling highlands, low coastal plain, savannah	Laberintos del Norte 2,775	83.90	8.64
Paraguay	98.0	Grassy plains, wooded hills low, marshy plain, dry forest, thorny scrub	Cerro Pero 842	37.75	55.08
Peru	86.7	Coastal plain, lowland jungle, rugged mountains	Nevado Huascaran 6,746	57.66	18.51
Suriname	94.8	Rolling hills, coastal plain, swamps	Juliana Top 1,230	98.26	0.56
Uruguay	99.7	Rolling plains, low hills, coastal lowland	Cerro Catedral 514	82.56	82.56
Venezuela	93.1	Rugged mountains, plains, lowlands, highlands	Pico Bolivar 4,978	52.74	24.49
Belize	99.5	Flat, swampy coastal plain, low mountains	Doyle's Delight 1,124	59.68	7.01
Costa Rica	97.8	Coastal plains, volcanic cones, rugged mountains	Cerro Chirripo 3,819	54.57	34.46
El Salvador	93.8	Mountains, narrow coastal belt, plateau	Cerro El Pital 2,730	12.58	76.45
Guatemala	92.8	Mountainous highlands, vast lowlands	Colcan Tajumulco 4,220	32.70	35.98
Honduras	91.2	Mountainous, narrow coastal plains	Cerro Las Minas 2,870	39.97	28.91
Mexico	96.1	Rugged mountains, low coastal plains, high plateaus, desert	Volcan Pico de Orizaba 5,636	33.93	54.65
Nicaragua	87.0	Coastal plains, mountains, volcanoes	Mogoton 2,085	25.88	42.09
Panama	94.7	Rugged mountains, rolling hills, upland plains, coastal plains	Volcan Baru 3,475	61.89	30.36
Cuba	94.9	Flat to rolling plains, rugged hills, rugged mountains	Pico Turquino 1,974	31.28	59.86
Dominican Republic	84.7	Rugged highlands, rugged mountains, fertile valleys	Pico Duarte 3,098	41.74	48.69
Haiti	57.7	Rough, mountainous	Chaine de la Selle 2,680	3.49	66.76

BIBLIOGRAPHY

1. "Colombian Geography." Colombia – SA, accessed September 6, 2019. https://www.colombia-sa.com/geografia/geografia-in.html.
2. "Encomienda."Encyclopedia Britannica, last modified 2019. https://www.britannica.com/topic/encomienda.
3. "How does the political and administrative organization work in Colombia?" ProColombia, last modified January 18, 2017. https://www.colombia.co/en/colombia-country/colombia-facts/how-the-colombian-state-is-composed/.
4. "The Bromeliads." University of California Berkeley, accessed October 10, 2019. https://ucmp.berkeley.edu/monocots/bromeliflorae.html.
5. "The Cretaceous Period." University of California Berkeley, accessed October 13, 2019. https://ucmp.berkeley.edu/mesozoic/cretaceous/cretaceous.php.
6. "Colombia." CRW Flags. Last modified May 20, 2019. https://www.crwflags.com/fotw/flags/co.html#first.
7. "Historia Moravia." G4moravia, May 2, 2007. http://g4moravia.blogspot.com/2007/05/historia-moravia.html.
8. "Manifesto Compromiso Ciudadano." El Independiente (2019). https://www.elindependiente.com/wp-content/uploads/2019/11/Compromiso_Ciudadano.pdf.
9. "Medellin, Colombia Population 1950–2020". Macrotrends, last modified January 2020. https://www.macrotrends.net/cities/20827/medellin/population.
10. "Metropolitan Medellín, Colombia." International Urban Development Association. INTA, accessed September 19, 2019. https://inta-aivn.org/en/481-inta/activitities/exchange/roundtables/20122013-inbetween/1686-metropolitan-medellin-en.
11. "Peasant Agriculture in Latin America, Asia and Africa," accessed May 16, 2019. http://cactus.dixie.edu/mahmud/econ333/fa98/Lecture27(333)fa98.html.
12. "San Lorenzo de Aburrá Cumple Cuatro Siglos." El Mundo, last modified December 22, 2016. https://www.elmundo.com/portal/pagina.general.impresion.php?idx=271560.
13. "The Nobel Prize in Literature 1982." The Nobel Prize. Nobel Media AB 2019, accessed December 21, 2019. https://www.nobelprize.org/prizes/literature/1982/summary.
14. "The Veronica Rudge Green Prize in Urban Design." Urban Design Prize. The President and Fellows of Harvard College, accessed October 1, 2019. https://urbandesignprize.gsd.harvard.edu/porto-medellín/about/.
15. "UVA Los Guayacanes." Fundación EPM, accessed August 4, 2019. 285. http://www.grupo-epm.com/site/fundacionepm/quehacemos/programas/uva/uvalosguayacanes.
16. A.L. "What is the Monroe Doctrine?" *The Economist*. February 12, 2019., accessed May 22, 2019. https://www.economist.com/the-economist-explains/2019/02/12/what-is-the-monroe-doctrine.
17. Adler, Veronica, et al. Vivienda ¿Qué viene?: De Pensar la Unidad a Construir la Ciudad. Banco Interamericano de Desarollo, 2018.
18. Aedes. "Medellín: Topography of Knowledge, urban Transformation Through Collective Processes." Berlin. Aedes, 2015.
19. Ahlert, Moritz, et al. Moravia Manifesto: Coding Strategies for Informal Neighborhoods. Berlin: Urban Lab Medellín, 2018. http://futurearchitectureplatform.org/projects/2130fb49-b316-41ba-96ce-f0a9d5688d97/.
20. Agudelo, L. *Indicadores Territoriales de Sostenibilidad y Ordenación del Territorio. Huella Ecológica y Ecosistemas Estratégicos en Medellín*, Colombia, 2002. https://sostenibilidadurbana.files.wordpress.com/2008/12/indicadoresdesostenibilidadyordenaciondelterritorio.pdf.
21. Agudelo, P. et al. *Identificación, Caracterización y Valoración Económica de los Servicios Ambientales Prestados por Ecosistemas Localizados en el Área de Influencia del Valle de Aburrá*. Medellin: Corantioquia-Unal, 2000.
22. Alcadía de Medellín. "Del Miedo a la Esperanza." Alcadía de Medellín, 2008. https://acimedellin.org/wp-content/uploads/publicaciones/del-miedo-a-la-esperanza-2014.pdf.
23. Alcaldía de Medellín. BIO 2030 Plan Director: Medellín, Valle de Aburrá. Medellín: Alcaldía de Medellín, 2011.
24. Alcaldía de Medellín. El Nuevo POT: Plan de Ordenamiento Territorial: Una Ciudad para la Gente, una Cuidad para la Vida. Medellín: Alcaldía de Medellín, 2014. https://acimedellin.org/wp-content/uploads/2017/06/RevistaPOT2014.pdf.
25. Alcaldía de Medellín. Medellín: una Ciudad que se Piensa y se Transforma. Medelln: La Alcaldía de Medellín, 2011. file:///C:/Users/ws_landscape/Downloads/Medellin_1960_-_2010._Una_ciudad_que_se.pdf.
26. Alcaldía de Medellín. Rehabitar la Montaña: Violencia Política en Colombia. Medellín: EAFIT, 2013.
27. Alcaldía de Medellín. *Síntesis del diagnóstico y diseño para el abastecimiento y distribución de alimentos para la ciudad de Medellín*. Medellín: PADAM, Universidad Nacional de Colombia sede Medellín, 2011. https://www.medellin.gov.co/irj/go/km/docs/wpccontent/Sites/Subportal%20del%20Ciudadano/Planeaci%C3%B3n%20Municipal/Secciones/Publicaciones/Documentos/PlanAbastecimiento/S%C3%ADntesis%20del%20diagn%C3%B3stico%20y%20dise%C3%B1o%20del%20PADAM.pdf
28. Alcaldía Mayor de Bogotá D. C. IDU. "Guía de Lineamientos Ambientales para Proyectos de Infraestructura en Bogotá D.C." Bogotá: Ecotono Ltda. 2006. p.95.
29. Alejandra Silva, Maria. "Alvaro Uribe: The Most Dangerous Man in Colombian Politics." Council on Hemispheric Affairs. Council on Hemispheric Affairs, October 20, 2017. http://www.coha.org/alvaro-uribe-the-most-dangerous-man-in-colombian-politics/#_ednref12.
30. Allen, Robert C. *The British Industrial Revolution in Global Perspective.* Cambridge: Cambridge University Press, 2009.
31. Aponte, G. y Escobar, L. "Miradas quebradas." En *Naturaleza Urbana, plataforma de experiencias*. Bogotá: Bogotá Instituto de investigación de recursos biológicos Alexander von Humboldt, 2016.
32. Applebaum, N.P. *Muddied waters: Race, region, and local history in Colombia, 1846–1948*. Durham: Duke University Press, 2003.
33. Ararat, Lisifrey et al. *La Toma: Historias de territorio, resistencia y autonomía en la cuenca del Alto Cauca*. Bogotá: Pontificia Universidad Javeriana, Observatorio de Territorios Étnicos, 2013.
34. *ArchDaily*. November 30, 2018. https://www.plataformaarquitectura.cl/cl/tag/latitud-taller-de-arquitectura-y-ciudad.
35. Ardao, Arturo. Genesis de la Idea y el Nombre America Latina. Caracas: Centro de Estudios Latinoamericanos Romulo Gallegos, 1980.
36. Área Metropolitana Del Valle de Aburrá. "Hacia una Región de Ciudadanö." Acuerdo Metropolitano, no. 15 (2006).
37. Área Metropolitana del Valle de Aburrá AMVA. "Inventario de emisiones atmosféricas del Valle de Aburrá, año base 2013." Convenio de Asociación No. CA 315 de 2014 Subdirección Ambiental. Medellín AMVA– UPB, 2015. https://www.metropol.gov.co/ambiental/calidad-del-aire/Documents/Inventario-de-emisiones/2013-Inventario-de-emisiones-atmosfericas.pdf.
38. Aricapa, Ricardo. "La Toma." Universo Centro, accessed October 10, 2019. https://www.universocentro.com/NUMERO63/LaToma.aspx.
39. Bailey, Norman A. "La Violencia in Colombia." *Journal of Inter-American Studies* 9, no. 4 (1967): 561-75.
40. Bauman Z. *Ética posmoderna*. Cambridge: Polity Press Ltd., 2005.
41. Bauman Z. *La cultura en el mundo de la modernidad líquida*. Cambridge: Polity Press Ltd, 2013.
42. BBC. "Colombia Profile – Timeline." BBC News, August 8, 2018. https://www.bbc.com/news/world-latin-america-19390164.
43. Becht, U. *La metamorfosis del mundo*. Cambridge: Polity Press Ltd., 2017.
44. Bedoya, Anamaría. *De oro están hechos mis días.* Medellín : Hombre Nuevo Editores, 2011.
45. Bedoya, M.R. ed. *Marmato: Disputa por el oro y el territorio*. Medellin: Biblioteca Vértices Colombianos, Universidad de Antioquia, 2017.
46. Bernal Franco, Lilian, and Claudia Navas Caputo. "Urban Violence and Humanitarian Action in Medellín." HASOW Discussion Paper 5 (2013): 1–36. http://www.cerac.org.co/assets/pdf/Other%20publications/Hasow_6_Urban%20violence%20and%20humanitarian%20action%20in%20Medellin_(6jun)_CN.pdf.
47. Berry, L. G. "Mineralogy: Concepts, Descriptions, Determinations." *Geological Journal* 2, no. 3 (1959): 282.
48. Betancur Hernández, Jason. "Intervención del río Medellín: la Sociedad de Mejoras Públicas y la Administración Municipal de Medellín, 1940–1956." *Revista de Historia Regional y Local* 4, no. 8 (2012). https://revistas.unal.edu.co/index.php/historelo/article/view/31715/41982.
49. Betancur, John. "Approaches to the Regularization of Informal Settlements: The Case of Primed in Medellín, Colombia." *Global Urban Development* 3, no. 1 (2007). https://www.researchgate.net/publication/265192365_Approaches_to_the_regularization_of_informal_settlements_The_case_of_primed_in_medellin_colombia.
50. Blaut, J. M. "Colonialism and the Rise of Capitalism." *Science & Society* 53, no. 3 (fall 1989): 260–96.
51. Brand, Peter, and Julio Davila. "Mobility Innovation at the Urban Margins." *City; Analysis of Urban Trends, Culture, Theory, Policy, Action* 15, no. 6 (2011): 1.
52. Brew, Roger. "El desarrollo económico de Antioquia desde la Independencia hasta 1920," *Anuario Colombiano de Historia Social y de la Cultura*, no. 9 (2000): 151-3.

53. Brillembourg, Alfredo, ed. *Torre David: Informal Vertical Communities*. Zurich: Lars Müller Publishers, 2012.

54. Brooke, James. "Vigilantes Fight Crime in Colombian Cocaine City." *New York Times*. February 16, 1992. https://www.nytimes.com/1992/02/16/world/vigilantes-fight-crime-in-colombian-cocaine-city.html.

55. Brown, Kendall W. *A History of Mining in Latin America: From the Colonial Era to the Present*. Albuquerque: University of New Mexico Press, 2012.

56. Burle Marx, Roberto. *Roberto Burle Marx Lectures: Landscape as Art and Urbanism*. Baden: Lars Müller Publishers, 2018.

57. Cabezas, Constanza. "Latitud, Primer Lugar del Concurso Público Internacional Parque del Río en Medellín." *ArchDaily,* accessed July 3, 2019. *https://www.archdaily.co/co/02-320551/primer-lugar-concurso-publico-internacional-de-anteproyectos-parque-del-rio-en-la-ciudad-de-medellin*

58. Capote Fernández, Raúl. "U.S. Military Presence in Latin America & the Caribbean." Granma. August 15, 2018. http://en.granma.cu/mundo/2018-08-15/us-military-presence-in-latin-america-the-caribbean.

59. Casas, Víctor. "Medellín aún Desconoce Desplazados Intraurbanos por Conflicto." El Tiempo, 2011.

60. Catalytic Communities. "Asset-Based Community Development." https://www.catcomm.org/abcd.

61. Catalytic Communities. "Why We Should Call Them Favelas." http://www.catcomm.org/call-them-favelas.

62. Ceballos, G. y Ehrlich, P. "The misunderstood sixth mass extinction." *Science, 2018,* https://www.sciencemagazinedigital.org/sciencemagazine/08_june_2018/MobilePagedArticle.action?articleId=1400889#articleId1400889.

63. Ceballos, G., Ehrlich, P., Dirzio, R. "Biological annihilation via the ongoing sixth mass ex-tinction signaled by vertebrate population losses and declines." *PNAS* 114, no. 30 (2017): E6089-E6096, https://www.pnas.org/content/114/30/E6089.

64. Chase, Arlen F., Diane Z. Chase, and Michael E. Smith. "States and Empires in Ancient Mesoamerica." *Ancient Mesoamerica* 20, (2009): 175–182.

65. CIA. "The World Factbook." Central Intelligence Agency, last modified October 22, 2019. https://www.cia.gov/library/publications/the-world-factbook/geos/ar.html.

66. Colombia Reports. "Medellín." Colombia Reports, 2019. https://colombiareports.com/medellin/.

67. Colombia. "Everything You Need to Know about the Silleteros in Medellín's Flower Festival." Colombia CO, July 28, 2018. https://www.colombia.co/en/colombia-culture/folklore/everything-need-know-silleteros-medellins-flower-festival/.

68. Cook, Thomas R. "The Financial Arm of the FARC: A Threat Finance Perspective." *Journal of Strategic Security* 4, no. 1 (Spring 2011): 22.

69. Cordy, Paul et al, "Mercury contamination from artisanal gold mining in Antioquia, Colombia: The world's highest per capita mercury pollution," *Science of the Total Environment* 410-411(2011): 154-160.

70. Coupe, Francoise. "Medellín Metropolitan, Colombia." Interview by IN-Between Metropolitan Strategies Programme, International Urban Development Association, 2013. https://inta-aivn.org/en/101 inta/activities/exchange/roundtables/20122013-inbetween/1686-metropolitan-medellin-en.

71. Cowgill, George L. *Ancient Teotihuacan, Early Urbanism in Central Mexico*. New York: Cambridge University Press, 2015.

72. Cuadros, Alex. "My Gang Is Jesus'," Harper's, February 2020. https://harpers.org/archive/2020/02/my-gang-is-jesus-brazilian-evangelicals/?fbclid=IwAR1OR-sXgzA3NIm9LAQpOdDtJPmjBlQrS0CqctMIRX3oF62Sp8IQ8vnJ4Lw.

73. Cuervo Calle, Juan José. "El Centro Cívico para Medellín: del Plan Piloto de Wiener y Sert al Centro Administrativo La Alpujarra." *Iconofacto* 13, no. 20 (2017): 208–210. https://revistas.upb.edu.co/index.php/iconofacto/article/view/7859/7175.

74. Dávila Ladrón de Guevara, Andrés. "Capítulo 2. El Frente Nacional: una Transición Democrática Reformista y Conservadora." Democracia Pactada: El Frente Nacional y el Proceso Constituyente de 1991 en Colombia. Lima: Institut Français D'études Andines, 2002. https://books.openedition.org/ifea/3975?lang=en#notes.

75. Dávila Ladrón de Guevara, Andrés. Democracia Pactada: El Frente Nacional y el Proceso Constituyente de 1991 en Colombia. Lima: Travaux de l'IFEA, 2002.

76. Dávila, Julio D. and Diana Daste. "Poverty, Participation and Aerial Cable-cars: A case study of Medellín." Paper presented at 12th NAERUS Annual Conference "The City at a Human Scale." Madrid, October 2011. https://www.ucl.ac.uk/bartlett/development/sites/bartlett/files/davila-daste-naerus-2011.pdf.

77. Departamento Administrativo Nacional de Estadística DANE. *Estimaciones dc población 1985 - 2005 y Proyecciones de población 2005 – 2020, total municipal por área*. DANE 2015, https://www.dane.gov.co/index.php/estadisticas-por-tema/demografia-y-poblacion/proyecciones-de-poblacion, accessed February 26, 2017.

78. Destler, I. M. "America's Uneasy History with Free Trade." Harvard Business Review. April 28, 2016. https://hbr.org/2016/04/americas-uneasy-history-with-free-trade.

79. DK Publishing. *Complete Atlas of the World*, 2nd Edition. New York, NY: DK, 2012.

80. Echeverri, A., and F. Orsini. "Informalidad y Urbanism Social en Medellín." in *Medellín Environment Urbanism Society*, 2012. 132-56. https://www.google.com/books/edition/Medell%C3%ADn_environment_urbanism_society/Si-jDwAAQBAJ?hl=en&gbpv=1&printsec=frontcover.

81. Empresa De Desarrollo Urbano–Edu. "Equidad Territorial en Medellín - La Empresa de Desarrollo Urbano (EDU)) como motor de transformación urbana," EDU and BID, Medellín: EDU, 2014. http://www.plataformaarquitectura.cl/cl/02-358933/equidad-territorial-en-medellin-edu-como-motor-de-la-transformacion/536a9a56c07a801713000037

82. Escobar Villegas, Juan Camilo. "La Historia de Antioquia, Entre Lo Real y Lo Imaginario. Un Acercamiento a la Versión de las Èlites Intelectuales del Siglo XIX." *EAFIT University Magazine* 40, no.134 (2012): 60. http://publicaciones.eafit.edu.co/index.php/revista-universidad-eafit/article/view/879.

83. FAO. "Water Resources." Food and Agriculture Organization of the United Nations, last modified 2016. http://www.fao.org/nr/water/aquastat/countries_regions/profile_segments/amazon-WR_eng.stm.

84. Felter, Claire and Danielle Renwick. "Colombia's Civil Conflict." Council on Foreign Relations, 2017.

85. Ferguson, Ben and Juanita Ceballos. "Police Are Killing with Impunity Inside Rio's Favelas," Vice, September 20, 2019. https://www.vice.com/en_us/article/xweavd/police-are-killing-with-impunity-inside-rios-favelas.

86. Fernández Vázquez, Esteban, Fernando Rubiera Morollón, ed. *Defining the Spatial Scale in Modern Regional Analysis: New Challenges from Data at Local Level*. New York: Springer-Verlag Berlin Heidelberg, 2012. https://books.google.com/books?id=gTZEAAAAQBAJ&pg=PA240#v=onepage&q&f=false.

87. Ferry, Elizabeth and Stephen Ferry. *La Batea*. Brooklyn: Icono Editorial/Red Hook Editions, 2017.

88. Ferry, David, and Elizabeth Ferry. "Batea," in *La Batea*. Brooklyn: Icono Editorial/Red Hook Editions, 2017.

89. Ferry, Stephen. *Violentology: A Manual of the Colombian Conflict*. Brooklyn: Umbrage Editions, 2012.

90. Fierro, J. *Políticas mineras en Colombia*. Bogotá: Ilsa, 2012. http://ilsa.org.co:81/biblioteca/dwnlds/taq/Taqpoliticas-m/completo.pdf.

91. Flint, Anthony. "Episode Four: Solutions in Slums," in Land Matters Podcast, Lincoln Institute of Land Policy. August 30, 2019. https://www.lincolninst.edu/publications/articles/land-matters-podcast-1.

92. Forero, Juan. "Medellin's Effort Against Crime Prove Fleeting." *Washington Post*. June 13, 2013. https://www.washingtonpost.com/world/medellins-efforts-against-crime-prove-fleeting/2013/06/12/4852323e-d374-11e2-b3a2-3bf5eb37b9d0_story.html.

93. Fox, Donald T., and Anne Stetson. "The 1991 Constitutional Reform: Prospects for Democracy and the Rule of Law in Colombia." *Case Western Reserve Journal of International Law* 24, no. 2 (1992): 144-148, accessed August 25, 2019. https://scholarlycommons.law.case.edu/cgi/viewcontent.cgi?article=1629&context=jil.

94. Furtado, Celso. *Economic Development of Latin America: A Survey from Colonial Times to the Cuban Revolution*. Cambridge: Cambridge University Press,1970.

95. Galeano, Eduardo. *Open Veins of Latin America*. New York: Monthly Review Press, 1997.

96. Garcia Marquez, Gabriel. "The Solitude of Latin America." The Nobel Prize, 1982. https://www.nobelprize.org/prizes/literature/1982/marquez/lecture/.

97. Gärtner, Álvaro. *Los místeres de las minas: crónica de la colonia europea más grande de Colombia en el siglo XIX, surgida alrededor de las minas de Marmato, Supía y Riosucio*. Manizales: Universidad de Caldas, 2005.

98. Geisinger, J. "Connective spaces and social capital in Medellin." The Architectural League NY. March 4, 2012. https://archleague.org/article/connective-spaces-and-social-capital-in-medellin-by-jeff-geisinger/.

99. Gomez Alvarez, Lilliam Eugenia. "La Historia de la Agricultura y de la Tenecia de Tierras en el Valle de Aburra." Repertorio Histórico de la Academia Antioqueña de Historia, 108, no. 26 (2014): 47.

100. Green, Peter S. "Cocainenomics-The Syndicate; How Cocaine Traffickers from Medellin transformed the Multibillion Dollar Global Drug Trade." *The Wall Street Journal* (2015). https://www.wsj.com/ad/cocainenomics.

101. Hanson, Victor Davis. *Carnage and Culture: Landmark Battles in the Rise of Western Power*. New York: Anchor, 2007.

102. Harvard Design Magazine. "Run for Cover!" *Harvard Design Magazine*, no. 42 (2016).

103. Hermelin Arbaux, Michel, Alejandro Echeverri Restrepo, and Jorge Giraldo. *Medellín: Environment Urbanism Society*. Medellín: Universidad EAFIT, 2012.

104. Hermelin, Michel. "Geología y Paisaje." in *Historia de Medellín*, 1996. 3–15.

105. Hermelin, M. "Valle de Aburrá: ¿Quo Vadis?." *Revista Gestión y Ambiente* 10, no. 2 (2007).

106. Hernández, Felipe, Peter Kellett, and Leah K. Allen. "Rethinking the Informal City: Critical Perspectives from Latin America." *Remapping Cultural History*, no. 11 (2009).

107. Hoyos-Patiño, Fabian. Glaciers of Colombia. January 25, 1999. USGS. November 11, 2019. https://pubs.usgs.gov/pp/p1386i/colombia/intro.html.

108. Interview with Moravia resident. August 8, 2019.

109. Jacobson, Joey. "How EPM Group is Reclaiming Medellín's Infrastructure as Public Space." *ArchDaily*, June 15, 2015. https://www.archdaily.com/642184/how-epm-group-reclaimed-medellin-s-infrastructure-as-public-space.

110. James Corner Field Operations. "The High Line." James Corner Field Operations, accessed December 21, 2019. https://www.fieldoperations.net/project-details/project/the-high-line.html.

111. James, George. "New York Killings Set a Record, While Other Crimes Fell in 1990." *The New York Times*. April 23, 1991, accessed June 10, 2019. https://www.nytimes.com/1991/04/23/nyregion/new-york-killings-set-a-record-while-other-crimes-fell-in-1990.html.

112. Jaramillo Ramirez, Marcelo. "El Desarrollo Económico En Antioquia Entre 1760 y 1830: La Formación de una Ciudad Como Centro Económico y Como Capital." Universidad EAFIT, 2005.

113. Jeremy, McDermott. "Revealed: The secrets of Colombia's Murderous Castaño Brothers." *The Telegraph*. November 7, 2008. https://www.telegraph.co.uk/news/worldnews/southamerica/colombia/3391789/Revealed-The-secrets-of-Colombias-murderous-Castano-brothers.html.

114. Kay, Cristobal. "Latin America's Agrarian Reform: Lights and Shadows." UN: Food and Agricultural Organization, 1992.

115. Lee, Richard. *Globalization, Language and Culture*. New York: Chelsea House Publishers, 2006.

116. Leite, C., Acosta, C., Militelii, F., Jajamovich, G., Wilderom, M., Bonduki, N., Somekh, N., Herling, T. *Social Urbanism in Latin America: Cases and Instruments of Planning, Land Policy and Financing the City Transformation with Social Inclusion.* Switzerland: Springer International Publishing, 2019.

117. Letelier, Orlando. "The Chicago Boys in Chile: Economic Freedom's Awful Toll." Libcom (blog). August 28, 1976. https://libcom.org/library/chicago-boys-chile-economic-freedoms-awful-toll.

118. Londoño, Camilo, Antoine Cleef, and Santiago Madriñán. "Angiosperm Flora and Biogeography of the Páramo Region of Colombia, Northern Andes." in *Flora - Morphology, Distribution, Functional Ecology of Plants*. Munich: Urban & Fischer, January 8, 2014. https://www.sciencedirect.com/science/article/pii/S0367253014000024.

119. Macias, Amanda. "10 Facts Reveal the Absurd Wealth of Pablo Escobar." *Business Insider,* September 21, 2015. https://www.businessinsider.com/10-facts-that-prove-the-absurdity-of-pablo-escobars-wealth-2015-9.

120. Maclean, Kate. "The 'Medellín Miracle': The Politics of Crisis, Elites and Coalitions." University of London, 2014.

121. Maclean, Kate. *Social Urbanism and the Politics of Violence*. Basingstoke: Palgrave Pivot, 2015.

122. Maderuelo J. "El paisaje urbano." *Estudios geográficos* LXXI, no. 269 (2010).

123. Mario Rodríguez, Carlos. "La Transformación de Medellín: Una Acción Social." Medellín: Alcaldía de Medellín, 2009.

124. Martinez E. "Mortalidad por enfermedades respiratorias crónicas y contaminación atmosféri-ca en Medellín." *Revista de la Asociación Colombiana de Alergia Asma e Inmunologia* 1, no.1 (2007): 108.

125. Marx, Karl. *Capital: A Critique of Political Economy, Chapter Thirty-One: Genesis of the Industrial Capitalist*. Translated by Samuel Moore and Edward Aveling. Moscow: Progress Publishers, 1887.

126. McFadden, Robert. "New York Leads Big Cities in Robbery Rate, but Drops in Murders." *The New York Times* (1991), https://www.nytimes.com/1991/08/11/nyregion/new-york-leads-big-cities-in-robbery-rate-but-drops-in-murders.html.

127. McGuirk, Justin. *Radical Cities: Across Latin America in Search of a New Architecture*. New York: Verso, 2015.

128. "Medellín, el Río." *Esfera Viva,* June 6, 2017, http://esferaviva.com/medellin-el-rio-tomas-carrasquilla/.

129. Mejia Botero, J.r. et al. "Mejoramiento Integral del Hábitat para la Región Metropolitana del Valle de Aburrá," Medellín: AMVA y UPB, 2007.

130. Moncada, Eduardo. "Urban Violence, Political Economy, and Territorial Control: Insights from Medellín." *Latin American Research Review* 51, no. 4 (2016): 225–43.

131. Monclús, Francisco-Javier. "El 'Modelo Barcelona' ¿Una Fórmula Original? de la 'Reconstrucció' a los Proyectos Urbanos Estratégicos (1979-2004)." *Planning Perspectives* 18, no. 4 (2003): 399–421. https://upcommons.upc.edu/bitstream/handle/2099/703/art03-3.pdf?sequence=2&isAllowed=y.

132. Montaner, Josep and Zaida Muxi. "Los modelos Barcelona, de la acupuntura a la prótesis." *Arizona Journal of Hispanic Cultural Studies* 6 (2002): 263-9.

133. Montoya Correa, Jonathan. "Cuatro Siglos de El Poblado de San Lorenzo de Aburrá: La Génesis de Medellín." Universidad EAFIT. *El Eafitense*, last modified February 28, 2017. http://www.eafit.edu.co/medios/eleafitense/110/Paginas/cuatro-siglos-de-el-poblado-de-san-lorenzo-de-aburra.aspx.

134. Montoya, N. "Urbanismo social en Medellín: una aproximación a la utilización estratégica de los derechos." *Estudios Políticos* 45 (2014). https://revistas.udea.edu.co/index.php/estudiospoliticos/article/view/20203.

135. Moore, J. "Ecological Footprints and Lifestyle Archetypes: Exploring Dimensions of Consumption and the Transformation Needed to Achieve Urban Sustainability." *Sustainability* 7, no. 4 (2015). https://www.researchgate.net/publication/276135867_Ecological_Footprints_and_Lifestyle_Archetypes_Exploring_Dimensions_of_Consumption_and_the_Transformation_Needed_to_Achieve_Urban_Sustainability.

136. Morfin, Mely. "Architecture Classics: Nonalco Tlatelolco/Mario Parni Housing Complex." *ArchDaily*, 2015. https://www.archdaily.mx/mx/772426/clasicos-de-arquitectura-conjunto-habitacional-nonoalco-tlatelolco-mario-pani.

137. Mundigo, Axel I., and Dora P. Crouch. "The Laws of The Indies," in "The City Planning Ordinances of the Laws of the Indies Revisited, Part I: Their Philosophy and Implications." *The Town Planning Review* 48, no. 3 (1977): 247-68. Translation of ordinances 92,102–7 by Ramon Trias.

138. Muñera Lopez, Luis Fernando. "Historia de Medellín a Cuentagotas 1." *El Mundo*, June 9, 2019. https://www.elmundo.com/noticia/Historia-de-Medellin-a-cuentagotas-1/376794.

139. Nates Cruz, Beatriz. Territorio y Cultura: Territorios de Conflicto y Cambio Socio Cultural. Colombia: Universidad de Caldas, Departamento de Antropoloía, Grupo de Investigación Territorialidades, 2001.

140. National Autonomous University of Mexico. "The Ways of Working in New Spain." Portal Academico, accessed January 14, 2019. https://portalacademico.cch.unam.mx/alumno/historiademexico1/unidad3/economianovohispana/formasdetrabajo.

141. National Geographic. *Atlas of the World, Tenth Edition*. Washington, D.C.: National Geographic Society, 2014.

142. NATO. "Relationships with Colombia." North Atlantic Treaty Organization. Last updated December 6, 2018. https://www.nato.int/cps/en/natohq/topics_143936.htm.

143. Nolen, Stephanie. "The illusion of Brazil's income equality," *The Globe and Mail*, January 8, 2018. https://www.theglobeandmail.com/news/world/the-illusion-of-brazils-incomeequality/article37536515/.

144. Observatorio de Políticas Públicas del Concejo de Medellín. "Planes de Desarrollo Local." Universidad EAFIT, 2017. http://www.eafit.edu.co/centros/analisis-politico/publicaciones/observatorio/Documents/investigacion-planes-de-desarrollo-local.pdf.

145. Olano García, Hernán Alejandro. "Historia de la Regeneración Constitucional de 1886." *Revista IUS* (2019). https://www.redalyc.org/jatsRepo/2932/293259573009/html/index.html.

146. Olmo, Rafael Mata and Munoz, Santiago Fernandez. "Paisajes y patrimonios culturales del agua; la salvaguarda del valor patrimonial de los regadíos tradicionales." *Scripta Nova* XIV, no. 337 (2010). http://www.ub.edu/geocrit/sn/sn-337.htm.

147. Orlando Melo, Jorge. "Espacio e Historia en Medellin." Colombia es un Tema, last modified October 2016. http://www.jorgeorlandomelo.org/espaciomedellin.htm.

148. Osorio Gaviria and Danny Andres. "Moravia: The Story of a Slum on a Hill of Garbage." Academia, 2014. http://www.academia.edu/10623171/Moravia_The_story_of_a_slum_on_a_hill_of_garbage.

149. Otis, John. The FARC and Colombia's Illegal Drug Trade. Wilson Center Latin American Program, 2014.

150. Palacios, Marco y Frank Safford. *Colombia, país fragmentado, sociedad dividida*. Bogotá: Editorial Norma, 2002.

151. Parque Arví. "'Que es el Parque Arví?'" Corporacion Parque Arví. 2016. https://parquearvi.org/.

152. Parsons, J.J. *Antioqueño Colonization in Western Colombia*. Berkeley: University of California Press, 1968.

153. Paschke, Jeff. "Is Medellín Safe? Security in Medellín and Safety Tips – 2019 Update." Medellín Guru, accessed September 19, 2019. https://medellinguru.com/medellin-security-safety-tips/.

154. Pérez Jaramillo, J.; et al. El Plan de Ordenamiento Territorial de Medellín 2014: Un Modelo Territorial para la Intervención Estratégica. Medellín: Departamento Administravito de Planeación DAP, 2014. https://upcommons.upc.edu/bitstream/handle/2117/80323/97BCN_PerezJorge.pdf.

155. Pérez Jaramillo, J., J.M. Patiño, G. Spera, J.C. García, D. Tarchópulos, and L. Cardona. "Plan De Ordenamiento Territorial De Medellín 2014: Un Modelo Territorial para la Intervención Estratégica." Medellín: Departamento Administrativo de Planeación DAP, Alcaldía de Medellin, 2014. https://upcommons.upc.edu/bitstream/handle/2117/80323/97BCN_PerezJorge.pdf.

156. Pérez Jaramillo, Jorge. "Medellín: A City for Life." Biophilic Cities Journal 1, no. 2 (2017): 34-38.

157. Pérez Jaramillo, Jorge. Medellín: Urbanismo y Sociedad. Colombia: Turner Publications, 2019.

158. Pianca, G. "Le Corbusier and Sao Paulo - 1929: Architecture and Landscape." Paper presented at Le Corbusier, 50 years later. November 2015. http://ocs.editorial.upv.es/index.php/LC2015/LC2015/paper/viewFile/937/1337.

159. Quinchía Roldán, Suly María, Luis Carlos Agudelo Patino and Armando Arteaga Rosero. Urbanismo en Medellín, siglo XIX: Aportes a la Discusión. Medellín: Universidad National de Colombia, 2018.

160. Ramirez, Loïc. "Peace is Trapped in the Networks of Betrayal." Le Monde Diplomatique, September 2018. http://mondediplo.com/2018/09/06colombia.

161. Reist, Stephanie. "Mapping the Slave Trade and Growing Black Awareness in Brazil," RioOnWatch, November 20, 2015. https://www.rioonwatch.org/?p=25458.

162. Restrepo, Vanessa. "Cuando Medellín Tenía una Playa Para Nadar." El Colombiano. August 10, 2019. https://www.elcolombiano.com/antioquia/que-habia-antes-en-la-avenida-la-playa-canalizacion-de-quebrada-santa-elena-IL11389414.

163. Rio 2016 Olympics: The Exclusion Games, Mega-Events and Human Rights in Rio de Janeiro Dossier. Popular Committee on the World Cup and Olympics, November 2015. (https://issuu.com/mantelli/docs/dossiecomiterio2015_eng_issuu).

164. Rodriguez Jimenez, Pablo. "Medellín: La Ciudad y su Gente." Banrepcultural. 2017. https://www.banrepcultural.org/biblioteca-virtual/credencial-historia/numero-230/medellin-la-ciudad-y-su-gente.

165. Rodriguez, Antonio. A History of Mexican Mural Painting. London: Thames and Hudson, 1967.

166. Rojas, B. "En Medellín Mueren al Año 3000 Personas por la Contaminación." Noticias Caracol, April 6, 2016. https://noticias.caracoltv.com/medellin/en-medellin-mueren-al-ano-3000-personas-por-la-contaminacion.

167. Ross, John. "Thugs, Not Freedom Fighters." Opinion, The Harvard Crimson (1986). https://www.thecrimson.com/article/1986/3/17/thugs-not-freedomfighters-pbjbudging-by/.

168. Russo, A. and Cirella, G. "Modern Compact Cities: How Much Greenery Do We Need?" International Journal of Environmental Research and Public Health 15, no.10 (2008), https://www.mdpi.com/1660-4601/15/10/2180/htm.

169. Sachs, Jeffrey D. "New Approaches to the Latin American Debt Crisis." Essays in International Finance, Princeton University, 1989. https://www.princeton.edu/~ies/IES_Essays/E174.pdf.

170. Sandoval, Mary Luz, "Habitus productivo y minería: el caso de Marmato, Caldas," Revista Universitas Humanística 74, no. 2 (2012): 145-172.

171. Sato, Mine. "A Fresh Look at Capacity Development from Insiders' Perspectives: A Case Study of an Urban Redevelopment Project in Medellín Colombia." JICA Research Institute, 2013. https://www.jica.go.jp/jica-ri/publication/workingpaper/jrft3q00000024w6-att/JICA-RI_WP_No.60_2013_2.pdf.

172. Sauer, Carl O. "La morfología del paisaje," Polis 5, no. 15 (2006). https://www.rodalyc.org/pdf/000/0001700001 9.pdf.

173. Sawe, Benjamin Elisha. "List of Presidents of Colombia." World Atlas, April 3, 2019. worldatlas.com/articles.

174. Schnitter Castellanos, P. José Luis Sert y Colombia: de la Carta de Atenas a una Carta del Hábitat. Medellín: AMVA and UPB, 2007.

175. Shifter, Michael. "Plan Colombia: A Retrospective." Americas Quarterly (2012). https://www.americasquarterly.org/node/3787.

176. Silva. "Alvaro Uribe." http://www.coha.org/alvaro-uribe-the-most-dangerous-man-in-colombian-politics/#_ednref12.

177. Smith, Adam. An Inquiry into the Nature and Causes of the Wealth of Nations. Scotland: William Strahan, Thomas Cadell Publishing, 1776.

178. Stewart, Stanley. "How Medellin went from Murder Capital to Hipster Holiday Destination." The Telegraph, January 2, 2018. https://www.telegraph.co.uk/travel/destinations/south-america/colombia/articles/medellin-murder-capital-to-hipster-destination/.

179. The Economic Times. "Definition of 'Gross Domestic Product'." The Economic Times, accessed April 1, 2019. https://m.economictimes.com/definition/gross-domestic-product.

180. The Library of Congress. "Primed Documents in American History: Monroe Doctrine." The Library of Congress, accessed May 22, 2019. https://www.loc.gov/rr/program/bib/ourdocs/monroe.html#bibliography.

181. The Nobel Prize. "Juan Manuel Santos." The Nobel Prize. Nobel Media AB 2020, updated January 28, 2020. https://www.nobelprize.org/prizes/peace/2016/santos/facts/.

182. Toledo, A. Agua, hombre y paisaje. Mexico City: Instituto Nacional de Ecología, 2006.

183. U.S. Census Bureau. "Statistical Abstract of the United States: 2011." United States Census Bureau, last modified September 26, 2015. https://www2.census.gov/library/publications/2010/compendia/statab/130ed/tables/11s0359.pdf.

184. UNESCO. "Records of the General Conference." UNESCO 27th Session, Paris (1993): 1-141.

185. United Nations Development Programme Colomia and Secretaría de Desarrollo Comunitario de la Alcaldía de Medellin. PRIMED; Integral Program of Subnormal District Improvement in Medellin. Medellín: UNESCO, 1996.

186. Universidad EAFIT and URBAM. "Metodología de Trabajo Colaborativo, Alrededor de la Transformación de Río Norte." Medellín: Universidad EAFIT.

187. Universidad Pontificia Bolivariana. "Paisaje de Borde el papel estructurante de las quebradas en las laderas de Medellín." Unpublished, 2013.

188. Valencia, Nicholas. "Presentan La Historia del Campamento de Chuquicamata, La Mina a Cielo Abierto Más Grande del Mundo." Plataforma Arquitectura. Plataforma Arquitectura, February 1, 2018. https://www.plataformaarquitectura.cl/cl/888156/presentan-la-historia-del-campamento-de-chuquicamata-la-mina-a-cielo-abierto-mas-grande-del-mundo.

189. Wackernagel, M. and Rees, W.E. Our Ecological Footprint: Reducing Human Impact on the Earth. Gabriola Island, BC. Canada: New Society Publishers, 1999.

190. Waldheim C. Landscape as Urbanism: A General Theory. New Jersey: Princeton University Press, 2016.

191. Ward, J. D. "The Industrial Revolution and British Imperialism, 1750-1850." The Economic History Review 47, no. 1 (February 1994): 44-65.

192. Weaver, Frederick S. The United States and the Global Economy. Plymouth, United Kingdom: Rowan & Littlefield Publishers, Inc., 2011.

193. West, Robert Cooper, "Folk mining in Colombia". Economic Geography 28, no. 4 (1952). http://www.jstor.org/stable/141970.

194. Williamson, Theresa. "Community Land Trusts in Rio's Favelas: Could Community Land Trusts in Informal Settlements Help Solve the World's Affordable Housing Crisis?" Land Lines, July 31, 2018. https://www.lincolninst.edu/sites/default/files/pubfiles/land-lines-july-2018-full_2.pdf

195. Williamson, Theresa D. "Favela vs. Asphalt: Suggesting a New Lens on Rio de Janeiro's Favelas and Formal City," in Comparative Approaches To Informal Housing Around The Globe, edited by Udo Grashoff. London: UCL Press, 2020.

196. Williamson, Theresa D. "Not Everyone Has a Price: How the Small Favela of Vila Autódromo's Fight Opened a Path to Olympic Resistance." in Rio 2016: Olympic Myths, Hard Realities. Cambridge: MIT Press, 2017. http://bit.ly/Vilaseries.

197. Williamson, Theresa D. "Rio's Favelas: The Power of Informal Urbanism." in Perspecta 50. Cambridge: MIT Press, 2017.

198. Williamson, Theresa D. "The Favela Community Land Trust: A Sustainable Housing Model for the Global South," in Critical Care: Architecture and Urbanism for a Broken Planet. Cambridge: MIT Press, 2019.

199. World Health Organization. "Homicide." WHO, accessed October 12, 2016. http://apps.who.int/violence-info/homicide/.

200. World Population Review. "Medellín Population 2020." World Population Review. Last updated 2019. http://worldpopulationreview.com/world-cities/medellin-population/.

201. Yagoub, Mimi. "Alvaro Uribe, When did it All Go Wrong?" Colombia Reports. Colombia Reports, January 22, 2014. https://colombiareports.com/uribe-go-wrong/.

202. Zambrano D. "Valle de Aburrá: insostenible y en deuda ambiental con resto de Antioquia." El Colombiano. (Medellín, Colombia) August 14, 2017. https://www.elcolombiano.com/antioquia/valle-de-aburra-no-es-sostenible-dice-estudio-DB7102445.

203. Zapata, Gustavo Ospina. "Vida y muerte fluyen en el río Medellín." El Colombiano. (Medellín, Colombia) February 26, 2017. https://www.elcolombiano.com/antioquia/el-rio-medellin-un-afluente-que-arrastra-vida-y-muerte-CX6033523.